"Pomfret's book is eye-opening in the best sense. . . . Colorful . . . disquieting." —*The Washington Post*

"Suspenseful . . . Well worth picking up—an engaging story of how spies on opposite sides of the Cold War came together, with plenty of riveting detail from participants in the events." —**NPR**

"An eye-opening account of America's relations with Poland and its intelligence service . . . A lively and insightful exploration of an over-looked international alliance." —*Kirkus Reviews* (**starred review**)

"Written in crisp, novelistic prose, this is an insightful study of the ins and outs of international spycraft." —*Publishers Weekly*

"In his revealing behind-the-scenes account . . . Pomfret draws strong portraits of principal spies and diplomats on both sides and recounts significant events, including Poland's daring rescue of six high-value American diplomats from Kuwait during the Gulf War. All in all, an important contribution to the study of US-European relations." —*Booklist*

"Utilizing countless former CIA, Polish, and US government sources, Pomfret masterfully describes . . . a fascinating and important story in a highly readable and compelling fashion. . . . A must-read not only for those interested in Polish-American relations but also for those interested in gaining a deeper and more profound understanding of intelligence liaison relationships and the idiosyncrasies inherent therein." —*The Cipher Brief*

"*From Warsaw with Love* is much more than a spy story. . . . It's a tale rich with historical accounts based on the highly regarded journalist's interviews of former agents and officials and declassified Polish archives as well as contemporary observations of US-Polish relations and the broader lessons of their secret partnership. . . . It's a masterpiece of historical investigative reporting." —*SpyTalk*

"Hold on to your hats for a journey of espionage, bravery, great escapes, and jolting change at the hands of Polish and American intelligence officers. John Pomfret's *From Warsaw with Love* takes you on a gripping roller-coaster ride through the final years of the Cold War and into the blinding sunlight of a new age. This is an odyssey not to be missed." —**David E. Hoffman, Pulitzer Prize–winning author of**
The Billion Dollar Spy: A True Story of Cold War
Espionage and Betrayal

"Put down your John le Carré, Pomfret's book is the real deal."
—**Alex Storozynski, chairman of the Kosciuszko Foundation**
and author of *The Peasant Prince: Thaddeus*
Kosciuszko and the Age of Revolution

"*From Warsaw with Love* is a real-life and riveting spy story. John Pomfret reveals how American spymasters seduced the Poles away from the embrace of the KGB and enlisted them in American adventures and misadventures from Iraq to North Korea to a CIA black site. The cast of characters comes wonderfully alive. I loved this book and learned so much." —**Barbara Demick, author of *Eat the Buddha:***
Life and Death in a Tibetan Town **and**
Nothing to Envy: Real Lives in North Korea

"*From Warsaw with Love* is more than an amazing piece of reporting. It deserves to be read by as many as possible."
—**Nicholas Meyer, author of *The Seven-Per-Cent Solution***
and director of *Star Trek II: The Wrath of Khan*
and *Time After Time*

"An astonishing account of one of the most consequential spy-agency collaborations since the Cold War. Fast-paced, with startling revelations and exquisite storytelling, *From Warsaw with Love* is a portrait of an unlikely and largely secretive relationship between Americans and Poles, spanning dozens of operations ranging from daring rescue missions to a black site prison for suspected terrorists. For Poland, the journey underscores the rewards and occasionally painful costs of loyalty."   —Joby Warrick, Pulitzer Prize–winning author of
Black Flags: The Rise of ISIS

"Sometimes former enemies make the best of friends. . . . Brilliant reporting that reveals a riveting and untold chapter of our modern history."   —Samuel M. Katz, *New York Times* bestselling
coauthor of *Under Fire: The Untold Story
of the Attack in Benghazi*

"In an age of cyberattacks and satellite surveillance, the central role of human intelligence can be lost and forgotten. Through spy tales riveting to experts and novices alike, John Pomfret reminds us of the harrowing and sometimes shocking work of operatives in the little-known but enormously impactful partnership between US and Polish Intelligence. From Iraq to Afghanistan to Europe and beyond, the former adversaries had thrilling victories, agonizing misses, and troubling betrayals."   —Jim Sciutto, anchor and chief national
security correspondent for CNN

"Great reporting once again from Pomfret."

—*National Catholic Reporter*

ALSO BY JOHN POMFRET

The Beautiful Country and the Middle Kingdom

Chinese Lessons: Five Classmates and the Story of the New China

FROM WARSAW

WITH LOVE

Polish Spies, the CIA, and the Forging
of an Unlikely Alliance

John Pomfret

A Holt Paperback

Henry Holt and Company

New York

Holt Paperbacks
Henry Holt and Company
Publishers since 1866
120 Broadway
New York, New York 10271
www.henryholt.com

The Library of Congress has cataloged the hardcover edition as follows:

Names: Pomfret, John, 1959– author.
Title: From Warsaw with love : Polish spies, the CIA, and the forging of an
    unlikely alliance / John Pomfret.
Description: First edition. | New York N.Y. : Henry Holt and Company, 2021. |
    Includes bibliographical references.
Identifiers: LCCN 2021022613 (print) | LCCN 2021022614 (ebook) |
    ISBN 9781250296054 (hardcover) | ISBN 9781250296061 (ebook)
Subjects: LCSH: United States. Central Intelligence Agency—History—
    20th century. | Spies—Poland—History—20th century. | Poland—Politics
    and government—History—20th century. | Espionage, Polish—United
    States—History—20th century. | United States—Politics and government—
    History—20th century. | Poland—Foreign relations—United States. |
    United States—Foreign relations—Poland.
Classification: LCC JK468.I6 P64 2021 (print) | LCC JK468.I6 (ebook) |
    DDC 327.1243807309/049—dc23
LC record available at https://lccn.loc.gov/2021022613
LC ebook record available at https://lccn.loc.gov/2021022614

ISBN 9781250848802 (trade paperback)

Our books may be purchased in bulk for promotional, educational, or
business use. Please contact your local bookseller or the Macmillan Corporate
and Premium Sales Department at (800) 221-7945, extension 5442, or
by e-mail at MacmillanSpecialMarkets@macmillan.com.

Originally published in hardcover in 2021 by Henry Holt and Company

First Holt Paperbacks Edition 2022

Designed by Omar Chapa

Map designed by Emily Langmade

Printed in the United States of America

1   3   5   7   9   10   8   6   4   2

To Dali, Liya, and Sophie

Liberty is nothing without a Pole. . . . His presence here is essential—The Illumination—the rockets—and the racket are lost without him.

—*Colonel Michael Jackson,*
8th Massachusetts Regiment, Continental Army, 1783

CONTENTS

FROM WARSAW

WITH LOVE

INTRODUCTION

One afternoon in late October 1990, on a dusty stretch of highway in the mountains of northern Iraq, a Polish intelligence officer pulled four bottles of Johnnie Walker Red out of his satchel and passed them to six new friends—from the United States.

Drink, came the command.

Although they hadn't had a bite to eat all day, the Americans—two US Army officers, three intelligence agency cryptanalysts, and a CIA station chief—obeyed, sipping and sloshing the fiery brew. The booze, along with six pairs of cheap khaki overalls and six fake passports, were meant to camouflage the Americans as drunken Poles on their way home from construction jobs in the Middle East. The alcohol had little effect. Stone-cold sober and clammy with sweat, the six officers approached the border between Iraq and Turkey at dusk.

The whiskey-soaked escapade capped one of the most remarkable clandestine operations of the Persian Gulf War—a mission of such significance that it opened the floodgates for an alliance between Washington and Warsaw and joint intelligence operations that would span the globe.

The twisted roots of this union stretch back to the dissolution of the USSR, when foe became friend; before that to the Cold War, when Polish spies infiltrated America and stole US secrets; and deeper still into the rubble of World War II, when America tossed Poland to the Russians in exchange for Josef Stalin's promise to level Soviet firepower at Japan. This unlikely alliance culminated when Poland led the Czech Republic and Hungary into NATO in 1999—a geostrategic earthquake that obliterated the boundaries of a divided Europe. The alliance with Poland didn't stop there; it continues to this day.

From Warsaw with Love reminds us how far allies go for America. They risk the lives of their operatives, their soldiers, and those of innocents, too. They bend morality. They break the law. All for the chance to be America's friend. For those friends, Uncle Sam provides security, counsel, technology, and an enormous market. But this account also warns of an America that can lead its allies down the garden path, leaving professed partners belittled and betrayed.

As Polish politician and journalist Radosław Sikorski has observed, an alliance with the United States is like marrying a hippo. At first, it's warm and cuddly. Then the hippo turns, crushes you, and doesn't even notice.

PART ONE

COLD WAR CAPERS

CHAPTER ONE

TINSELTOWN ESPIONAGE

On February 1, 1977, Marian Zacharski, a Polish salesman, rolled into the late-afternoon light of Los Angeles in a Pontiac Catalina with his wife and daughter. At the end of a four-day drive from wintry Chicago, their destination was a tidy apartment complex within earshot of Los Angeles International Airport.

A rangy tennis player with a big serve and an easy smile, Zacharski exuded the entrepreneurial chutzpah of a fresh-faced immigrant answering the long pull of the California dream. But Zacharski would not become an American; instead he'd become a spy. As an agent from the Soviet-led Warsaw Pact, Zacharski robbed the United States of its most closely held military secrets. In so doing, he achieved a legendary status among the FBI agents and CIA officers who tracked him down.

As he guided the Catalina into the parking lot of Cross Creek Apartments, Zacharski wasn't yet a master of espionage tradecraft. He wasn't even an intelligence officer. Zacharski had been sent to America for the mundane task of selling lathes. He represented an outfit called the Polish American Machine Company, or POLAMCO, which was founded in 1975 as Poland's Communist government sought to stabilize its tottering economy with exports to the capitalist world. Between 1970 and 1977, Poland borrowed $20 billion from Western banks and institutions in a failed bid to put money in people's pockets and food on empty shelves. Poland counted on increased exports through state-run firms like POLAMCO to repay its debts.

POLAMCO was a subsidiary of Metalexport, the trading wing of the Ministry of Machine Building. Zacharski had joined Metalexport in 1973, after graduating from the University of Warsaw with a degree in law. At six-two with sandy blond hair and an engaging if somewhat narcissistic personality, Zacharski impressed his bosses as an ambitious man on the make.

Zacharski had been born into, as he put it, "a respectable" Polish family. During World War II, his father, Wacław, served in the underground resistance forces known as the AK, the Armia Krajowa, or the Home Army, which battled the occupying German Wehrmacht. Over the summer of 1944, Wacław fought in the Warsaw Uprising, which sought to liberate Poland's capital from German occupation.

The Warsaw Uprising failed. German forces massacred thousands of Poles, obliterated the AK, and gutted Warsaw while the Soviet Red Army watched and waited on the east bank of the Vistula River. For the remainder of the war, Wacław and thousands of other prisoners were confined to a slave labor camp in Bavaria. After the Allied victory, Wacław returned to Poland. With Warsaw in ruins, he opted for a small city on the Baltic Coast near Gdańsk, where he met Zacharski's mother, Czesława.

The Soviet-installed government of the newly minted People's Republic of Poland mistrusted those who'd served in the anti-Communist AK. For years, Wacław was monitored by the secret police. Still, he succeeded in building a modest manufacturing business allowing Czesława to stay at home to raise Marian and his younger brother, Bogdan. Small firms, like small private farms, were fixtures of Poland's socialist economy. Communism never took root in Polish soil, as it had in the neighboring USSR. The heft of the Catholic Church and the cussedness of the Polish peasantry were mostly to blame. Imposing Communism on Poland, Soviet leader Josef Stalin once quipped, "is like saddling a cow." He mocked Polish Communist comrades as "radishes," red only on the outside.

Zacharski's parents gave their son opportunities that many of his peers could only dream of. Thanks to study in England, his English was practically fluent. He'd backpacked around Europe, too. So, when POLAMCO began operations in the United States in 1975, Zacharski, barely twenty-four years old, was tapped as one of the firm's reps. Zacharski's wife, Basia, and ten-month-old Małgosia joined him in America in the fall of 1976.

The Polish government based POLAMCO in Elk Grove Village, near Chicago's O'Hare International Airport, banking on a warm embrace from a metropolitan region home to a million and a half Polish Americans. But after suffering through the winter of '76, the third coldest in Chicago's history, Zacharski wanted out of Illinois. He hadn't come all the way to America just to endure Warsaw-like iciness in the Windy City. He'd also found promising leads for POLAMCO's products among US aeronautics firms on the West Coast. California made sense for a satellite office. Besides, the tennis was better in L.A.

At the end of January 1977, Zacharski and his family packed the Pontiac to the gills and headed west. The day they left Chicago was so blustery it felt like minus fifty. Zacharski had never seen so much snow, which says a lot for a Pole from the shores of the Baltic Sea. Through Nebraska and Wyoming, there wasn't an automobile in sight, just the vast, white emptiness of the Plains. The weather finally broke in Utah. At a gas station outside Provo, little Małgosia wouldn't get back in the car because it'd seemed like forever since she'd seen the sun. Four days after bidding goodbye to Chicago, the family rolled up to Cross Creek Apartments on Redlands Street in Playa del Rey, a

thirty-minute stroll from the shores of the Pacific. "California!" Zacharski recalled in 2018 gazing up at the green hills above Switzerland's
Lake Geneva, where he resides. "I have been searching for California
ever since."

Back home in Poland, the economy reeled from shortages. Initially, Western bank loans had boosted living standards, but persistent
mismanagement by the Communist government made things worse.
Poland exported meat to the USSR, but meat was unavailable in Polish
stores. In 1976, the government raised the price of staples and insti-
tuted rationing. Workers in two industrial towns, Ursus and Radom,
went on strike. Food riots erupted; strikers were fired, beaten, and
imprisoned. A team of dissidents formed the Workers' Defense Committee to stitch together an alliance between Poland's working class
and its Western-leaning intellectuals. In June 1979, the new Polish-
born pope, John Paul II, visited his homeland to a tumultuous welcome, further galvanizing hope for political change. In August 1980,
now schooled in civil disobedience and aware of their basic rights,
more than seven hundred thousand workers at shipyards, steel mills,
coal mines, and factories went on strike, forcing the Communist government to recognize the independent labor union that would come
to be known as Solidarity.

Halfway across the world, Zacharski mailed care packages to his
parents while he eased into the life of a Southern California executive.
He swapped the office Pontiac for a Chrysler Cordoba. A friend advised
him to avoid living by the ocean and working downtown because he'd
have to fight the sun both ways on his commute. Zacharski stayed in
Playa del Rey. "I need the sea," he said. "I was born there." He bought
sunglasses instead.

POLAMCO's machine tools found a market in America. The
technology was adequate and the prices were good. Zacharski sold
to a who's who of American capitalism: McDonnell Douglas, United
Airlines, and Standard Oil. Lockheed employed the tools in its skunk

works projects for the US Department of Defense. POLAMCO's machinery was used to manufacture the Trident nuclear submarine and was sold to EG&G, which made nuclear weapons. This was all despite a ban on Warsaw Pact products in US weapons plants. In 1981, when Rockwell was preparing to restart production of the B-1 bomber, an executive invited Zacharski to submit a bid.

Zacharski tapped into the Polish American network on the West Coast. He befriended a physics professor at Stanford and engineers in Los Angeles. He spent time with a Polish American expert on rocket fuel who'd flown for the Royal Air Force during World War II. He hiked the canyons around Southern California with a renowned metals inventor, wielding sticks to ward off rattlesnakes. Zacharski's clients called him Marian or Marion, Walter or Walt—an Anglicized version of his tongue-twisting middle name, Włodzimierz.

Being Polish in America, especially in Southern California, hundreds of miles from the nearest Polish diplomatic mission, meant that Zacharski escaped the scrutiny that the FBI brought to bear on Russians and other Eastern Europeans elsewhere in the United States. Americans just couldn't conceive of Poland as a foe. Poles were the brunt of jokes but never an enemy. The FBI could be forgiven for its inattention. On October 6, 1976, no less than President Gerald Ford, in his second campaign debate with challenger Jimmy Carter, erroneously declared that Poland was a member of the free world. Ford's gaffe helped cost him the White House.

At Cross Creek, Zacharski and Basia fell in with a group of eight couples, all of whom had lived overseas or were married to foreigners. They called themselves "a little United Nations." There were barbecues and trips to Disneyland, tennis and cocktails. Zacharski was a fixture on the courts and at drinks afterward. As a boy, Zacharski had yearned to play soccer, but his father forbade him. Studies, not sport. Tennis was acceptable, however, because the "right kind" of people played. Marian, Basia, and Małgosia settled in nicely in Southern

California. Before they knew it, June 1977 had come and it was time
for home leave.

Several days after returning to Warsaw, Zacharski received a call from
a colleague at the machine-building ministry who invited him to meet
for coffee on Saturday morning, June 11. At the café was a man who
introduced himself as Zdzisław Jakubczak. Zacharski vaguely recognized Jakubczak as a functionary at the ministry. Leaning toward
Zacharski and dropping his voice, Jakubczak explained that in reality he was a captain in Department I—Foreign Intelligence—of the
Służba Bezpieczeństwa (the Security Services). The SB was Poland's
version of the Soviet KGB.

Zacharski had never met a spy. He'd gleaned his understanding of
espionage from his mother, a big fan of thrillers, who passed that passion on to her son. Zacharski had grown up on stories of the exploits
of Polish intelligence officers against the German occupation in World
War II and the Polish mathematicians who'd first broken Germany's
secret Enigma codes. Captain Jakubczak probed Zacharski's familiar-
ity with intelligence operations. "Complete ignorance," he concluded
in a report to his superiors in Department I.

Jakubczak had come with a proposal. Zacharski's presence in
Los Angeles, he said, was of interest to Polish Intelligence. Jakubczak
asked Zacharski whether he'd be willing to spy for Poland. Zacharski
blushed. He was already having a hard time grasping that Jakubczak
was an undercover intelligence officer detailed to his ministry. And
now this spy was recruiting Zacharski to be his agent? "He could not
see himself in that role at all," Jakubczak observed in his report to
Department I, "due to his very hazy understanding of what intelligence actually does."

Jakubczak massaged the young man's ego. He told Zacharski that
he was an ideal candidate: he spoke great English and clearly had a
knack for making friends. Jakubczak steered the conversation to the
Cuban Missile Crisis and other developments in world affairs. After

about an hour, Zacharski warmed to the idea. Zacharski had a request, Jakubczak noted: "Due to his unfamiliarity with this subject, he would like to receive exact instructions on what to do and how to do it." Jakubczak felt it was premature to have Zacharski sign a contract to spy for the SB. The pair agreed to meet again.

Zacharski walked out of the café on a cloud. "I felt like a character in one of the books I'd been reading so avidly," he recalled in a 2009 memoir. "All my lifelong dreams as a twenty-something had been leading to this moment: I'd been noticed!" To Zacharski, intelligence officers belonged to "an elite club" and he was being given the chance to "measure myself against the best."

"I didn't know if I would win," he wrote, "but I wanted this test. I wanted a job that required me to move mountains because I felt that I was capable of moving mountains!"

Zacharski's fantasy conveniently ignored the specifics of Jakubczak's proposal. He wasn't actually being offered the chance to become the Polish James Bond. Zacharski would merely be a source, run by a case officer, Captain Jakubczak. But Zacharski never let facts get in the way of a good story. In a nod to 007, he'd title his memoirs *The Name Is Zacharski, Marian Zacharski.*

Jakubczak and Zacharski met again on June 21 as Zacharski prepared to return to California. Zacharski signed a contract with the SB and promised to keep his activities secret. Jakubczak gave Zacharski a code name, "Pay." He took out two identical calling cards and gave one to Zacharski. The other would be sent to a courier in the United States who'd contact Zacharski after Zacharski signaled he had intelligence to share. Jakubczak directed Zacharski to focus on obtaining American commercial technology.

More than the Russians or other Eastern Europeans, the Poles specialized in industrial espionage. Poland's economy relied on secrets pilfered from the West. Its pharmaceutical industry was built on stolen patents. Its electronics industry depended on technology purloined from the United States and Japan, as did its automotive and shipbuilding assembly lines. During a posting in West Germany, urban legend has it that a colonel from Foreign Intelligence named Henryk Jasik stole the formula for what became one of the most popular brands of laundry detergent in the Eastern Bloc, IXI (pronounced ik-see).

The Polish service was respected in the West. A 1978 "Spy Guide" by *Time* magazine ranked Poland's intelligence agency fifth in the world behind the United States, the Soviet Union, Israel, and Britain. Polish spies didn't favor murder, or "wet work," like the Bulgarians or the KGB. In fact, Polish Intelligence is believed to have carried out only one overseas assassination, in 1960, of an officer who'd defected to France. "Poles," *Time* noted, "tend to move and mix better internationally."

Returning to Los Angeles, Zacharski fell back into the busy life of a salesman. In early December 1977, Zacharski had just finished a tennis match when his partner pointed out William Bell, a resident at Cross Creek who was entering the courts. "He's a big shot in aerospace, a genius, I tell you, a genius!" the man whispered. Zacharski took note of his neighbor: late fifties, six-two, sideburns, thickening middle, followed by an attractive, much younger wife, named Rita. "I pricked up my ears," Zacharski wrote. "I just watched."

CHAPTER TWO

TENNIS, ANYONE?

William Bell, fifty-seven, and his wife, Rita, thirty-three, were members of Cross Creek's "little UN." Rita was from Belgium. They'd met in Europe when Bill, recently divorced, had been posted there and she was the office secretary. Rita had brought her six-year-old son from another marriage to live with them in the United States and was applying for a job as a flight attendant with Pan American Airlines.

On the evening of December 10, Zacharski, already curious about Bell, sidled over to Rita at a Saturday night party in a neighbor's apartment. Rita introduced Zacharski to her husband, Bill.

Bell had the air of an absentminded professor. Zacharski stood there wondering how he could crack him. He figured alcohol would do the trick. "In Poland you start a friendship with vodka," Zacharski announced. "I've got a bottle in my fridge." He took Bill's empty glass, sprinted home, and returned with it filled. The two clinked glasses and drank. Rita told the story of Bill at a restaurant where he'd kicked off his shoes under the table. After the meal was over, Bill asked a waiter to call him a cab, and only noticed that his shoes were missing after he'd returned home. Bill beamed whenever Rita called him a scientist.

When it was time to go, Zacharski pulled Bill aside and told him he needed a tennis partner. Bill eagerly agreed. That night Zacharski dashed off a report to Jakubczak. "I accidentally met a gentleman in my apartment complex who I believe is the vice president of a company called Hughes," he wrote. "In the near future I will probably have the opportunity to play tennis with the gentleman and find out more about his work."

A few days later, they played. Bill was terrible; Zacharski let him win a few points. After the match, Zacharski invited Bell over and the pair drank again. It was then that Zacharski discovered Bell was a weapons engineer at Hughes Aircraft Company, one of the most important defense contractors in the United States.

Feeling his way into his new role as a spy, Zacharski drew up a list of several contacts, including Bell, and passed them to Jakubczak. In a report on February 7, 1978, Jakubczak told the leadership at Poland's Foreign Intelligence Bureau that he'd directed Zacharski to focus on Bell, who was given the nickname "Pato." But, Jakubczak cautioned, "We must not allow Pato to realize that via Pay he's dealing with Polish Intelligence."

Zacharski learned that Bell had graduated from UCLA in 1951 with a degree in applied physics and, after specialist courses in the US Navy, had worked in the defense industry ever since, mostly for Hughes. Bell had been posted abroad twice in the 1960s and mid-1970s but had returned to the United States after the second tour in deep financial straits. He'd come out the wrong end of an audit by the Internal Revenue Service and had been through a nasty divorce. He'd filed for bankruptcy. What's more, in 1975, Bell's nineteen-year-old son, Kevin, died in a camping accident in Mexico after his bug repellent caught fire and he suffered severe burns. Friends at Hughes took up a collection to pay for some of Kevin's medical expenses. Still, Bell was in a very deep hole.

Bell told Zacharski he dreamed about solving his financial woes by penning spy novels. In his drawer was a rough draft of a potboiler starring a swashbuckling arms dealer named Peter K. Peach, who, like Bell, had married his secretary and sported a mustache. Peach loved gourmet food, beautiful women, and, naturally, danger. Bell had asked a friend who covered Hollywood for the *Burbank Daily Review* to spice up the manuscript with bodice-ripping sex scenes.

Although well liked at Hughes, Bell felt like an outsider upon his return home from Belgium. A younger group had taken charge of his department and he sensed he'd been shunted off to a quiet back office to waste away. He began to drink copiously. Bell was being oversensitive. Even in that back office, Bell was working on incredibly important stuff. Under his direction, a team of engineers was developing an early iteration of stealth technology. It was called low-probability-of-intercept radar. The Pentagon planned to deploy it in tanks, helicopters, bombers, and fighter planes.

Brilliant techie that he was, Bell still craved respect and praise. Zacharski lavished attention on him and Bell took comfort in his companionship. There was something of Bell's lost son, Kevin, in Zacharski's jaunty demeanor. Kevin and Zacharski were close in age and practically the same height. "He slowly became my best friend," Bell would later say.

Jakubczak instructed Zacharski to probe Bell for weaknesses, and asked for more information about "character traits, interests, addictions, political beliefs, attitude toward Poland, morale, material and family situation, etc." When Zacharski visited Warsaw again near the end of February 1978, Jakubczak ordered a crash course for Zacharski on espionage. By this time, Basia was pregnant with their second child. Karolina would be born in the United States.

Back in Warsaw, with Basia and Małgosia ensconced at her parents' place, Zacharski holed up in a ministry safe house. Jakubczak personally oversaw his instruction in everything from Foreign Intelligence's organizational structure, to how to detect counterintelligence activity, to psychological issues involving espionage, to methods of source cultivation and interviews. Specialists taught Zacharski how to use a miniature camera to photograph documents. The training wasn't always relevant. In one session, he had to practice how to lose a tail on foot. "Great!" he wrote in his memoirs. "In LA, nobody walks!"

Zacharski was an enthusiastic student. He "showed great initiative and commitment," Jakubczak wrote, and had turned out to be "a conscientious and disciplined collaborator" with "a high predisposition for operational work." In short, Zacharski was a natural. Reflecting on Zacharski's motivations to spy, Jakubczak observed that "elements of adventure" dwarfed patriotism. Zacharski was in it for the game.

Jakubczak recommended that the ministry hire Zacharski as a contract employee, increasing his total pay package by 20 percent, and bring him into the service full-time when he and his family moved back to Poland. Jakubczak suggested that Zacharski begin parceling out "beer money" to Bell to judge his receptiveness.

Soon after Zacharski returned to Los Angeles, he asked Bell for contacts at Hughes and other companies for POLAMCO's products. Bell gave Zacharski the name of a purchasing manager at Hughes along with executives at Lockheed and Northrop. Zacharski dipped into his "beer money" funds and paid Bell $200 here, $200 there. Zacharski and Basia took Bill and Rita to the Christmas ball on board the *Queen Mary* in Long Beach in 1978. When Bell offered reimbursement for the tickets, Zacharski waved him off. "Don't worry," he said. "My firm is paying." After tennis, the two would retire to Zacharski's house for drinks. Zacharski downed water and plied Bill with vodka as Bill whined about his financial troubles. Zacharski presented Bill with books about Polish history and coffee mugs from Warsaw. Bill would often stop himself in the middle of a sentence to say, "Oh, but that's classified." Zacharski had a stock reply: "No, no, you're just helping me with my technical English."

Zacharski floated the possibility of Bell becoming an adviser to POLAMCO. Flattered, Bell opened up more, bringing home documents to share with Zacharski. He started with declassified reports, Hughes's in-house newsletter, and publicity materials. Bell told himself he was just trying to help out his new friend.

Zacharski played the role of an interested, younger apprentice. "Bill," Zacharski recalled saying at one point, "you're using terms I don't understand. You need to bring me something that explains it." That was how Zacharski opened the gate. "Gently, gently I got him into the relationship," Zacharski explained. "He was a scientist. He wanted a sounding board. I played along." For a while, Bell maintained the fiction that Zacharski was paying him to help POLAMCO sell tools. But soon Zacharski's requests veered into classified territory and Bell didn't flinch. Bell even upped the classification of some documents he gave Zacharski to make them appear more secret than they actually were.

Zacharski came to the United States with no knowledge of espionage. Intelligence Command had directed him to fish for minnows. In Bill Bell, he landed a whale. Zacharski started giving Bell thicker envelopes stuffed with dollars. "He hooked me, you're damn right, he did," Bell would admit.

Zacharski furnished Bell with a camera and special high-resolution film that simplified the process of photographing confidential documents. He also gave Bell concealment devices, including a tie rack and a large wooden chess piece that opened only if turned upside down for forty-five seconds and then gently tapped.

In Warsaw, Zacharski's haul of classified material swamped Department I. In addition to early US stealth technology research, he obtained information on West Germany's radar control system and the Patriot antimissile system; details of the Amram, Phoenix, and Hawk missiles; and classified material on the Apache attack helicopter. Zacharski stole the whole radar setup for the F-15 Eagle and the F-18 Hornet combat jets along with plans for a new radar used by the US Navy. When an experimental US aircraft crashed at the Nevada Test and Training Range, Zacharski got the report.

Zacharski provided his minders with the classified American analysis of the defection of Soviet fighter pilot Viktor Belenko, who flew his MiG-25 Foxbat to Japan in September 1976. "It was a helluva book, what he told the Americans," Zacharski recounted. "They were drinking from a firehose." He was given the proceedings to conferences held by the Pentagon's Defense Advanced Research Projects Agency, which managed cutting-edge weapons research. Zacharski handed over US plans to fly a Lockheed SR-71 Blackbird along the East German border to wake up its radar and study the Warsaw Pact's ability to recognize a threat. An official Polish accounting of the secrets Zacharski obtained went on for seven pages. A 1982 CIA report, declassified in 2006, said Zacharski and Bell passed to their handlers at least twenty secret reports on future US weapons systems. It estimated that Warsaw Pact forces saved hundreds of millions of dollars in research and development and "put in jeopardy existing weapons and advanced future weapons systems of the United States and its allies."

US investigators in the 1980s believed that Zacharski's espionage harvest was limited to information provided by Bell. It now appears that he had other contacts. Americans felt comfortable discussing sensitive programs with Zacharski. He attended classified briefings at Rockwell as it tooled up to resume producing the B-1 bomber. Polish Americans in the aeronautics business routinely shared details of their work with him. "When someone says, 'This is top secret,' they forget the human element," Zacharski observed. "I had friends, and friends help friends."

Zacharski's requests for information from Bell were also suspiciously precise. Zacharski knew system designations and individual document numbers. When Bell asked him how he had found those, Zacharski just smiled. "Bell wasn't the only show in town," Zacharski said in 2018. "He wasn't my only source."

The idea that Zacharski had help elsewhere is further bolstered by a document from Poland's Intelligence Command dated June 24, 1985. "Apart from Bell," it reads, "Zacharski provided other information on the operational situation in California, on military plans and personal data which continue to be used for operational purposes."

When Zacharski was ready to pass documents to the Polish government, he called the Polish consulate in Chicago and announced, "I suspect my daughter has pneumonia." A courier was then dispatched to Los Angeles. After only one visit, the chief intelligence officer at the consulate, known as the *rezydent*, told Warsaw that he no longer wanted to go to L.A. He worried about being tracked by the FBI, especially because he was flying.

Zacharski began stuffing documents into suitcases and transporting them to Chicago himself. He had a decent cover: meetings at PO-LAMCO's headquarters in Elk Grove Village. A frequent first-class flier on American Airlines, Zacharski lugged the suitcases directly on board.

Zacharski was juggling increasing responsibilities: the birth of his second daughter, Karolina, in Los Angeles, the need to service PO-LAMCO's machine-tools throughout the American West, a demanding Bill Bell, and a confusing series of instructions from Intelligence Command in Warsaw. "There were moments when I was going completely crazy. We had two young children at home and I was managing a full-time job *and* full-time espionage," Zacharski recalled.

In late 1978, Cross Creek's owners announced that the apartment complex was converting to condominiums. Bill and Rita wanted to buy their place but they were strapped for cash. Zacharski stepped in. In February 1979, he handed Bell $12,000 in two envelopes. Bell used a portion of the money for a down payment and to pay his back taxes.

Bell took what was left and went on a spending spree. He swapped his medium-sized Chevrolet for a red Cadillac with a white vinyl top and sunroof. He began sporting a Panama hat and designer shades, à la Bell's novelized character, Peter K. Peach. Zacharski worried that Bell's showboating would raise eyebrows among the security officers at Hughes. He started giving Bell gold coins instead of cash to make it harder for Bell to burn a hole in his pocket.

Following direction from Warsaw, Zacharski suggested that Bell travel to Europe to meet directly with officers from Department I. In November 1979, Bell brought a suitcase full of documents to a park in Innsbruck, Austria. He was approached by a man who asked him, "Aren't you a friend of Marian's?" The man introduced himself as "Paul." His real name was Anatoliusz Inowolski, a longtime Polish intelligence officer who'd served undercover at the Polish consulate in New York. Bell made two more trips to Austria and one to Geneva, passing reams of files to Paul and other handlers. Altogether, the Poles paid Bell more than $100,000 in cash and $60,000 in gold Kruger-rands.

From 1978 into early 1980, Zacharski conducted espionage unmolested by any US law enforcement agency. He was good at it. He was also lucky. A close shave occurred one morning before dawn. Zacharski was driving to his office to photocopy a batch of Bell's documents, when an LAPD officer pulled him over for speeding. The officer searched Zacharski's car, overlooking two hundred pages of highly classified reports piled in the backseat.

In Poland, Zacharski's documents revealed a vast knowledge gap between the Warsaw Pact and the United States. A Polish radar specialist spent three days studying one group of files and emerged to say that he couldn't fathom the science. When Zacharski passed along US plans to use stealth technology to conceal US warships, one Polish official asked, "How can you hide a boat?" In his memoirs, Czesław Kiszczak, the former Polish minister of interior and spy chief, observed that "even our most outstanding scientists had no idea how to deal with the material supplied by Zacharski, not to mention how to put it to practical use."

KGB experts on US technology traveled to Warsaw and had a better time analyzing Zacharski's harvest. Yuri Andropov, the general secretary of the Communist Party of the Soviet Union, personally

thanked Kiszczak for Zacharski's contributions to the defense of the
Warsaw Pact. Still, to Zacharski and his Polish minders at Intelligence
Command, the documents served as a wake-up call that they were on
the wrong side of a race for military supremacy. As Zacharski put it:
"It showed us that we had no chance to catch up."

CHAPTER THREE

THE AMERICAN BEAR

Espionage is a two-way street, and the CIA had spent years penetrating the Polish government. Take the case of Polish army colonel (and CIA agent) Ryszard Kukliński. Kukliński worked in the heart of the Warsaw Pact's military command. In the 1970s, Kukliński passed the CIA thirty-five thousand pages of classified documents that revealed Moscow's strategic plans for its use of nuclear weapons, details of its weapons systems and spy satellites, and the whereabouts of hidden antiaircraft installations and bunkers used by the Warsaw Pact's command.

Horrified by the Soviet invasion of Czechoslovakia in 1968, Kukliński volunteered to spy for the CIA. Kukliński did so because he feared that the Soviet Union's growing superiority in conventional weapons might tempt Moscow to invade Western Europe. The only effective way for NATO to counter such an assault, Kukliński surmised, would be with nuclear weapons, which would turn his homeland into a nuclear wasteland. Kukliński saw Poland as enslaved by the Soviet Union. His main handler at the CIA said Kukliński never asked for money.

Kukliński was the most important of the many Polish agents who worked for the United States. The CIA recruited a Polish spy who was the world's greatest fencer. Another asset served as a triple agent for Poland, the Soviets, and the CIA. (Later in life, he claimed to be descended from the last Russian czar.) Another was a member of Poland's secret police who was so notorious for torturing political prisoners that they nicknamed him "The Butcher." Zacharski's first office mate at Metalexport, Leszek Chróst, had been working for the CIA since 1964.

One CIA officer was at the center of an extraordinary number of Polish recruitment operations. Over the course of a thirty-five-year career, John Palevich managed eighteen agents and recruited even more, a remarkable juggling act in a profession where many successful CIA case officers never conscript a single spy.

Palevich's grandparents were Polish, although when they immigrated to America at the end of the nineteenth century, Poland didn't exist. One branch came from territory held by Prussia; another from a region that belonged to the Austro-Hungarian Empire. Like many Polish arrivals, they made their way to coal country in northeastern Pennsylvania. There, the men found employment in the mines.

At thirteen, Palevich's father had already begun work as a "breaker boy," picking slate out of the coal. He was prepared to follow his dad underground. But as phone ownership spread across the United States, a job as a lineman for AT&T kept him aboveground. He spent the rest of his life working for Ma Bell.

John's mother also left school early, to labor in a silk mill. When his parents married, she became a housewife. The family moved to the central Pennsylvanian town of Bloomsburg, along the banks of the Susquehanna River. Born in 1934, John was the second of three brothers and a sister.

John's elder brother, Edward, was a standout student, the first in his family to graduate from high school and go to college—on a scholarship to Princeton. John didn't share Edward's academic bent.

He'd rather spelunk in the caves on the outskirts of town. In 1950, at sixteen, John tried to enlist in the US Army to fight in Korea— but he was too young and the army found him out. A year later, he enrolled at Pennsylvania State University, joined a fraternity, and settled on geology as a major. After tangling with organic chemistry, the trenches of Korea began to look even more inviting. Dropping out of Penn State in his sophomore year, John enlisted, this time legally, in 1953.

John had his heart set on an armored division, even though he'd never gotten close enough to a tank to see whether his beefy six-one frame could squeeze into the hull. The army had other plans. After a battery of tests, the army sent John to its language school in Monterey, California. "Palevich, what type of name is that? Yugoslav?" asked an officer as Palevich stepped off the bus from the East Coast. "Polish," Palevich replied. "We've got an opening in the Polish section," the officer said.

Palevich studied Polish for a year. Only three out of ten students, including John, passed. The army assigned Palevich to the Army Security Agency, part of the growing national security architecture being built in the emerging Cold War.

"I didn't know what intelligence operations were but they sounded pretty sexy," he recalled. By the summer of 1954, John found himself detailed to a secret location in a small forest in West Berlin where he spent eight hours a day with a set of headphones listening to the chit-chat of Polish pilots and tank operators.

John's agency shared its intelligence with other members of the North Atlantic Treaty Organization, the world's largest peacetime military alliance, which had been founded in 1949 and included the United States, Canada, and, initially, ten Western European nations. NATO faced off against the Warsaw Pact, which grouped the USSR with seven Eastern European Communist-run countries. Palevich served three years in Germany, returning to Penn State in early 1956.

Palevich left America a boy and returned a staff sergeant in the US

Army. He withdrew from the fraternity, became an RA in a dorm, and switched his major from geology to political science with a Russia area specialization. He planned on a career as a diplomat.

After finishing midterms at the end of his first semester, Palevich was loafing around campus when a friend, the son of a German rocket scientist, offered to drive him down to Washington if he'd split gas money. His friend had an interview with the CIA. John was game. In DC, John accompanied his pal to the CIA personnel office located in a nondescript building on the Mall. An attendant handed Palevich a stack of forms. "As long as you're here, you might as well apply," the man suggested. Palevich got a job offer; his friend did not.

At Penn State, Palevich met a bright education major named Bonnie Jones and the pair began dating. John graduated in August 1958 and joined the agency the next month. He was soon sent to The Farm, the CIA's training facility, in Williamsburg, Virginia. For Thanksgiving that year, Bonnie's parents invited John to their home outside Baltimore. John had already told Bonnie he was going to be an intelligence officer. It wouldn't have been fair otherwise. After dinner that night he asked her to marry him. They fixed a wedding date for the fall of 1959 after Bonnie was set to graduate.

John Palevich was an easy fit for the CIA. He already spoke Polish, which the US government considered a strategic language. He had a security clearance thanks to his military service. His political science degree meant that he could operate comfortably under State Department cover. In addition, John was a gentle giant. His nicknames were "Big John" and the "Bear." (Well into his eighties, he maintained a collection of ursine knickknacks.) Graced with an avuncular personality, Palevich displayed the natural bonhomie that the CIA sought to instill in its case officers who were charged with recruiting spies. Early on, Palevich mastered the skill of talking engagingly without saying anything. He was, as he put it, chatty.

In 1961, the agency sent Palevich back to Berlin for his first overseas posting. He witnessed the East Germans building the Berlin Wall and the standoff between US and Russian tanks near the Brandenburg Gate. Bonnie gave birth to their first child, John, in 1962.

From Berlin, the Paleviches moved to Warsaw, where John worked undercover as a consular officer at the embassy. John, Bonnie, and son John lived in an apartment building with World War II bullet holes in its facade. In a report on Palevich, a Polish intelligence officer noted his Polish heritage and his improving Polish but appeared to have no inkling that he was a spy.

John and Bonnie hung out with Western reporters at the US embassy bar and played matchmaker between *New York Times* correspondent David Halberstam and his soon-to-be bride, Polish actress Elżbieta Czyżewska. "It was love at first sight," Bonnie recalled. "But communication was challenging so John translated." Warsaw social life was enlivened by visits from Hollywood stars Omar Sharif and Kirk Douglas and by Marlene Dietrich's first concert east of the Iron Curtain. In 1964, Bonnie had a second child, Matthew.

Palevich's next foreign posting took the family to Laos during the Vietnam War; he worked across the region cultivating Polish sources. Indochina was a rich hunting ground for the CIA. Polish military officers made up one-third of the International Control Commission set up in the 1950s to monitor the partition of Vietnam. The CIA recruited Polish army officers and trade officials, such as Marian Zacharski's colleague Leszek Chróst, who became an American agent when he was stationed in Thailand. In some cases, the CIA would prepare what was known in the business as *kompromat*; they'd set up the men with prostitutes, photograph them in compromising situations, and use the threat of informing their wives to get the officers to spy for the United States. Palevich had little truck with that type of tradecraft. "If you blackmail your target, he's going to spend most of his time thinking how to screw you rather than work for you," Palevich said. "I always found it easier to become their friends."

While the family was posted in Vientiane, Matthew fell ill. Bonnie took him to a US military hospital in the Philippines, where he was diagnosed with childhood leukemia. Despite treatment at the National Institutes of Health, Matthew didn't make it past his sixth birthday. A hole opened up in the family.

Tragedy followed Palevich to his next posting in Athens. After a Christmas party in 1975, leftist gunmen murdered his boss, CIA station chief Richard Welch. In 1976, Palevich and the family returned to the United States for good. Bonnie needed to care for her aging mother. By that time, several writers had already identified Palevich as a CIA officer.

At Langley, John served in a few leadership positions but itched to get back into the game of recruiting spies. In a highly unusual move, the agency appointed Palevich special assistant to the chief of Soviet/Eastern European operations. He essentially became a freelancer, roaming the globe roping in Polish agents. The Bear referred to himself as a "paladin," like the medieval French knights who served Charlemagne's court. His colleagues called him "Mr. Poland."

John was one of only two CIA officers to make "super grade," a CIA rank equivalent to that of an army general, without having spent years as a manager. Palevich wasn't interested in administration. "He didn't like worrying about the Sams and Marys," recalled Burton Gerber, a senior CIA officer who'd joined the agency around the same time as Palevich. "He liked being a case officer. And he made super grade anyway. The agency never had anyone like him." John had his flamboyant side. He was proud of his "sweetheart," a 1986 white Jaguar XJ6, the first one in the CIA's parking lot. That sweetheart got him into a pickle in the early 1990s, when US authorities received a tip that a Jaguar-driving CIA officer was spying for the KGB. Palevich was investigated; the turncoat turned out to be Aldrich Ames, a former CIA counterintelligence officer who was sentenced to life in prison in 1994.

Dots on a map on the wall of John and Bonnie's condo outside Seattle show the places where Palevich recruited agents: the Middle East, the Balkans, North America, Western Europe, Latin America,

Southeast Asia, Africa. He used seven different passports and seven different names. "You have these situations where our case officers could sense that maybe a guy was a good target but they didn't have the self-confidence to reel him in, so they called me," he said. Palevich became one of the best recruiters in the agency's history. "I never had the bureaucracy," John said, noting the reams of paperwork and questionnaires that can squeeze the life out of an ordinary spy. "I had the fun."

There are as many clichés in espionage as there are spy movies. But one cliché that rang true to Palevich was the first lesson he learned at The Farm: "Never fall in love with your agent." The idea behind it was that if you weren't suspicious enough, you could be double-crossed. It also meant something else. In a life-and-death business where intelligence agencies on the Warsaw Pact side had no compunction about executing traitors, getting too close to an agent could be devastating if he or she were to be unmasked. To the Bear's enduring relief, he never lost an agent. "If I had," he said, "I don't know what I would've done."

Palevich had a great appreciation for Polish history and, partially due to his ethnic background, was deeply sympathetic to the Poles. He also respected the expertise of his Polish foes. "They were a good service," he said. "They weren't a bunch of goons like the KGB or the Bulgarians. Of course, they had baddies in internal security. But as far as foreign intelligence, their CIA types, I found them very, very decent."

Palevich described his Polish agents as lovable. One senior Polish intelligence officer whom John had recruited checked himself out of a hospital in order to make a rendezvous with John. "Talk about dedication," Palevich said.

Another Palevich recruit sympathetic to the United States was Jerzy Koryciński, a nondescript, balding man who favored Clark Kent glasses and skinny ties. Koryciński had joined Polish intelligence in the early 1960s, and from the outset his personnel file was riddled with lackluster reports. His evaluations were consistently negative and several times he almost lost his job.

When Koryciński was posted to the Polish consulate in Chicago from 1973 to 1975, he pulled a series of stunts that alarmed his bosses. He disappeared for days on end; he set his wife up with a job working for the state of Illinois; and he maintained contacts with US government officials that seemed, to his superiors, overly chummy. Plus, according to an evaluation from Intelligence Command, Koryciński basically refused to spy.

In 1975, Koryciński was recalled to Poland. Back in Warsaw, he was assigned to a team charged with analyzing the weapons industry and Western military technology just as Zacharski's gusher began to swamp Department I. He shared an office with Zdzisław Jakubczak, Zacharski's handler.

Koryciński's new boss in Warsaw tried to get him fired. "The complaints made to date against Jerzy Koryciński disqualify him as an intelligence officer and argue for his removal from the Center," he wrote. His report was ignored. In 1979, Koryciński was sent to Stockholm. He had no more success there than elsewhere and would again vanish for days.

Palevich probably recruited Koryciński in Sweden if not earlier. In January 1980, Koryciński informed Palevich that a Polish spy was operating in Los Angeles. Three years later, Koryciński and his family would defect to the United States. In all, he'd out more than one hundred Polish officers and spies.

There were reasons why Polish officers were open to working for the United States. Something intangible drew Americans and Poles together. Things worked between the two cultures, a natural fellowship, an ease of understanding. "Ameryka" was a magic word, and world, to the Poles. There was also something else. During the Cold War, as Polish historian Przemysław Gasztold has noted, the "black-and-white" narrative of the CIA on one side of the Iron Curtain and the spy services of the Warsaw Pact on the other didn't fit the complicated reality of the day. Even back then, between the American and

Polish spy agencies, there was no shortage of contact and backdoor deals.

In the 1980s, for example, the CIA bought millions of dollars of Polish weapons from the state-run Polish arms dealer CENZIN and shipped them to the Nicaraguan "contras" and the Afghan mujahideen. So, while Poland's political authorities feted Nicaragua's leftist president Daniel Ortega during a May 1985 visit to Warsaw—and cheered the Soviet Union's occupation of Afghanistan—American-backed rebels in both countries killed Communists with Polish-made guns. The CIA also purchased advanced Soviet weaponry from Polish intermediaries, allowing US weapons experts to devise countermeasures against the arsenal of Warsaw's ostensible ally, the USSR. The CIA remembered its Polish partners; when two Polish arms dealers who'd done business with the agency in the 1980s were indicted in a US weapons smuggling case in 1993, the CIA persuaded the Justice Department to drop the charges against them.

The camaraderie between spies wasn't confined to Polish defectors or collaborators. Competition between the intelligence services, although serious, was often oddly good-natured. Sometimes they even had each other's backs. In November 1979, at the height of the American hostage crisis in Iran, Polish counterintelligence filmed a CIA officer retrieving a dead drop in a Warsaw park. The dead drop, a hollow rock, contained information on Poland's air defense system. The officer was expelled but the Polish government didn't publicize the case until January 1982, a year after Iran released the last of the fifty-two hostages. The Americans had requested the Poles not give Iran any additional fodder with which to attack the United States; the Poles complied.

Around the same time, an Athens-based Polish Intelligence officer, Waldemar Markiewicz, had a problem. He wanted to know whether he should take seriously a death threat he'd received from a man who carried a Jordanian passport. Markiewicz asked Warsaw for guidance but no one replied to his urgent request. Desperate, Markiewicz approached a Polish American CIA officer named Ksawery

Wyrożemski, who because of his almost unpronounceable name was universally known as "Ski." Ski ran the Jordanian's name by Langley and learned that he was, in fact, a major financier of the Palestine Liberation Organization.

"The opportunity of being shot is not an everyday occurrence," Markiewicz noted. "Ski did his best to make sure I understood the risks." Even in the spy-v.-spy days in the systemic battle between Communism and capitalism, "we had a feeling," Markiewicz recalled, "that we could count on the Americans." Added Ski, "We just couldn't see the Poles as the bad guys."

In early 1980, Palevich passed Koryciński's tip that the Poles had a spy in Los Angeles to the FBI. The bureau had been blind to the presence of a Polish businessman at the heart of the aeronautics industry in Southern California. After searching for several months, the CIA found Zacharski in April and began surveillance. Two months later, FBI agents started tailing Bill Bell.

Zacharski notified Warsaw on May 4 that he was being followed. He responded to the surveillance in a manner that worried Department I. In Poland, he'd been taught to lose a tail. Instead, Zacharski confronted the G-men who were doing the tailing. Zacharski motioned over an FBI agent in an L.A. mall to tell him he wasn't doing a very good job. He boasted to another FBI agent, "I could leave this country in a matter of hours and you people would never know it." On November 10, 1980, at the Fox Hills Mall in Culver City, he approached FBI agent Don Ligon.

"I guess you fellows will be at my daughter's birthday party next week," Zacharski said.

"Yes," Ligon said. "We'll get her a present."

"What kind of present?" Zacharski asked.

"I don't know," Ligon said; "we don't make too much money." They ended up bringing miniature American flags to Małgosia's party at a local Burger King. Zacharski gave the agents mechanical pencils from POLAMCO in return.

"I know you guys take a tremendous amount of notes," he quipped.

Zacharski complained to the FBI that an agent had been following too close in his car. "If I brake suddenly, he's going to rear-end me and my daughter could be in the back seat," Zacharski griped. "Take him off me and I promise I'll be less difficult." The agent was removed.

Department I wasn't pleased with Zacharski's gall. His minders worried that he was cracking under the pressure of FBI surveillance. During one of Bell's trips to Europe, his Polish handler suggested that Bell stop contacting Zacharski and communicate directly with Warsaw via the *rezydent* in Chicago. Bell wasn't interested; Zacharski was his friend. In early 1981, Department I considered ordering Zacharski's ministry to pull him out of Los Angeles. All the while, more American documents wended their way to Warsaw.

Under the noses of a bevy of FBI agents, Bell took three of his four trips to Europe. Zacharski continued to bring suitcases stuffed with classified material out of L.A. The FBI had Zacharski under surveillance for more than 250 days and, throughout, Zacharski passed classified information to Poland's Intelligence Command.

Arriving on one trip to Chicago with two suitcases of classified files, Zacharski found the *rezydent* so spooked about handling the goods that he refused to touch the bags until they were safely inside a consular office in a downtown office building. Zacharski even surprised Jakubczak in Warsaw, bringing a load direct to Poland. Jakubczak told Zacharski off for having the nerve to travel to Poland without informing him beforehand. Zacharski blew up and threatened to take the files back to the United States.

Zacharski complained that his bosses were idiots. He was disgusted with what he called "talentless, vulgar drunks." A newbie to espionage, Zacharski thought he knew the business better than the pros.

CHAPTER FOUR

TRUE CONFESSIONS

At ten o'clock on Tuesday, June 23, 1981, three FBI agents arrived at Hughes Aircraft's headquarters on East Imperial Highway in El Segundo. A corporate security officer had been expecting them. He summoned Bill Bell.

The agents spoke with Bell for two hours at Hughes, then suggested lunch. Bell agreed. After sandwiches at a deli, they asked Bell to accompany them to a room at the Holiday Inn on Century Boulevard where they could talk more. Bell agreed again. The agents interrogated Bell throughout the afternoon. It was all very civil and businesslike.

Special Agent James Reid showed Bell a translation of a Polish newspaper article on a Polish diplomat assigned to the United Nations in New York who'd defected to the United States. Reid claimed that the defector had given the FBI details on Polish intelligence activities in the United States.

"Did he mention me?" Bell asked. Without waiting for an answer, Bell said, "This is very serious. I would like to talk with an attorney."

Reid suggested a public defender or a private lawyer. Bell then slumped in his chair and announced, "I did it. I do not need an attorney."

"We know everything," Special Agent James R. Pace replied.

In fact, the bureau didn't know much. They might have known that the UN diplomat who was the subject of the Polish article wasn't actually the source of any information about Bell. They definitely didn't know that the real source was Palevich's agent, Koryciński, because the CIA kept these details to itself. Indeed, ever since the CIA was formed during World War II as the Office of Strategic Services, it'd maintained a testy relationship with the FBI. The two organizations competed bitterly and cooperated poorly. The FBI was appalled at what it saw as the CIA's bad judgment in operations around the world; CIA officers called FBI agents "cops."

The same held true in the Zacharski case. After 250 days of surveillance, FBI agents had gathered hardly any evidence to prove that espionage had taken place and, after Palevich's tip, the CIA had provided nothing more. While the bureau had been playing cat and mouse with Bell and Zacharski, the pair had boarded airplanes with reams of classified documents that they spirited behind the Iron Curtain—via Chicago, Geneva, and Vienna or direct to Warsaw. Talk about slamming the barn door shut after the horse had bolted. And the FBI had barely enough to bring Bell in.

The FBI's decision to interrogate Bell appears to have been prompted less by evidence than by word that Zacharski had gotten a promotion and would soon be leaving L.A. While he was masterminding an intelligence collection operation on a massive scale, at PO-LAMCO Zacharski had also churned out $30 million a year in sales. He'd been promoted to president of the company and the family was relocating back to chilly Illinois.

The FBI interrogators were lucky that their gambit to break Bell paid off. The only way to explain their success, one participant later acknowledged, was that Bell was "weak." On the same afternoon that he was first questioned, Bell dictated a six-page confession.

Done at five in the afternoon, the agents accompanied Bell back to his office, where he handed them a red notebook that contained lists of the documents that the Poles had requested. Then they went to Bell's apartment to retrieve more files, along with a camera and film. By the late evening, they were back at the Holiday Inn, where Bell signed his confession. The agents told Bell that in exchange for his cooperation they would recommend a lighter sentence. Bell handed over twenty-two gold coins that he'd stored in a safe deposit box at a Bank of America branch.

A federal prosecutor was brought in. Reviewing the evidence, US Attorney Robert Brewer, a former army captain and Vietnam vet, was unimpressed. What if Bell was mentally disturbed or just making stuff up, he wondered. To build a decent case, Brewer determined, Bell would have to wear a wire and record Zacharski implicating himself.

Three days after their initial hello, the FBI brought Bell to a room in the Brentwood Motor Inn. There a FBI technician Velcro'ed a one-pound tape recorder to Bell's back with wires running down his limbs. In those days it was state-of-the-art, yet it felt like a Rube Goldberg contraption. Bell worried that it was going to fall apart. "I hope this damn thing works," he was recorded saying to no one in particular as he fumbled with the machine.

Bell spent the night at home at Cross Creek Apartments, trying to sleep with the device appended to his back. The next day, Bell came to Zacharski's door three times. Finally, at 9:20 in the evening, Zacharski answered. He steered Bell onto the second-floor landing. "The bloody guys are all over me," Zacharski complained. Bell tried to lead the conversation in an incriminating direction. "Didn't I get you that secret. . . . What was it? Secret F-15 data?" Bill asked. "Partially, I guess. Yeah," Zacharski responded.

The next day, Sunday, Bell returned the recorder to the FBI and was formally arrested. That afternoon, a dozen FBI agents led a phalanx of TV and print reporters to Zacharski's door. Zacharski was home with Basia and their daughters. The agents rolled into his apartment, ordered that nothing be touched, and escorted Zacharski out in handcuffs: a perp walk the likes of which Cross Creek Apartments had never seen. Zacharski was denied bail and locked in the maximum-security section of the Federal Correctional Institution at Terminal Island.

Several days later, Zacharski and Bell were arraigned at the First Street Courthouse in downtown L.A. They spent a few minutes in a holding cell together. Bell cowered in a corner like a child, staring at Zacharski with tears in his eyes. Zacharski walked over to him. "Bill, they know nothing," Zacharski said. "Bill, Bill, let's shake. I am your friend." From jail, Bell called his contact at the *Burbank Daily Review* and urged him to find a publisher for his novel so he could pay his legal fees. There were no takers.

The trial of *United States v. Marian Zacharski* began on October 13, 1981. It marked a rare prosecution of an Eastern European intelligence agent on US soil. Most other cases had ended with expulsions. But the United States had a new president, Ronald Reagan, who wanted to be seen as tougher on Communism than his predecessor, Jimmy Carter. Zacharski made a good target. As a businessman, he had no diplomatic immunity. He was what is known as an "illegal." Judge David Kenyon, a longtime Hollywood attorney whom Carter had appointed to the federal bench, presided.

Robert Brewer was the ideal prosecutor. In Vietnam, he'd been involved in highly classified missions so he was comfortable when Department of Justice officials told him that many of the details of the case had to remain secret—in particular its genesis: the defection of Jerzy Koryciński. The Justice Department sent out John Dion, the head of its counterintelligence section, a standoffish presence who worried Brewer initially. As Brewer noted, Dion was "aware of so many facts in this case that he, (a) can't tell me about, and (b) can't tell me that he can't tell me about." Dion turned out to be a tremendous asset, offering expert counsel as Brewer sought to fashion a workable prosecution out of the evidentiary slim pickings provided by the FBI.

When Brewer heard Bell's tape, he realized it was a thin reed on which to build his case. "God, it's not as good as I had hoped," he remembered thinking. As *60 Minutes* and other nationwide TV news shows clamored for a piece of the story, Brewer began to have the waking nightmare of a prosecutor as his high-profile case wobbled toward collapse. The FBI agents worried Brewer. "They were bad," he recalled. "They had no concept of the rules of evidence, of the pressure of a trial. Of proving a case beyond a reasonable doubt. And they were terrible witnesses." Brewer did, however, have an ally: history.

Zacharski's trial unspooled against a backdrop in the United States of increasing fears of the Soviet threat. Two espionage cases had recently erupted: a first lieutenant in the air force who'd worked on the Intercontinental Ballistic Missile program had pleaded guilty to spying for the USSR, as had a warrant officer at the US embassy in Paris. Just days before the trial began, Egypt's leader, Anwar Sadat, a bulwark against Russian influence in the Middle East, had been assassinated. Then there was the internal situation in Zacharski's homeland. Even casual readers of newspapers at the time could not escape news about Communist Poland. Since August 1980, Poland had been rocked by strikes that would soon lead to the creation of the independent Solidarity trade union. Solidarity would mount the most serious challenge to Moscow's domination of Eastern Europe since 1968's "Prague Spring," when Czech leader Alexander Dubček's modest attempt to attain "socialism with a human face" was met with a Soviet invasion. Just a month before Zacharski's trial commenced, Edward Gierek, Poland's Communist leader, had been purged from the Polish United Workers' Party because of the economic crisis and the resulting mass protests.

On October 13, 1981, the day the trial commenced, the local daily, the *Los Angeles Times*, ran a front-page story in which Polish farmers accused their Communist overlords of being worse than their Nazi occupiers during World War II. Five days later, a soldier, Minister of Defense and General Wojciech Jaruzelski, was appointed chief of

Poland's Communist party. Jaruzelski's ramrod posture, bald pate, and dark glasses became an internationally caricatured symbol of Communist intolerance. Outside Poland, Solidarity's foreign affiliates staged rallies and marshaled international public opinion. In L.A., potential jurors at Zacharski's trial were asked if they cracked Polish jokes, had heard of Frédéric Chopin, or knew the nationality of Polish pope John Paul II.

Zacharski's defense attorney, Edward Stadum, noted in his opening remarks that this case differed from other espionage cases "in which people have been caught entering the Soviet embassy in Mexico City with a microfilm in their pockets." Basically, he argued, there was no proof. Other than a few murmurings by Zacharski on the tape, he was right. Still, Stadum felt that the weight of current events—specifically, the increasing exposure of Poland as an international bad actor—had already determined the outcome. "It was," he later said, "like arguing against an oncoming steamroller."

Brewer called forty-eight witnesses and did his best to make a case based on the flimsy evidence provided by the FBI. Bill Bell spent several days on the stand, admitting guilt and fingering Zacharski. Brewer wasn't shy about venturing some courtroom razzle-dazzle. Brewer had Major General Richard Larkin, the former head of the Defense Intelligence Agency, testify in full dress uniform although Larkin had already retired, On November 16, the jury found Zacharski guilty of conspiring with Bell to obtain and deliver national defense documents.

At the sentencing hearing, on December 15, Judge Kenyon addressed defendant Marian Zacharski from the bench. For the defense, the timing could not have been worse. Two days earlier in Poland, General Jaruzelski, declaring that "our homeland is at the edge of an abyss," had imposed martial law and had ordered the arrests of thousands of Solidarity activists.

While an audience of men and women waiting to be sworn in as US citizens looked on, Kenyon told Zacharski that the United States "will not tolerate spies." Zacharski believed his case was being used to warn those in line to become Americans—"Don't become spies!"—and send a message to Poland, too. Kenyon then sentenced Zacharski to life in prison. Figuring that he'd probably be exchanged at some point, Zacharski didn't appeal. Basia and the two girls returned to Poland. A week later, President Reagan devoted his Christmas address from the Oval Office to the martial law crackdown in Poland. He urged Americans to place a candle in their windows as a sign of support for the Poles.

At the Federal Correctional Institution in Memphis, Zacharski, now Prisoner No. 73820–012, was visited on occasion by FBI Special Agent James Reid, who tried to convince Zacharski to defect. He showed Zacharski a paper signed by the president. "The only thing missing was the number of millions they were going to pay me to talk," Zacharski claimed. "I didn't sign."

In late October 1984, in the middle of Zacharski's third year in prison, Reid vowed that Zacharski was never getting out. "We never negotiate with people who kill priests," he told No. 73820–012, even though Reid was there to do exactly that: negotiate. The reference was to Jerzy Popiełuszko, a Roman Catholic priest who'd been murdered by Polish secret police earlier that month. "Why are you such a patriot?" Reid asked. "I don't have the genes of a traitor," Zacharski replied.

Zacharski's case made waves throughout the American national security establishment; his refusal to flip only added to his élan. In a speech, then FBI director William Webster labeled Zacharski's exploits "a textbook example of espionage." Over the next few years, numerous confidential US government reports lauded Zacharski's tradecraft. The Defense Department called him "a skilled salesman and master persuader and well-equipped for his task." A congressional report praised Zacharski for his "extreme caution and practiced subtlety." The Senate's Select Committee on Intelligence observed that a focus on Bill Bell's credulity "can lead us to ignore Zacharski's skill." An unnamed "federal spy hunter" called Zacharski a "real pro."

US Senate investigators were less professional than Zacharski. They concluded, incorrectly, that Zacharski had been involved with Polish Intelligence from the start. They claimed that Zacharski came to the United States "fitted with suitable camouflage" of a salesman. No one seemed to realize that he was an accidental agent. In the assessment of America's intelligence community, Marian Zacharski was a superspy.

Zacharski's prosecution came to a head in Los Angeles just as another spy faced his own life-and-death crisis in faraway Warsaw. Ryszard Kukliński, the aforementioned Polish army colonel and asset for the CIA, was in danger of being outed and needed to flee Poland. In early November 1980, just as Judge Kenyon was preparing to sentence Zacharski, Kukliński's American handlers packed him, his wife, and their two sons up in a car, covered them with rugs and Christmas presents, and drove them across Communist Poland and East Germany to safety in the West. In 1984, a Polish military court sentenced Kukliński to death in absentia. His crimes: treason and desertion.

At the CIA, the exploits of both men reinforced an image of the excellence of Polish spies; both were seen as courageous, creative, bold, and professional despite the fact that Zacharski served the Warsaw Pact and Kukliński was, as the great Polish American strategist and former national security advisor Zbigniew Brzeziński put it, "the first Polish officer in NATO." One had spied *for* Poland out of a love of adventure. The other had spied *on* Poland out of a love of Poland. Still, in the minds of many CIA officers and among many Poles, as well, the fates of these two agents became intertwined.

At the CIA, John Palevich reviewed Zacharski's case files and was deeply impressed. Zacharski had worked alone as an "illegal" without diplomatic immunity, thousands of miles from a Polish mission. He had an instinctive feel for espionage and, in the Pole, John saw a reflection of his younger self. "He was on his own for years. There wasn't anyone giving him any guidance. He did it himself,"

Palevich said. The pair were connected in another way. Palevich had always befriended his agents; the same was true for Zacharski with Bill Bell. "If we hadn't had a source, he would've gotten away with everything," Palevich noted. "He had excellent tradecraft, really, really impressive." Palevich promised himself that if the opportunity presented itself, one day he would like to work with, not against, the likes of Marian Zacharski.

CHAPTER FIVE

THE BRIDGE OF SPIES

Inside Warsaw's Intelligence Command, Zacharski's reputation was less stellar than it was in the United States. Once FBI surveillance began, Zacharski's handler, Jakubczak, insisted that Zacharski become "passive" but Zacharski taunted the FBI instead. His minders ordered him to leave the United States but he ignored them. Now Zacharski had been sentenced to life.

Zacharski's comrades were split over the results of his espionage. Some were convinced that the materials were fake and that the Americans were running what the Soviets called a *dezinformatsiya* campaign, designed to make US military technology appear more imposing than it actually was. By far the most intriguing, if not far-fetched, theory was postulated by Zbigniew Twerd, the deputy head of the US Desk at Polish Counterintelligence at the time. "There was no doubt that it was all authentic," he said of Zacharski's haul. However, Twerd believed that the FBI preyed on Zacharski's inexperience to conduct "a strategic provocation," an elaborate game to deliberately hand over genuine

American military secrets to spook Soviet experts and lead the USSR into an economically debilitating arms race. "The Americans knew that if they showed the Russians how much they'd achieved, they'd give them a fright," Twerd said. "The objective was to force Moscow to raise defense expenditures at the expense of other things. In this way, the Soviet Union's internal stability could be affected. And it worked." Twerd said the Keystone Cops aspect of the FBI's investigation was a telltale sign that the case was a setup. The Americans left the barn door open on purpose, he argued. "It is hard to believe that errors so laughable were really made," he said of the FBI's handling of the case. Twerd's theory displayed a typical Eastern Bloc view of American intelligence operations that assumed the omniscient US services could do no wrong.

Inside prison, Zacharski's life was hard. When *60 Minutes* aired a segment on his case in March 1982, just a few months into his jail term, an inmate approached him at lunch and muttered, "If I wasn't going to leave in a few days, you'd be dead." Zacharski tried to associate only with those who were convicted of nonviolent offenses: white-collar criminals, drug dealers, grifters, and check kiters. "But it wasn't easy," he said. Visitors from the Polish consulate in Chicago advised him to ignore the many petty slights he faced. Longtime State Department official John Kornblum recalled that the bad treatment was by design. "The FBI threw him in the worst prison they could find, filled with murderers and rapists, and no air conditioning," he said. "They hated him."

In his spare time, Zacharski tried to keep fit but he ended up losing more than seventy pounds. He studied Spanish and books on flying. On June 12, 1983, Zacharski's father, Wacław, died. There was, of course, no question of this affecting his sentence. FBI agents continued to press Zacharski to defect and offered no promises that he would ever be exchanged. While he sat in federal prison, as a way to lift his spirits and show that he'd been forgiven for mishandling the FBI, Polish Intelligence Command formally commissioned Zacharski as an officer of Department I.

For Zacharski, hope arrived in the form of another bungled American operation. In the early 1980s, a US Army intelligence cell outside Frankfurt came up with the rather Monty Python-esque idea of giving cameras and $500 to West German sources who traveled back and forth between East and West Germany on family visits. US Army officers asked the Germans to snap pictures of Warsaw Pact military installations and troop movements. Inside East Germany, however, agents from its feared Stasi secret service arrested them as soon as they took out their cameras. Within weeks, some twenty West German citizens were facing espionage charges in East German jails.

Rozanne Ridgway, then a high-ranking State Department official, was livid that so many people had been put at such risk. In 1983, after she was confirmed as US ambassador to East Germany, negotiations began via an East German lawyer, Wolfgang Vogel, to secure their release. Talks continued for a year until the Soviets, pressured by Warsaw, made freedom for Marian Zacharski a condition of the deal. The Justice Department and the FBI, however, didn't want to let Zacharski go.

The decision went all the way to the White House. Helmut Schmidt, who'd recently stepped down as Germany's chancellor, lobbied Secretary of State George Shultz in favor of the swap. Defense Secretary Caspar Weinberger opposed it, as did the Department of Justice. The Americans pushed the Soviets to include two prominent dissidents, Andrei Sakharov and Natan Sharansky, in the exchange. Moscow didn't agree. (They'd be released later.) Finally, President Reagan decided to allow Zacharski to walk free in exchange for the West Germans, minus their cameras. Reagan granted Zacharski executive clemency on June 7, 1985, and commuted his sentence to time served.

In Memphis, Zacharski had little inkling of what was transpiring until Wolfgang Vogel, the East German lawyer, visited him. On June 10, federal marshals arrived at Zacharski's cell and told him to collect his things. He knew he was going home when they reminded him to make sure he had his passport. Zacharski was escorted to a room filled with secondhand clothes and told to pick something. Zacharski chose jeans. After an hour, he was told to return the jeans and pick out a suit. The only pants he could find were too short and the shoes were three sizes too big. He looked like a clown.

From Memphis, Zacharski boarded a plane for New York. The next afternoon, after a night in the Metropolitan Correctional Center in downtown Manhattan, Zacharski was taken to McGuire Air Force Base, outside Trenton, New Jersey. He was placed in chains, hands and feet, and escorted onto a waiting C-5 Galaxy. Eight hours later, at two thirty in the morning local time, after one toilet break, a stale sandwich, and cup of room-temperature orangeade, Zacharski landed at Ramstein Air Base in West Germany. For the next two hours, he sat on a weight-lifting bench in a racquetball court next to the runway.

Among the dozens of Department of Justice and State Department types accompanying Zacharski from the United States, one man stood out. He was tall, burly, and silent. "He stared at me throughout the flight, looking straight into my eyes. When we got to Germany in the middle of the night, and he saw that I was thirsty and hungry, I am sure it was he who arranged for a coffee," Zacharski recalled. What a strange guy, Zacharski thought. "Every occasion that our faces met there was nothing but eye contact," he said. Zacharski made a note to include a description of this man in his report to Intelligence Command.

The silent traveler was John Palevich, the CIA's representative to the exchange. John was banned from speaking with Zacharski unless Zacharski made it known that he wanted to defect. As this was an official prisoner exchange, Palevich was traveling under his real name and didn't want it casually revealed to a Polish spy.

At Ramstein, Palevich, Zacharski, and the rest of the crew switched to a Hercules for the short flight to Berlin. From the airport they traveled in vans to the Glienicke Bridge, the Bridge of Spies, that spanned the Havel River. The bridge had first been used in 1962 to exchange U-2 spy plane pilot Gary Powers for Soviet agent Rudolf Abel.

The bridge was the only crossing into East Germany where the Soviets maintained a permanent presence. The USSR had a facility there and always flew a flag. The United States was loath to deal with the East German authorities; in fact, the US government had only recognized East Germany's existence in 1974, following West Germany's lead. The Glienicke Bridge was chosen because it provided a place where Americans could liaise directly with the Soviets and pretend East Germany didn't exist.

Scores of journalists had been milling around the bridge since early morning to cover the exchange. Temperatures were in the sixties with a slight breeze. Zacharski arrived to the staccato sound of clicking cameras. While the Justice and State Department guys played it up for the publicity, Palevich's chief concern was to avoid appearing in any of the pictures. He succeeded. Palevich got a video of the event and passed it up the chain. President Reagan had asked to see it.

The prisoner swap took place at noon on June 11. Four Eastern Europeans—Zacharski, a Bulgarian secret service officer, an East German spy, and an elderly courier—were exchanged for twenty-five individuals whom US officials, to avoid exposing details of the ill-conceived photography escapade, described as "friendly to the United States." Four Poles crossed into the West. Among them was Zacharski's old office mate, Leszek Chróst, who'd been sentenced to twenty-five years for spying for the United States.

Arriving on the other side of the Iron Curtain, Zacharski was hailed as a hero. The next evening the Polish embassy in East Berlin held a reception in his honor, attended by fabled East German foreign intelligence chief Marcus Wolf, the Cold War spymaster known in the West as "the man without a face." The festivities continued in Warsaw, where Communist party boss Jaruzelski's right-hand man, Minister of Interior Czesław Kiszczak, welcomed Zacharski home. Writing to Jaruzelski, Zacharski gushed that the day he crossed the Bridge of Spies "was the happiest day of my life." Zacharski pledged to fight for the security of "the motherland, People's Poland." His greatest desire, he wrote, was to "lay my small brick in the foundation of this honorable goal."

Zacharski returned to a Poland racked with social, economic, and political turmoil. Jaruzelski's regime had lifted martial law in 1983 but in

June 1985 hundreds of political prisoners remained in jail. On the economic front, abandoning fealty to socialist ideology and desperately trying to improve living standards, the Communist party introduced modest market-oriented reforms. The number of private businesses jumped, but the entrepreneurial bustle failed to offset the collapse of lumbering state-owned firms. Interest payments on Poland's ballooning foreign debt swallowed up the nation's limited cache of foreign currency. Rationing and long lines for everything from meat to vegetables to toilet paper became a fixture of life. Still, Zacharski seemed proud to be an officially recognized hero in a country where everyday heroes were behind bars.

Zacharski had hoped to be named president of the Polish airline, LOT. Instead, he was offered a job as a junior executive at Pewex, a retail chain that had a monopoly on selling goods like stereos, video cameras, cigarettes, and wine, imported from the capitalist world. Zacharski tried wielding his Yankee business acumen to jazz things up at Pewex's drab outlets. "This is not America," one board member snapped at a meeting. "It's a pity," Zacharski shot back, "because we have to make it into America."

In the summer of 1986, Minister Kiszczak sent a cable to Polish spies in the United States, asking what the Polish government could do to ease American pressure on Warsaw. US economic sanctions that had been slapped on Poland in 1981 with the onset of martial law were still in place. Krzysztof Smoleński was the *rezydent* in Chicago at the time. "The answer was simple," he recalled. "Release all political prisoners and begin talks with Solidarity."

In September, Kiszczak emptied the jails of the remaining political prisoners and loosened some restrictions on freedom of speech. The Jaruzelski regime didn't officially legalize the opposition but, when Solidarity resumed organizing, Kiszczak's secret police didn't crack down. At the CIA, analysts labeled these gambits "Poland's American offensive." To a certain extent, the offensive worked.

Following the prisoner release, President Reagan lifted US

economic sanctions and Poland rejoined the World Bank and International Monetary Fund. Solidarity's leader, the charismatic, walrus-mustachioed shipyard worker from Gdańsk Lech Wałęsa, pronounced 1986 the "turning point" in Poland's quest for freedom. "While the government was still baring its teeth," he observed, "those teeth were already showing numerous signs of decay."

After relaxing sanctions, the Reagan administration leaned on the Polish government to help the United States achieve some of its policy goals. One involved international terrorism. Like other Eastern European countries, the Polish People's Republic had cultivated a cozy relationship with Arab militant groups. Polish military intelligence was particularly close to the Abu Nidal Organization (ANO), a radical Palestinian group that competed with the more mainstream PLO.

Since the 1970s, Polish weapons had been turning up in terrorist attacks across Europe linked to Abu Nidal: a submachine gun in a series of assaults on Syrian diplomatic missions in Europe in 1976; a pistol linked to the murder of a prominent Austrian Jew in May 1981; another submachine gun at a rampage on a Jewish restaurant in Paris in August 1982 that killed six. The ANO was also responsible for terrorist attacks that had killed Americans in Rome, Vienna, and Karachi.

The CIA learned that Abu Nidal himself had decamped to Poland in the early 1980s to recuperate after heart surgery. ANO operatives studied at Polish universities. Samir Najmeddin, the head of the ANO's financial wing, established a business in Warsaw, the SAS Investment Trading Company, that made hefty profits marketing more than $100 million in Polish weapons to regimes in the Middle East. Abu Nidal himself had reportedly deposited $10 million in a Polish bank.

The Poles initially denied US charges that Poland was aiding and abetting terrorists. Then they flipped. During a visit to Warsaw by then vice president George H. W. Bush in September 1987, Jaruzelski acknowledged the connection and agreed to sever it. But progress was slow. By all accounts Samir Najmeddin was still in Poland as late as November 1989.

None of these baby steps in an improving relationship with Washington would've been possible without changes in Poland's overlord, the USSR. There a transformation was underway. On March 10, 1985, Konstantin Chernenko became the third Soviet Communist Party leader to die in office in four years. His passing paved the way for a younger generation of Communists, led by Mikhail Gorbachev, who took the reins of power a day after Chernenko died. Gorbachev believed that reforms were essential to save the Soviet system. Accelerating after the Chernobyl nuclear disaster in April 1986, Gorbachev launched the policies of glasnost, to relax restrictions on speech, and perestroika, to decentralize economic decision-making. Gorbachev embarked on a series of summits with President Reagan and ordered Soviet troops out of Afghanistan. Liberal winds from Moscow reverberated across the Eastern Bloc.

At the CIA, Director William Casey called on his analysts to consider what Eastern Europe might look like if the USSR failed to stop the changes in Poland and elsewhere. "One threshold after another in Poland has been crossed and the Soviets have been unable to bring themselves to pay the costs of halting Polish liberalization," Casey observed in a memo to the National Foreign Assessment Center on May 4, 1987.

Casey noted that there remained a chance, "and perhaps a good one," that Communists would resume their crackdowns. Throughout martial law, the shock troops of Poland's Ministry of Interior, motorcycle-riding, leather-clad toughs called ZOMO, had been notorious for their brutality. Scores of Poles had died at the hands of the SB. But the Soviets had yet to get directly involved. Casey called on his analysts to consider the possibility that the Soviet Union was going to stand aside. "With each passing day," he noted, "the cost of intervention rises even further." What would the world look like, Casey asked, if the USSR and its Polish minions let the changes unfold?

Within Department I, Poland's Foreign Intelligence officers were pondering the same question. They, too, sensed that a transformation was coming, but they were divided over how to react. Some defected.

"We are observing many cases of betrayals and refusals to return to the country," read one report from Intelligence Command. Others continued to hold desperately to the catechism of the Warsaw Pact: that Poland could only find security in the arms of Mother USSR. But a growing number of them, especially the ones who'd been posted in the West, began to advocate, at first quietly and then with increasing confidence, that the job of Polish intelligence was no longer to protect socialism but rather to ensure the security of the Polish state. Thus did they embark on the road to blasphemy—the first sin being doubts about the benefits of Poland's continued loyalty to the Soviets.

Hailing from a family of farmers, Krzysztof Smoleński, Department I's man in Chicago, had joined Foreign Intelligence in 1974 after taking classes at two colleges, an unproductive foray as a math teacher, and a year as a cop. An evaluation from Foreign Intelligence noted that he was soft-spoken, highly strung, skinny, and prone to ulcers. It found him not particularly intelligent, with a "low cultural level." On the plus side, Smoleński was also "more than normally perceptive." Apparently, Smoleński's superiors didn't take into account the possibility that before joining Foreign Intelligence, he might've been bored. Soon after he entered Department I, his evaluations improved and by the time he was posted to Chicago he was running at least nine agents in the United States. Intelligence Command tagged him as "a model intelligence officer."

Smoleński had been in the Midwest since 1985. He'd prepared to serve as the main contact for the imprisoned Zacharski but then Zacharski was exchanged. Before Chicago, Smoleński had been posted to Canada, also as a diplomat assigned to cultivate Americans. Living for years in North America, it was clear to him that Poland had no option but to transform itself into a freer, more open place. In Poland, Smoleński's friends and relatives had to line up to eat. In the West, there was an abundance of every possible material good. That obvious difference said a lot about the relative strength of the two systems.

The FBI did its best to make Smoleński's life miserable. Three months after Smoleński took over the Chicago station, the US government warned the Polish embassy that it would expel Smoleński if he didn't stop his "illegal activities."

On February 8, 1989, the FBI tried to recruit him. On a flight from Chicago to Las Vegas, Smoleński found himself sitting next to an FBI counterintelligence officer. The officer revealed that the recruitment operation was being carried out in conjunction with the CIA. Smoleński declined the offer. But after landing in Las Vegas, Smoleński asked the FBI agent to pass a message of encouragement to the CIA. "Knock on the door of Polish Intelligence when the time is right," he said. Eventually, the CIA would come knocking—not to recruit a single agent but to recruit the whole service.

"We felt that without dramatic change in Poland, we'd be in real trouble," Smoleński recalled. At the same time, the presence of tens of thousands of Soviet troops and Soviet nuclear weapons on Polish soil was a constant reminder that Poland remained an occupied nation. "It was," Smoleński observed with typical reserve, "a very delicate game."

As crises brewed in Poland and in the USSR, Poles knew that in its centuries-long search for security, their homeland had been playing—and often losing—this "delicate game." Awareness of this tragic history and of Poland's place in the world informed the psychology of Poland's spies.

Take geography. Poland's great forests and rivers, broad plains, and manifold lakes cannot mask the fact that the nation sits on a well-trod invasion route, as welcoming to cavalry in the eighteenth century as to tanks in the twentieth. Most of the country is flat, with an average elevation of six hundred feet above sea level. Barely 3 percent of the land exceeds fifteen hundred feet. Unlike mountainous Switzerland, there are no natural barriers to a conquering horde. Little wonder God's Playground is the title of the leading history of Poland in the English language.

Then there was politics. Every Pole knew that Poland's constitution of 1791 was Europe's first. The ruling houses of Poland's imperial neighbors feared its democratic ideas and responded by attacking the young republic, splitting it in three. Poland stayed divided until the end of World War I in 1918, when it won its independence at the Paris Peace Conference. But a mere two years later, Vladimir Lenin, the head of the newly formed Soviet government, ordered the invasion of Poland in an attempt to export world revolution to the rest of Europe. Miraculously, Polish forces beat the Red Army as it massed along the eastern banks of the Vistula River overlooking Warsaw. One Soviet officer, Josef Stalin, never forgot that ignominious defeat; he was the chief political commissar on the Red Army's southwestern front.

Poland's victory in 1920 was called "the miracle on the Vistula," but Polish spies knew that espionage played a role. From the first days of independence in 1918, Poland's government had devoted time and money to building a professional intelligence service with two main targets: Russia and Germany. In 1920, Polish ciphers broke Soviet codes, allowing them to pinpoint the positions of Soviet forces, which led to Stalin's mortifying retreat. A decade later, a team of Polish mathematicians built their own Enigma machine and began decoding German cable traffic. In 1939, Polish spies supplied allies France and Britain with copies of that machine, without which England wouldn't have succeeded in cracking Germany's codes during World War II.

Poles knew that Poland's history had long been determined in foreign capitals. So it was again on August 23, 1939, in Moscow when German foreign minister Joachim von Ribbentrop and his Soviet counterpart, Vyacheslav Molotov, signed a pact to partition Poland. Poland disappeared in 1939, with the Nazi blitzkrieg from the west on September 1 followed by the Soviet invasion from the east sixteen days later. "The Polish state and its government have virtually ceased to exist," Molotov declared in a statement carried by the Soviet news agency TASS.

Over the course of World War II, divided between Russia and Germany, Poland lost almost 20 percent of its population, the highest percentage of any nation in the war. About six million people, including three million Jews, died of disease, in massacres, in combat, and in concentration camps—Auschwitz, Treblinka, Birkenau, and others—run by the Nazis. Poland lost all its minorities: Jews in the Holocaust and Ukrainians and Germans due to shifting borders and massive population transfers. Polish society was decimated. One-third of all urban residents were listed as missing. Fifty-five percent of all lawyers, forty percent of doctors, one-third of university professors and Catholic clergy were killed. Soviet authorities executed some twenty-two thousand Polish army officers and leading intellectuals, burying them in mass graves in the Katyn Forest of western Russia. Still, Poles kept alive the flame of their nation. They fought valiantly—in the air during the Battle of Britain and on land in Italy. Poland's Warsaw Uprising in September 1944 that resulted in the death of two hundred thousand Poles constituted the largest mass action against the Nazis in the war. Some of the earliest intelligence received on the Nazi genocide of the Jews came from Polish resistance fighter Jan Karski.

As the war drew to a close, Poles pinned their faith on the inherent justice of the world, the ideals of President Franklin D. Roosevelt, and the moral influence of the great democracies of the United States and Britain. "Poland is the inspiration of the world," FDR had said at the height of Poland's suffering. Many Poles took this to be a commitment that when the war was over Poland wouldn't be treated as an expendable pawn in a game played with the USSR.

But it was. At the Yalta Conference of February 1945, Roosevelt and Churchill abandoned Poland into the Soviet sphere of influence. Stalin argued that the USSR had to be repaid for its losses, which in truth—some twenty-six million dead—were huge. Roosevelt needed Russia in the Pacific fight against Japan. America's atomic bomb was as yet unproven. FDR and Churchill made half-hearted efforts to ensure democracy in Poland. But those efforts were in vain.

In September 1939, Poland had been the first victim of World War II to stand up to the Nazis. In April 1945, Poland became the first victim of the Cold War. That month, when representatives of fifty-one nations gathered in San Francisco to establish the United Nations, Poland's flag wasn't among them because the Soviets refused to allow

Poland to participate. The Polish-born pianist Artur Rubinstein, performing at the UN's inaugural, was so outraged by the exclusion of his homeland that he played Poland's national anthem, "Poland Is Not Yet Lost," to thunderous applause.

At the Potsdam Conference during the summer of 1945, Churchill and President Harry Truman, who had succeeded the late FDR, recognized Stalin's puppet regime in Poland. They also signed off on changes that shrank Poland's territory by 20 percent. Poland lost a strip two hundred miles wide on its eastern flank while its western border was pushed miles into what had been Germany.

The shifting borders precipitated a population transfer of catastrophic proportions. Twelve million people, including Germans, Poles, Ukrainians, and other groups, were forced to move. Breslau had been the third-biggest city in the German Reich. It became Wrocław. All seven hundred thousand of its German inhabitants moved to Germany, while Poles from Lviv, which was given to Ukraine, were uprooted and transported west to take their place. Same for the Prussian port city of Stettin, which became Szczecin. It lost four hundred thousand Germans, replaced by Poles from Vilnius, which was made capital of the Lithuanian Soviet Socialist Republic. Issues of German sovereignty and permanently fixing Poland's borders were left for the future.

Poland's Communist government used fears of German revanchism to generate support for a forced alliance with Moscow. Poles were taught to distrust West Germany and to believe that, if given the chance, a unified Germany would seek to reclaim the territory it had lost. Even after Poland and West Germany signed the Treaty of Warsaw in 1970, in which Bonn accepted the existing border, powerful German political interests, representing German expellees, continued to assert that the territories that Germany had ceded to Poland would one day be returned. So while Gorbachev's rise to power in Moscow potentially presaged more freedom in Poland, it also forced Polish strategists and spies to be sensitive to any sign that the Soviet Union and Germany, in a repeat of 1939, were negotiating behind Poland's back.

PART TWO

AN UNLIKELY ALLIANCE

CHAPTER SIX

PLAYING FOOTSIE

Andrzej Derlatka was one of the brainier officers in Poland's Foreign Intelligence. Smarts and an almost perfectly round head sitting atop a medium build won him the nickname "Globus." Derlatka had gone to the University of Warsaw wanting to study history but had fixed on law because with a law degree he could find a job. Still, he believed that his appreciation of history could animate his work and help Poland find safety in a dangerous neighborhood. A German speaker, Derlatka joined Foreign Intelligence in 1980. He'd been working undercover as a diplomat in the Netherlands when a Polish defector fingered him as an intelligence officer and he was called home in June 1988.

Captain Derlatka returned to Warsaw to find the political ground shifting under his feet. A wave of strikes that summer hit a dozen coal mines, Poland's two biggest ports, and its largest steel mill, threatening to bring the economy to a standstill. Faced with a determined resistance and a collapse of will within Communist ranks, the party decided to open talks with the opposition. CIA director Casey's musings were coming to life; neither the Soviets nor Poland's Communists could bring themselves to stand in the way of history.

On August 31, Minister of Interior Czesław Kiszczak met with Solidarity leader Lech Wałęsa to discuss political reforms. US ambassador John Davis, who'd served three tours in Poland, played a key role in bringing the two sides together. During the summer of 1988, Davis hosted quiet soirées between Solidarity and Communist officials at his residence. It was there that influential dissidents got to know their jailers. Davis was so deeply involved in pushing talks that at one point Jaruzelski quipped: "There is no Solidarity. It's just a group of people Davis keeps inviting over to dinner."

Beginning in February 1989, representatives from the opposition and the government gathered at a holiday resort in Magdalenka near Warsaw to undertake long and painful preparations for the historic Round Table negotiations. Those talks would spell the end of Communism in Poland and set an example for the rest of Eastern Europe, too.

During this time, Foreign Intelligence had assigned Derlatka to Department I's Section XII, which specialized in disinformation, media manipulation, and analysis. It was a dead-end job, a punishment of sorts. In addition to having been outed as a spy, Derlatka had returned home under a cloud. His boss, the *rezydent* in The Hague, had been a drunk and Derlatka hadn't been shy about chiding him for coming to work sloshed. The *rezydent* exacted revenge by inserting a lousy evaluation into Derlatka's file.

Derlatka assumed that, with political changes coming, he would soon be out of work. "Some people were waiting to see what was going to happen but not me," he said. "I was convinced that I had no future in intelligence. I'd received a bad evaluation and I'd been exposed." Derlatka started studying English during office hours as he prepared for life after government service. At thirty-five, he figured he was still young enough to have a second career.

At work, while learning English, Derlatka read Western

newspapers, which were kept from ordinary Poles but open to analysts in Department I. Derlatka noticed tidbits in the West German
press about envoys from Moscow traveling to West Germany to
speak with German contacts. He began to suspect that something
unusual was going on: West German representatives seemed to be
conducting talks with their Soviet counterparts without involving
Germany's Western allies. Derlatka caught wind that various pro-
posals were being floated between representatives of Gorbachev and
Helmut Kohl, the West German chancellor. Among the emissaries
were Bernd Schmidbauer, then serving as the West German intelligence coordinator, and Georgy Arbatov, a longtime foreign policy
adviser to Soviet leaders.

From the few, fragmentary leaks to the West German press, Derlatka came up with a theory. It seemed that the USSR, faced with a
desperate economic situation, was willing to consider a rapid unification of Germany in return for extensive economic support. Under
the potential deal, the united Germany would become a neutral state,
belonging to neither East nor West.

Of particular interest to Derlatka was Moscow's consent to the
unification of Germany without the new Germany first agreeing to
recognize its eastern border with Poland. If Germany wasn't forced to
accept this border, Derlatka surmised, the Soviet government would
remain the sole guarantor of Poland's territorial integrity. That would
relegate Poland to "the Soviet sphere of influence in practice forever,"
observed Henryk Jasik, the laundry detergent–swiping spy who was
now Derlatka's boss.

Derlatka believed that if West Germany's negotiations bore fruit,
Poland would have no choice but to stay a client state of the Soviet
Union. Warsaw's shops might be stocked with goods but its security
would be in Moscow's hands. Poland might boast a freer economy but
it would be a freer economy inside a Soviet cage.

Derlatka was aware that he wasn't the only one concerned by

back-channel talks between the West Germans and the Soviets. Several years earlier, in June 1986, senior representatives from the US embassy in Bonn met with Wolfgang Schäuble, then the minister for special affairs for West Germany and one of Chancellor Kohl's closest advisers. Schäuble showed them a piece of paper that indicated talks were ongoing between the West Germans and the Soviets over the status of Berlin and relations between East and West Germany. The talks appeared to the Americans to violate the Four Powers agreement made following Germany's defeat in World War II. That agreement essentially granted the Four Powers—the United States, Britain, France, and the Soviet Union—sovereignty over Germany, which could only be relinquished if they all agreed. No special deal between West Germany and the Soviets over East Germany could be made without the approval of the other three powers.

The American diplomats reported what they took to be West Germany's trial balloon back to Washington and, as John Kornblum, the highest-ranking US diplomat in Berlin at the time, recalled, "all hell broke loose." Kornblum convinced the State Department to turn President Reagan's trip to Berlin, scheduled for June 1987 to celebrate the 750th anniversary of the city, into a political event. In a speech at the Brandenburg Gate with the Berlin Wall at his back, Reagan declared, "Mr. Gorbachev, tear down this wall!" Analysts at the time thought the intended audience was Gorbachev, newly installed in the Kremlin. In reality, Kornblum said, Reagan had a second target in mind. Reagan was putting the West Germans on notice that the United States wouldn't accept any German side deal with the Soviets—especially one that guaranteed the neutrality of a future united Germany or recognized a Soviet sphere of influence in Eastern Europe. That mistake had already been made once, in Yalta in 1945, Kornblum said. It would not be made again.

In Warsaw, Derlatka read with increasing interest mentions in the German press that the West Germans were continuing to play footsie with Gorbachev. He'd seen Reagan's speech. And he began to contemplate something he would later call "crazy."

In the late summer of 1988, Derlatka drew up a proposal for what he called Operacja Jedność, or Operation Unity. It would consist of a messaging campaign of four parts. First, Foreign Intelligence officers and Polish diplomats would be directed to inform their Western contacts that West Germany and Russia were conducting secret talks about conditions for reunification. Second, given these developments, they were authorized to report that Poland was willing to pursue alternate means to guarantee its security. Poland might even be interested in joining the North Atlantic Treaty Organization or the European Economic Community. Third, if Warsaw entered either organization, Poland would fully accept the leading role of the United States. And finally, Poland was uncomfortable allowing Moscow to serve as the guarantor of its western border with a united Germany.

Derlatka was right. It was crazy. Here was a Polish intelligence officer in 1988, still technically employed by a Communist regime, suggesting that Warsaw dump its alliance with Moscow to pursue one with the "imperialists" of the United States. Derlatka figured that one of two things would result from his proposal: he would get fired or his bosses would ignore him.

For almost a year nothing happened. Then a senior officer wrote a rebuttal that extolled the fraternal relations between the Soviet Union and Poland. Derlatka concluded that Operation Unity was dead and he was in for almost certain punishment.

But changes were afoot inside Department I. In November 1989, Henryk Jasik, considered more of a technocrat than an ideologue, took over Foreign Intelligence. Jasik was a careful spy, not one to rock the boat. Still, he was impressed with Derlatka's theory. He ordered a special intelligence cell to verify Derlatka's charges. The analysts bickered, Jasik noted. But in the end, they acknowledged that Derlatka had been correct. The USSR and West Germany were negotiating in secret.

Jasik gave Operation Unity the go-ahead soon after he took control of Department I. He took the decision "alone," he said, "without consulting anyone, without permission from my superiors," including Jaruzelski or Czesław Kiszczak, Jaruzelski's right-hand man. There'd be a lot more freelancing to come.

Jasik directed Poland's spies and diplomats who worked for the service to approach some five hundred foreign contacts, among them diplomats, journalists, spies, and businessmen, with the message that Poland knew about the secret talks and wasn't happy. "The goal," Jasik said, "was to provoke a reaction from Germany and the Soviet Union and to alarm the Western powers responsible for Germany's post-war status."

Polish Intelligence informed old comrades in the KGB that, in the view of Poland's Intelligence Command, the Soviets were betraying Poland by considering German unification—without getting Germany to formally recognize Poland's western border. The second message was a bombshell: Polish officials intimated that they were considering "membership in NATO and the European Economic Community and open to recognizing the leadership role of the United States."

Derlatka was surprised that Jasik authorized the operation. "I dug up information on the secret talks," Derlatka said. "It was my obligation to convince my bosses to work against it. I was amazed that they agreed."

In his application to join Department I, there was nothing to suggest that by his midthirties, Derlatka would be advocating an about-face of Poland's geostrategic orientation. Derlatka had been, he claimed in a personal statement accompanying the application, "patriotic from childhood." He'd even won a prize for knowledge of the Soviet Union. He'd decided to join Foreign Intelligence in December 1980 during the height of the first wave of Solidarity-led protests and public discontent with the Communist system. He didn't share those sentiments. Like his father, also a party member, Derlatka had been a loyal Communist, although whether that was out of a genuine love for Poland or cynical opportunism was another question.

Still, just like Americans had a hard time imagining Poles as enemies, so it was ingrained in Poles, and especially in history buffs like Derlatka, that the United States had never given Poland any grief. Derlatka's grandfather had fought in the bloody Battle of Monte Cassino during World War II and had come home with tales of brave American GIs. Everyone in Poland seemed to have an uncle in the United States or know someone who did. Millions of Poles had immigrated to America. Even under Communism, Poles learned that as far back as the birth of the American republic, Poles and Americans had an innate capacity to get along.

Derlatka knew that Poles and Americans had a shared history. Both nations had been oppressed by imperial overlords. The Americans had won independence from the British, while the Poles battled Russians, Prussians, Austrians, and Swedes. Poland's first constitution was inspired by America's, and Americans supported Poland's protracted struggle to remain a country during the nineteenth century. "For our freedom and yours" was Poland's unofficial motto since 1831. At the Paris Peace Conference in 1918, after World War I, the United States helped Poland regain independence from Germany, Austria, and Russia. The thirteenth of President Woodrow Wilson's famed Fourteen Points called for an independent Poland with access to the sea. (A central Warsaw traffic circle bears Wilson's name.) Many Poles, including intelligence officers, privately applauded the fact that the Solidarity trade union had been backed by the AFL-CIO and the CIA. So there was a certain logic to Derlatka's crazy idea: using the threat of NATO membership and a complete reversal of Polish foreign policy to rein Moscow in.

In May 1990, after political changes had rocked Poland, Intelligence Command not only didn't fire Derlatka, it gave him a cash bonus, recognizing "his personal engagement and his extraordinary contribution in working out the outlines of a great operation."

Derlatka and Henryk Jasik showed it was possible for the Communists to evolve with the times. In fact, they were ahead of the curve. Back then, the leaders of Poland's opposition didn't voice openly their hopes for NATO membership or an alliance with the United States. Many of them supported neutrality, squeezed between Poland's old archenemies, Russia and Germany. Some advocated a defense pact with Czechoslovakia and Hungary. Others embraced pacifism. But once the blasphemy of an alliance with America had been uttered by the likes of a Communist intelligence officer, it wormed its way into Poland's body politic, where it would utterly transform its host. To be sure, Poland's ex-Communist spies weren't the main ones bringing Poland in from the cold. But, as they floated new ideas and later undertook bold missions for America, they helped pry open the door.

The Round Table talks that would result in the dismantling of Communism in Eastern Europe began on February 6, 1989, in Warsaw. Twenty-eight representatives of the Communist regime, led by spymaster and deputy prime minister Czesław Kiszczak, sat down with thirty-two members of the opposition, captained by Solidarity leader Lech Wałęsa.

Participants recall numerous moments when a deal was hanging by a thread. Some dissidents showered and packed an overnight bag in expectation of imminent arrest. But on April 5, an agreement was announced that transferred political power from the Polish United Workers' Party to a cabinet of ministers, a president (a post that hadn't existed since 1952), and a bicameral National Assembly. Political parties were legalized. Elections were called. It'd be the first partially free vote in Poland—and across Eastern Europe—since the 1930s.

Under the rules, 65 percent of the seats in the lower house of parliament, the Sejm, would be reserved for Communists and their allies. The remaining 35 percent would be freely contested. The agreement restored the upper house of parliament, the Senate, and decreed that all of its seats would be up for grabs.

If the Communists were hoping to co-opt the opposition into a deal that would make only cosmetic changes to Poland's system of government, they were mistaken. In elections on June 4, Solidarity's candidates and its allies—known as "the Wałęsa team"—won in a landslide. They took all one hundred seats in the Senate, save one, and all of the 35 percent of the seats in the Sejm that had been competitive. Poland's balance of power was changed forever.

In Washington, the administration of George H. W. Bush, who'd entered the White House in 1989, wanted a slow but steady transformation in Poland. Bush had a particular fondness for Jaruzelski; it'd sprouted during his trip to Poland as vice president in 1987 and grown when President Bush arrived again in July 1989 in the midst of Poland's democratic rebirth. Bush saw Jaruzelski as a patriot, he wrote, "caught between his love for his country and the subservience to the Soviet Union demanded of him by geopolitical realities." Bush believed that Jaruzelski's continued participation in Poland's transition was essential to its success because it would calm concerns in the Soviet Union and assure Poland's Communists that they wouldn't be tyrannized in the new Poland.

The opposition's big win at the June 4 polls complicated the process of electing a president. Under the Round Table deal, the new president was to be chosen by majority vote of the National Assembly. With 65 percent of the seats in the lower house reserved for the Communists and their allies, the assumption was that Jaruzelski would get the job. But with Solidarity and its allies taking so many seats, it was an open question whether Jaruzelski could muster enough votes to win. Not wanting to be humiliated by a defeat, the old general declared he wasn't running. When Bush met Jaruzelski on July 10, he found himself in the paradoxical position of encouraging the architect of Poland's martial law to reenter the race. Moderate Polish intellectuals, such as Adam Michnik, the editor of *Gazeta Wyborcza*, the leading daily at the time, also supported the general's candidacy. "Your President, Our Government" read the headline in the newspaper's July 3 editions. On July 18, Jaruzelski threw his hat back in the ring. A day later Poland's parliament elected him president. Final tally: 270 to 233.

On August 2, Jaruzelski appointed Czesław Kiszczak—Poland's security chief—as prime minister. Then two smaller political parties abandoned the Communists and joined Solidarity, giving it a majority in the Sejm. After seventeen days in office, Kiszczak had little choice but to step down. Jaruzelski then tapped Tadeusz Mazowiecki, a journalist and famed dissident, to take his place.

Poland could have taken a different path. On June 4, 1989, the same day that Poland held its historic vote, Chinese troops slaughtered unarmed protesters around Beijing's Tiananmen Square. Closer to home, ethnic factions in Yugoslavia had begun stockpiling weapons for a war that would cost the lives of a quarter of a million people.

Instead, in his address to the Sejm on August 24, his first day in office, Prime Minister Mazowiecki called for the drawing of a "thick line" between Poland's future of freedom and its Communist past. Mazowiecki appealed to his countrymen to focus on the challenges of tomorrow rather than on recriminations over yesterday. As the first prime minister of a free Poland, Mazowiecki made the historic decision to unite, not divide, what people called the Third Polish Republic. Mazowiecki's "thick line" served other purposes. It avoided what could've been a bloody civil war by assuring Communists that they, too, had a home in their new country. And it sidestepped the potential unmasking of those among Solidarity's ranks who'd secretly collaborated with the security services during Communist rule. The Bush administration was pleased.

As part of the deal that allowed Mazowiecki to take the helm of government, Kiszczak stayed on as minister of interior. The control over the "force ministries," which also included the Ministry of Defense, guaranteed the support of many Communists for Poland's transition. In addition, by including the Communists in the government, Solidarity avoided having to fully own the economic catastrophe that was unfolding in Poland. Responsibility, like power, would be shared.

The young Polish government inherited two interlocking crises: a failed planned economy and a macroeconomic mess of hyperinflation, shortages, budgetary deficits, and foreign debt. The task it faced was unprecedented: to return from socialism to capitalism. It was, Wałęsa said, like "going from an omelet back to whole eggs."

Almost immediately, Kiszczak began to reorganize the SB. He cut the number of officers responsible for internal security and changed the ministry's mandate from defending socialism to protecting the Polish state. He also oversaw a massive destruction of ministry files to remove evidence of secret operations, Communist Poland's close relations with terrorist organizations, and the identity of collaborators.

Mazowiecki and the rest of the democratic forces walked a tightrope between fashioning the pro-Western Poland of the future while struggling to resolve issues of Poland's pro-Soviet past. When Mazowiecki took office, tens of thousands of Soviet troops were stationed in his country. Stockpiles of Soviet nuclear weapons were scattered on Soviet bases throughout the Polish countryside. Economically, Poland was part of COMECON, the Soviet-led trading bloc, and thus constituted a key cog in the economies of the Communist world. Disassembling these structures without making enemies demanded a scalpel, not a hammer.

Inside the ranks of the Solidarity movement, there were those who pushed for a radical new beginning at a hypothetical "Year Zero." Meanwhile, some Communists tried to preserve as much of the ancien régime as possible. Mazowiecki's government hewed to the middle. It moved to rid the government of officials who had violated human rights, but it kept the bulk of the bureaucracy and the secret services intact. To Mazowiecki and his team, the reason was clear. Wojciech Brochwicz was a lawyer and senior adviser inside Department I who played a crucial role in this process. "We had to take into account incipient threats," he said. "We were still surrounded on all sides by 'people's democracies,' with Soviet troops on our territory. We didn't know how long our adventure with freedom and democracy would last. It was all the more reason to avoid a witch hunt."

Mazowiecki was mindful of Soviet interests. He had to be. He went out of his way to assuage Soviet concerns. The first visiting dignitary he met wasn't a Western leader, it was Vladimir Kryuchkov, head of the KGB, who flew into Warsaw four days after Mazowiecki took office. Mazowiecki told Kryuchkov two things: that Poland would be friendly to Moscow and that Poland would be "sovereign." Translated, that meant that Poland promised not to harm Soviet strategic interests but it would not be pushed around. Still, until the German question was solved, the Solidarity-led government was not eager for the Red Army to fully withdraw. In fact, Mazowiecki proposed that the Russians keep some troops in Poland, which later surprised US president George H. W. Bush, who believed that a full pullout would be better. Mazowiecki also floated the idea for some type of Central European security organization, independent of NATO and the Warsaw Pact. Speaking to reporters after they met, Kryuchkov called Mazowiecki "a solid man."

As Poland's leaders groped for a way forward, the once-warring spy agencies in the Eastern Bloc and the West began to take steps to end their Cold War, giving politicians on both sides a sense of what cooperation could achieve.

On February 15, 1989, Boris Gromov, the commander of the Soviet 40th Army, crossed the Soviet-Afghan Friendship Bridge, marking the end of Moscow's nine-year-long occupation of Afghanistan. Milton Bearden, a veteran CIA officer, had played a key role in the agency's campaign to arm the Afghan mujahideen resistance against the Soviets. Now that the Soviets had been defeated, Bearden found himself spirited back from the Afghan battlefield to Langley. In

June, he assumed command of the clandestine service's Soviet/Eastern Europe Division.

Bearden returned to witness a revolution. It wasn't just the Poles who were on the march. On May 2, Hungarians cut the barbed wire fence that separated them from Austria. By October, with a constitutional amendment, the Hungarian People's Republic officially became the Republic of Hungary. In East Germany, demonstrators began to gather in Leipzig. By early November, the protests had mushroomed and, on November 9, the Berlin Wall crumbled as thousands took sledgehammers to that symbol of Soviet domination. A day later, Bulgaria's Communist leader Todor Zhivkov was ousted. By the end of November, the wave had reached Czechoslovakia, culminating in a demonstration of 750,000 in Prague's Wenceslas Square and, on December 29, in the election of playwright and dissident Václav Havel as president. In Romania, after security forces fired on demonstrators, dictator Nicolae Ceaușescu was overthrown and executed on Christmas Day. "I was watching the changes in my office, welling up with tears," Bearden recalled. "I wondered, 'Is this how it's going to go?'" The world turned upside down. Channeling CIA director William Casey, the question Bearden, his deputy Paul Redmond, and special assistant John Palevich asked themselves was, "Now what?"

In the midst of the chaos and the jubilation, someone suggested reaching out to the intelligence agencies behind the rapidly disintegrating Iron Curtain. Bearden, Palevich, and Redmond all claim to have come up with the idea, proving the adage that success has many fathers. Despite that disagreement, they concur on two points. As Redmond observed, nobody else in other parts of the federal government was much interested in reaching out and the CIA "would've been stupid if it hadn't tried."

A Harvard man with a thick Boston accent and a fondness for Anglo-Saxon swear words, Redmond understood that Eastern Bloc intelligence agencies had a lot to offer the United States. They knew the

Soviet Union, including the positioning and condition of its nuclear arsenal, in ways that Western agencies did not. They were familiar with the inner workings of the Communist Party of the Soviet Union. They or their counterparts in other parts of their governments had sold weapons to terrorist organizations. They had cooperated with drug traffickers and had dirt on Middle East despots with whom Soviet Bloc engineering firms had long done business. They operated in nations— Iran, North Korea, and Cuba—that were closed to US diplomats. The Eastern Bloc was also littered with Soviet military and eavesdropping equipment, presenting the technical side of the CIA and the Pentagon with tantalizing targets. And, in the United States and across the West, Eastern Bloc spies ran agents whom the FBI wanted rolled up.

The CIA tried Hungary first. Redmond laid out a formula. The approach would be discreet, and it would take place on neutral ground. Talks began with Hungarian intelligence in Vienna. In Warsaw, the American overture to Hungary didn't go unnoticed.

In November 1989, a Polish intelligence officer based in Budapest picked up word of the CIA's interest in working with Hungary's spies. That month, a delegation from the US Senate Select Committee on Intelligence traveled to Budapest. According to the Polish report, US senators demanded that Hungary stop gathering intelligence against the United States. The senators suggested that a good place to start would be to end surveillance of the US embassy in Budapest. The Hungarians had been eavesdropping on the embassy from the Hungarian National Bank building next door. The senators also griped to the Hungarians about Poland's espionage in America, another indication that they considered Warsaw's Foreign Intelligence, after the KGB, to be the most nettlesome of the Eastern Bloc.

The Hungarians countered that the United States should keep its nose out of their affairs and complained about the CIA's aggressive recruitment operations. Reporting to Warsaw, the Polish *rezydent* observed that the Hungarians were trying to find a middle road between their old allies in the Warsaw Pact and their new friends in the West. The Hungarians did agree to one American request. They expelled Edward Lee Howard, the only CIA officer who'd ever defected to the Warsaw Pact. Howard had been living in Budapest.

What happened next, according to the Polish intelligence officer, came straight out of a spy story. Unwilling to accept a neutral Hungary, the CIA set out to purge Hungary's Ministry of Interior officials who'd balked at cooperation with the CIA. They did so, the officer alleged, by fabricating a scandal.

On January 5, 1990, Hungary's two leading opposition parties released evidence that the government's secret services had been wiretapping Hungarian dissidents in the run-up to parliamentary elections scheduled for March 5.

Hungary's amended constitution outlawed such surveillance. The news sparked protests and the resignations of the Communist-era minister of interior along with other security officials. By the end of the month, Hungary dropped its opposition to working with the CIA. The two intelligence services exchanged liaison officers, initiating cooperation against terrorism, drug trafficking, and illicit arms sales. Hungary also froze collaboration with the KGB.

In reports back to Warsaw, the Polish *rezydent* in Budapest alleged that the CIA had cooked up the scandal. He claimed that the CIA had encouraged Hungarian intelligence officers to supply Hungary's democratic opposition with proof of the surveillance. Many officers in the Hungarian service, he wrote, "have no doubt that the US and the CIA knew about the provocation."

Was the CIA involved? Probably not. To be sure, most US documents on the 1989 transition in Eastern Europe remain classified. But Polish Intelligence reports from Budapest are riddled with errors. The *rezydent* identified every US official in Hungary as a closet CIA officer, which beggars belief. Other assumptions, such as the notion that US officials masterminded Hungary's transition to democracy, are equally far-fetched. But in Warsaw, in January 1990, Department I took the events in Hungary as a warning. There was only one conclusion:

the leaders of Poland's secret services had better accede to the CIA's
requests for cooperation or find themselves in trouble as well.

In January, Department I chief Henryk Jasik predicted in a report
to President Jaruzelski, Prime Minister Mazowiecki, and Minister of
Interior Kiszczak that the Americans would soon come knocking on
Poland's door. If Poland agreed to stop spying on the United States
and cut its ties to the KGB, Jasik believed, Polish companies would
be given access to American technology and Polish diplomats would
be allowed to travel freely in the United States. Based on intelligence
gleaned from Department I's network of sources in the United States,
Jasik foresaw that the CIA outreach would occur before Mazowiecki's
trip to Washington, scheduled for March 20–23. "Expect the Americans," Jasik wrote, to reach out "through normal diplomatic channels
at as high a level as possible."

CHAPTER SEVEN

THE BEAR COMES KNOCKING

Henryk Jasik was at least partially right. The Americans were coming. But not through the front door.

In late January 1990, John Palevich walked into Paul Redmond's office in the Soviet/Eastern European Division at the CIA with a question. "Why don't you reach out to the Poles?" he asked. "You know, they're the most important. What'd be the approach?"

Redmond looked up from his desk. "You're so fucking smart, John, why don't you figure it out?" Palevich did a mental tour of the horizon. Tokyo wouldn't work because the Polish *rezydent* there was "a real Commie, too close to the Russians." Scandinavia? The *rezydent* in one of its countries was a boozer so no one would believe him in Warsaw. Rome or Lisbon? Aleksander Makowski, the Polish *rezydent* in Italy, had studied at Harvard and attended the old Western High School in Washington when his dad was a spy in the United States. But, Palevich complained, "the geography" was difficult; Poland's embassy in Rome was on an alley and watched closely by Italian counterintelligence.

The Polish mission in Lisbon, however, sat on a wide boulevard. And Portuguese counterintelligence was notably sleepy. Palevich knew Lisbon's *rezydent* was trusted in Warsaw. Palevich chose Portugal.

On March 1, shortly before one in the afternoon, a man rang the bell at the Polish embassy on Avenida das Descobertas 2 in Lisbon and asked to see Ryszard Tomaszewski. The man had come to the embassy earlier that morning but Tomaszewski had been out. Tomaszewski peeked from his office to see standing in the reception area a fleshy middle-aged individual with an oval face, a bulbous nose, and dirty blond hair, combed to the right and graying about the temples. The man's baggy off-the-rack suit made his already robust frame look even thicker.

Tomaszewski, who, to fit in, had adopted the Portuguese name Ricardo, emerged from his office. The pair shook hands. Ricardo made a mental note of the man's sweaty palms. The man handed Ricardo a US diplomatic passport and said he'd come on official business. Ricardo steered him into his office.

"The passport in your hand is my true identity document and you can copy it to have a record. My home telephone number is in there, too," John Palevich announced in English once they were alone. "I am a CIA officer and I want to have a serious conversation with you." Seeing Ricardo rise and take a step toward the door, Palevich added rapidly: "No, no, I don't want to recruit you. I want you to pass a message to Warsaw." Ricardo sat down and Palevich continued.

"You're a colonel in the service. You're serving under cover in Portugal in the consular department," Palevich declared. He then requested that Ricardo inform Minister Kiszczak and several other high-ranking intelligence officers whom he mentioned by name that "the United States wishes to initiate liaison with Department I . . . with a view to cooperation on maintaining stability in Europe in the context of the ongoing changes in the Warsaw Pact countries and the approaching unification of Germany."

Ricardo pretended not to know the officers mentioned and asked

Palevich to write down their names, which he did without (to Ricardo's surprise) a single misspelling. Looking at the list, Ricardo interrupted Palevich to announce that John had chosen the wrong man and the wrong channel. "I'm just a Polish diplomat!" he hissed. "You can contact the Polish side directly."

"We have the right channel and the right person," Palevich insisted. "We have been tracking your career in this profession for a long time. You served in Libya, India, and Mexico; you have two sons from both marriages; the elder is studying in Moscow. You speak English, Spanish, Portuguese, and a little Arabic." Palevich then rattled off more details of Tomaszewski's postings, his aliases, and how Ricardo, based in Mexico City in the early 1980s, had managed the case of a Silicon Valley engineer. The engineer, James D. Harper Jr., had given the Poles a treasure trove of secrets about the US nuclear arsenal and the Minuteman intercontinental ballistic missile. Palevich even apologized for the CIA's bungled attempt to recruit Tomaszewski at the time.

John told Ricardo that he'd considered approaching other *rezydents*, including Foreign Intelligence's man in Washington, but decided that Ricardo's standing in Warsaw, his reputation as an excellent officer among his erstwhile foes at the CIA, and the fact that Portuguese counterintelligence was famously inept had led him to his door.

"Can I smoke?" Palevich asked.

"I do not expect the conversation or your stay to last that long," Ricardo replied. He left the office to give his secretary Palevich's passport to photocopy. Returning, he declared, in fluent but heavily accented English, "Mr. Palevich, what you are saying is a load of piffle and sounds like a silly joke."

"I appreciate that you may not trust me and you don't wish to talk openly so as not to blow your cover, but here in Portugal and in this embassy," Palevich said, motioning to the walls, "you can talk without worry. What I've communicated to you is the honest intention of the CIA. Poland lies between the Soviet empire and a reemerging great

Germany and for that reason has suffered a lot. Please trust me, I'm known to your service. In the sixties I worked for three years in Poland."

"What is your role within the CIA?" Ricardo asked.

"I am a senior officer," Palevich said. "You know, there are junior officers and senior officers." He smiled.

Ricardo stood up again, signaling the conversation's end. Palevich apologized for shocking him. "Shocking indeed," Ricardo said, "is the arrogance of this CIA provocation against men at an embassy of a country that is currently friendly toward the United States. We're done here."

"So you'll not pass on my message and I'm to go back to Washington empty-handed?" Palevich asked.

"That's your problem," Ricardo replied. "The whole affair is grotesque."

"By the way," Palevich added sheepishly, "can you call me a cab?"

"Let your backup do it," Ricardo snarled. But Palevich had come alone. By one fifteen, he was back on the street.

"I was really surprised," Ricardo said years later, "but I couldn't shut him up. He went on jabbering into the microphones of Portuguese counterintelligence." Ricardo said it would have been safer had Palevich approached him outside the embassy. "Times were changing," he said. "We knew that. None of us were Communists anymore." But Palevich's decision to barge into Poland's embassy was too risky. "It wasn't professional," Ricardo said. "It wasn't careful tradecraft." Palevich might've also been right. It didn't seem that Portuguese intelligence had been listening after all.

Time has altered Ricardo's view of Palevich's dangle. In a report to the Intelligence Command filed immediately after Palevich's visit, Tomaszewski found two plausible explanations for Palevich's approach. One, the CIA was trying to punish him for his involvement in the Harper operation by outing him to Portuguese counterintelligence and getting him expelled from Portugal. Or, two, the CIA was working with Poland's Solidarity-led government to expose Poland's spies overseas and help Solidarity purge them from Department I. There was "little logic," he said, to a third possibility, that Palevich had actually been sincere. Ricardo reacted like any Warsaw Pact intelligence officer could've been expected to react during the Cold War. The problem was that the Cold War was ending and the rules were in flux.

At Langley, John stuck his head in Redmond's office. "Did you hear what happened?" he asked. "The guy threw me out." Redmond looked up from his desk. "I guess I'm going to Rome then." Redmond figured he could use old school ties to open a door to Aleksander Makowski, the *rezydent* and fellow Harvard alum.

In Warsaw, Palevich's Lisbon visit touched off a flurry of cables among the officers at Intelligence Command and concern that Poland had blown its chance. Director Jasik had forecast that the CIA's advance would come through the highest channels but he recognized it via lowly Lisbon nonetheless. Jasik's boss, Minister Kiszczak, responding to Ricardo's cable, declared that he supported talks with the CIA. He suggested that the conversation be continued in Switzerland. Jasik proposed Washington. Someone realized that if it was Washington, the CIA would have to inform the FBI, which meant that FBI agents would be crawling all over the Poles. Someone else noted that Switzerland's counterintelligence service would probably get wind of the meetings and wouldn't be happy. The Poles concluded, as Palevich had, that Lisbon was the best choice. On March 5, a cable winged its way back to Ricardo instructing him to contact Palevich and invite him and other CIA representatives back to Portugal. "Palevich is known to us as a CIA operative," it ended.

At seven fifteen on the morning of March 6, John Palevich had just showered and was shaving at his comfortable four-bedroom split-level in Bethesda, Maryland, when the phone rang. Bonnie answered. John hustled out of the bathroom.

"This is Lisbon," the caller said.

"I recognize your voice. Please carry on," Palevich replied.

Before calling, Ricardo had walked around downtown Lisbon for two hours to ensure that there was no tail. From a phone booth on Rossio Square, Ricardo told Palevich that Intelligence Command had decided to accept the CIA's offer and could meet as soon as several of its officers obtained Portuguese visas. Ricardo apologized for "being inhospitable." Palevich laughed. "That's quite all right," he said. At work that day, Palevich stuck his head in Redmond's office again. "Did you hear what happened?" he asked. "They called." Redmond smiled: "I'll cancel Rome."

Palevich and Ricardo set the meeting for May 2 at three in the afternoon in the lobby of the Tivoli Hotel, a popular tourist spot on Avenida Liberdade. In his note to Warsaw, Ricardo reported that Palevich "communicated clear interest, excitement." Kiszczak informed both President Jaruzelski and Prime Minister Mazowiecki of the arrangements.

Although he'd been running Poland's government since August 1989, Mazowiecki had been cautious around Kiszczak and the rest of the security officials from the old system. He'd waited months before he appointed a Solidarity man to the Ministry of Interior. That man was Krzysztof Kozłowski, an influential columnist for *Tygodnik Powszechny*, a Catholic weekly that had stood as a bulwark against Communism for years. Mazowiecki appointed Kozłowski as Kiszczak's deputy five days after John Palevich entered the Polish embassy in Lisbon. New on the job, Kozłowski remembered Kiszczak asking him whether Poland should take up the CIA's offer. "It's always worth talking," Kozłowski said.

On March 20, 1990, Mazowiecki, the first freely elected Polish prime minister since the 1930s, arrived in Washington to meet President George H. W. Bush. Despite the economic hardship facing his nation, when he met Bush the following morning, Mazowiecki focused on the looming unification of Germany and the security of Poland's borders. The shadow of World War II and the Yalta Conference hung over this inaugural meeting between an American president and the leader of the newly democratic Republic of Poland.

Mazowiecki had been briefed about Operation Unity. He shared with Poland's Intelligence Command a concern that a powerful, reunited Germany might attempt to reclaim land ceded to Poland at the end of World War II. After all, when Solidarity won its electoral victory in June 1989, West German finance minister Theo Waigel still questioned the legality of Poland's western border. Following the demolition of the Berlin Wall in November, German chancellor Helmut Kohl's "Ten-Point Plan" for the unification of Germany notably left out any mention of borders.

Mazowiecki sought assurances that Washington would not let Poland be carved up by its neighbors as it had at Yalta. "The Polish people are paranoid about agreements being made over their heads," he told Bush soon after the two sat down in the Oval Office.

Alluding to another core point of Operation Unity, Mazowiecki made it clear that Poland didn't want the security of its western border with Germany to be Moscow's responsibility. Poland wanted out of the Warsaw Pact. Mazowiecki had yet to embrace the prospect of Poland's membership in NATO, but he did stress the need for a security arrangement that could protect Poland from both Russia and Germany. As he told Bush, "It is crucial to us to ensure that our western territories are not just a gift from Stalin—that they are guaranteed by all the powers, not just a unilateral act by one."

Bush, too, was focused on righting the mistakes of the past. When Mazowiecki expressed his fear that the big powers would again decide Poland's fate, Bush immediately made the connection to World War II: "There is similar thinking in this country on Yalta," he assured his Polish guest.

Mazowiecki asked the US president to push Germany to recognize the Polish border along the Oder and Neisse Rivers. President Bush agreed to lean on his friend, German chancellor Kohl. And, indeed, by June, the parliaments of both Germanies acknowledged the Polish border. A peace treaty followed soon after Germany united on October 3. As Mazowiecki declared in a toast to Bush on the occasion of the state dinner on March 21, "The era of Yalta is becoming history."

The next morning, Mazowiecki was in meetings at Blair House, across the street from the White House, when a man not on the public schedule walked in. CIA director William Webster had left his job as head of the FBI to lead the agency in 1987. Webster and Mazowiecki exchanged pleasantries. Webster noted the upcoming meeting in Lisbon. Was Mazowiecki happy about the idea of cooperating with the CIA? Webster asked. The prime minister nodded. "So are we," Webster declared.

Soviet penetration of Poland concerned Webster. He told Mazowiecki that it'd be difficult for the United States to move forward with intelligence cooperation and ease restrictions on technology transfers to Poland without weeding out Soviet influence and Moscow's collaborators. "We appreciate Poland's efforts to gain independence from the KGB," Webster noted, "but they will not give up their efforts to obtain technology through Poland. Poland is going to need to go through a quarantine." Webster steered the conversation to Lisbon and noted that Poland and the United States had a common interest in fighting terrorism. Again, Mazowiecki agreed.

Mazowiecki's interest in counterterrorism cooperation wasn't just talk. On March 26, in an address to the American Jewish Congress, Mazowiecki announced, to a standing ovation, that Poland was committed to facilitating the transit of Soviet Jews through Poland to Israel.

In 1989, a liberalizing Soviet Union under Gorbachev had relaxed controls on exit visas and opened direct flights for Soviet Jews to Israel. From November on, more than eleven thousand Jews had flown direct from Moscow to Tel Aviv and hundreds of thousands more were expected. But Arab states were livid at the Soviets and lobbied Moscow to turn off the tap. Worried about terrorist attacks and its waning influence in the Middle East, the Soviet government suspended direct flights in March 1990 and put a freeze on what had been warming ties with Israel. The Israeli government, with the help of the Bush administration, searched for another nation through which Soviet Jews could pass. Hungary volunteered but its state airline, Malev, dropped out after threats from terrorist groups.

Mazowiecki's motivation to step into the breach was threefold. First, Yalta was not the only ghost in need of exorcism. Anti-Semitism was another. On the eve of World War II, Poland, next to the United States, had been home to the second-largest agglomeration of Jews in the world. Ten percent of Poland's population considered themselves Jewish, including one-third of all urban residents. In Warsaw, Yiddish was spoken by more than 30 percent of the inhabitants.

The Nazis butchered Poland's Jewish community. From an original population of three million, by the end of the war, barely ninety thousand Jews remained. The official Polish line on World War II framed Poland and the Poles as victims, along with the Jews. But historians such as Jan T. Gross have noted that while Poland didn't participate in the annihilation of European Jewry in the way the French Vichy government had, some Poles contributed enthusiastically to the slaughter. Poles were involved in massacres of Jewish residents in a few Polish towns. And individual Poles informed on Jews hiding in their midst. Other Poles harbored and saved Jews. The Poles were, Gross has written, both "victim and a victimizer."

This recognition pushed leaders like Mazowiecki to make amends. In his speech to the American Jewish Congress, Mazowiecki expressed remorse for Polish anti-Semitism and looked forward to a new era in Polish-Jewish relations. He vowed that Poland would undertake the tangled task of returning property that had been expropriated—first by the Nazis and then by the Communists—to its rightful Jewish owners. Two months before he spoke, Poland and Israel had exchanged ambassadors for the first time since the Six-Day War in 1967.

A second reason to aid the Jews was that it was the right thing to do. As noted by Kiszczak's new deputy at the ministry, Krzysztof Kozłowski, the decision to help Soviet Jews was at root a moral one, a chance to draw a clear line between the past and the present and to argue, through action, that the new Poland shouldn't be blamed for the sins of the old.

Finally, in volunteering to help Soviet Jews find a new home, the young Polish government indicated that it understood the expression "The road to Washington leads through Tel Aviv." Jan Dowgiałło, Poland's new ambassador to Israel, had made this very observation on the floor of Poland's parliament. Mazowiecki was willing to chance a terrorist attack to bind Warsaw more closely with Washington.

Still, it was a controversial decision. Many Poles opposed the idea of aiding the Jews. For centuries, Catholic Poles had held on to deeply ingrained prejudices against the Jews living among them. Even in the 1940s, there were those who still believed the myth that Jews used the fresh blood of Christian children to prepare matzoh for Passover. Even though Mazowiecki was a devout Roman Catholic, when he later ran for president, right-wing Polish nationalists accused him of secretly being a Jew.

There was opposition in the Muslim world as well. No sooner had Mazowiecki vowed to help the Soviet Jews than threats against Poland surfaced in newspapers in Lebanon, signed by a group calling itself the Islamic Army for the Liberation of Palestine. On March 30, four days after the speech, masked gunmen toting Kalashnikovs shot a Polish couple outside Poland's commercial offices in Beirut. Both were seriously wounded but survived. Planning for the airlift continued apace.

On April 6, soon after Mazowiecki returned home, his government established a new intelligence agency to replace both the ministry's old Department I, responsible for foreign intelligence, and its Department II, which dealt with counterintelligence. Kozłowski was put in charge of the new service, which was renamed the Urzad Ochrony Państwa, the Office of State Protection, or UOP.

The UOP quickly established a coordination committee for

anti-terrorism. General Zdzisław Sarewicz was a longtime operative with vast experience in the USSR and the Middle East, including regular contacts with terrorist organizations. He was chosen to lead the group, with veteran Warsaw Pact spies Bronisław Zych and Gromosław Czempiński as his deputies. Experts from the Israeli spy agency Mossad and the CIA traveled to Poland to help the UOP set up security, organize the flights, and protect Soviet Jews. The Mossad would serve as a key link between Polish Intelligence and the CIA and as a model for an espionage relationship with America that the Poles sought to emulate.

To lessen the chance of a terrorist attack, the Polish Ministry of Foreign Affairs also reached out to Yasser Arafat, head of the Palestine Liberation Organization, to plead for understanding. Softening the blow of Poland's shift toward Israel and the United States, Polish arms dealers continued to sell to Arab middlemen, like they had during the Cold War.

At CIA headquarters in Langley, Paul Redmond, the deputy director of operations for Soviet/Eastern Europe, searched for something dramatic to convey the historic nature of the upcoming meeting in Lisbon. Redmond wanted to let the Poles know that the Americans respected Polish tradecraft and didn't view themselves as, he said, "the big, bad CIA."

"I didn't give a rat's ass whether they were commies or Buddhists," Redmond said. "We knew enough about their operations that we could compliment them." Redmond had an assistant dig into the CIA's archives, where she found an old carbon copy of a five-page undated memo on the Polish involvement in breaking Germany's Enigma codes before World War II. The document contained the names of a dozen Polish mathematicians, code breakers, and spies. During the war, several had fled Poland via France and made it to safety in Britain. But four stayed behind in Poland and were tortured by the Gestapo. Redmond memorized all the names.

CHAPTER EIGHT

SHALL WE DANCE?

On May 2, 1990, at three in the afternoon, John Palevich met three Polish spies in the lobby of the Hotel Tivoli in downtown Lisbon. Paul Redmond had rented a suite and Palevich invited the Poles upstairs to sit on overstuffed chairs as Redmond lounged on a sofa in the center of the room. With his shoes off and his stockinged feet perched on an ottoman, Redmond launched into a monologue on the triumphs of Polish Intelligence.

The American delegation consisted of Redmond, Palevich, and Fred Turco, a legendary CIA officer and the father of counterterrorism operations in the United States. Turco had served overseas for almost twenty years as a case officer in Pakistan, Africa, and elsewhere. On the Polish side there was Lisbon's *rezydent*, Ricardo, Colonel Bronisław Zych, the deputy director for operations, and Major Krzysztof Smoleński, the former *rezydent* in Chicago who now ran the American division of the UOP.

"I started my schtick that we weren't big and bad," Redmond remembered. "I said, 'We want to know whether the service that had broken the Enigma code wants to work with us.'" In a chair next to Redmond, Zych teared up. Like many Poles, he'd grown accustomed to people belittling Poland's contribution to winning World War II. "The rest," Redmond said, "was a lovefest."

Well, not exactly. Smoleński remembers both sides being tense. Palevich and Zych cleared the air by trading war stories of operations to recruit each other. Palevich showed off his knowledge of the Polish service and of Zych and Smoleński in particular. He detailed their careers and when and where they'd entered the United States.

The gist of the first round of talks was simple. "We concluded the time had come to stop fighting and to open a new era," Smoleński said. Then, "we started to look for common interests to work together."

The men stayed in Redmond's room for four and a half hours that afternoon. They agreed that Poland and the United States would collaborate to fight terrorism, especially now that Poland had decided to be a stopover for Soviet Jews on their way to Israel. Turco offered Poland intelligence, training, and other support. He also reiterated Washington's demand that Warsaw ensure that terrorist organizations, like the one run by Abu Nidal, cease operations in Poland.

Redmond asked the Poles if the United States could open an office for the Foreign Broadcast Information Service, making Poland one of the fifteen centers worldwide where the CIA's language experts compiled reports from open-source broadcasts. The center would require the installation of massive antennae, Palevich noted. The Poles expressed some willingness but were concerned that the Soviets would notice those antennae and figure out that the two sides had not simply stopped being enemies; they were becoming friends. Anyway, even more eye-catching American antennae would be coming to Poland soon.

Palevich requested that Poland stop gathering intelligence in the United States. Redmond mentioned that Zacharski's skullduggery had left a "residue of trauma" at the Pentagon and the FBI. But, Redmond added pointedly, "we trained professionals understand."

The Poles came to Lisbon with intelligence that indicated an impending collapse of the USSR. "The issue of who would control Soviet nuclear stockpiles was foremost in the minds of all of us," Smoleński recalled. The Poles shared information on the emerging movement for independence in Lithuania and the rest of the Baltic states and offered to facilitate CIA operations there. "We knew the USSR was going to fall apart but we didn't know whether it was going to be peaceful or violent," Smoleński said. Redmond requested briefings on the political situation in Cuba, where the Poles had a strong diplomatic presence, and on the Middle East, where thousands of Poles worked as engineers on infrastructure projects and in secret weapons plants.

After the talks, Palevich invited the Poles to dinner. At a few minutes after nine, they said their goodbyes. The Americans stressed again that they viewed the meeting as highly important and highly secret. Only President Bush, Secretary of State James Baker, National Security Advisor Brent Scowcroft, and the US ambassador to Poland, John Davis, would be informed. Zych invited the Americans to continue talks in Warsaw. Redmond and his colleagues were pleased. In his report to Warsaw summing up the day, Ricardo Tomaszewski noted that there was no sign that Portuguese counterintelligence had any inkling what had transpired.

In early June, after building an ad hoc terminal to process Jewish passengers, Poland's LOT Airlines began flying Soviet Jews from Warsaw to Israel. Arab diplomats in vehicles with diplomatic plates probed the area but were scared off by heavily armed Polish officers. In all, an estimated forty thousand Jews transited Poland to Israel. The Poles called it Operacja Most, or Operation Bridge: a bridge to Israel, and to Washington as well.

On June 28, five CIA officers arrived in Warsaw on two flights, one from Frankfurt, the other from Vienna. The American delegation of Redmond, Palevich, and Turco had been expanded to include a celebrated special operations officer named Wilfred "Squeak" Charette, who pioneered the high-altitude, low-opening parachute drops still used by special forces around the world today. In addition, Karen Rozbicki, a counterterrorism analyst, joined the team as one of the only women involved in fashioning the alliance. The Polish side was led by Krzysztof Kozłowski, the head of the UOP and soon to be minister of interior. Kozłowski was the sole member from the former opposition at the talks; he was joined by nine Communist-era intelligence officers. Their old boss, Czesław Kiszczak, the longtime Communist-era spy chief, did not attend.

At the US embassy the next morning, Redmond collected station chief Bill Norville. Together they and the other CIA officers headed to the very same resort in Magdalenka where the new Poland had been born in talks between the opposition and the Communists. A bearded, brainy type who favored motor scooters over fast cars, Norville was a Cold War veteran who'd been posted to Warsaw in the 1970s. There he'd helped manage the high-stakes case of superspy colonel Ryszard Kukliński. Norville had also worked against the Warsaw Pact out of Japan in the early 1980s. In 1986, he'd been expelled from Moscow during a bout of spy wars with the Soviets.

Norville, too, was a believer in the unique bond between Americans and Poles. In Tokyo at the height of the Cold War, Norville befriended Janusz Omietański, a Japanese-speaking, Soviet-educated Polish spy. In a report to Intelligence Command on August 25, 1980, Omietański described Norville as someone "who quickly and easily starts an acquaintance." Intelligence Command directed Omietański to deepen the relationship. The pair, one from America and one from the Warsaw Pact, joined forces to establish what Omietański called "a young diplomats club," which would convene at a Chinese restaurant in Tokyo. Both of them used the group to recruit agents. "That's what I loved about the Poles," Norville recalled. "You could be on opposite sides but still be friends." The Poles gave Norville a codename: Naughty.

Norville and his wife, Maggi, who later became a CIA officer herself, cemented a family bond with Poland when they became the first American diplomats granted permission to adopt a child, a son they named Matthew. "Terribly satisfying" was how Norville described the adventure of managing America's transition from Warsaw's foe to Warsaw's friend.

At the Magdalenka resort, talks between the CIA and the UOP began on June 29 in the same room as the preparations for the Round Table negotiations in February 1989. Redmond was asked to sit in the very chair that had been occupied by Lech Wałęsa. "Now that," Redmond recalled, "was cool."

Welcoming the Americans, Kozłowski struck a cautious note. He formally announced that Poland had halted its espionage activities in the United States. He framed Poland's interest in cooperation with the CIA as part of Poland's "return to Europe." Poland was building a new intelligence agency and needed the CIA's help, he said. Operation Bridge was teaching Poland that it required assistance countering terrorism and that it lacked the technical equipment to adequately monitor the large population of Arab students studying in Poland.

Kozłowski told the Americans that the new government would be refocusing its foreign intelligence gathering operations "on the region of eastern and central Europe," a not-so-subtle reference to the USSR and the uniting Germany. He finished by declaring that the tide of Poland's history was ineluctable but that Poland needed to proceed with caution. The Soviets were watching Poland's every move. Done with his speech, Kozłowski left the spies to work out the details. The tenor of the conversation immediately changed.

It was as if Kozłowski had his foot on the brake. The minute he was gone, the CIA and the UOP floored the accelerator. Out went caution. In came an eagerness to build an alliance. Redmond asked for Poland's evaluation of the situation in the USSR, and in particular the Baltic republics, which were angling for independence. To the CIA, those regions were black holes, he acknowledged, given the aggressive counterintelligence regime in the USSR. He asked for details about developments in Iran. In Libya, he was interested in what appeared to be a chemical weapons plant near Tripoli. Turco and Rozbicki requested information on the business activities of terrorist organizations in Poland and pressed the Poles to cut whatever ties remained. In exchange, Redmond and Turco committed to train the Poles in counterterrorism methods and to help Poland build the structure of its new intelligence agency, the UOP.

The Polish team signed on to America's search for loose nukes and other weapons of mass destruction from the remnants of the Soviet Union. Ukraine, to Poland's east, was of particular concern. The Soviets had based more than fifteen hundred nuclear weapons there during the Cold War.

Where it had once specialized in stealing secrets from the Western world, Intelligence Command told the Americans that Poland could be counted on to share intelligence from what remained of the USSR. For years, Polish Intelligence had maintained a bureau in Moscow to liaise with the KGB. It also ran a special unit, the Wisła Group, to spy on Polish nationals living in the USSR. The Poles revealed that Zdzisław Sarewicz, who had been heading up the counterterrorism team, would soon be deployed to Moscow to reorient the group toward espionage *on*, not *with*, the Soviets.

After the formal meetings concluded, Palevich requested an audience with Marian Zacharski. By this time, the American ex-con had risen to be a senior executive at the Pewex retail chain. He'd soon become its CEO. On the side, he continued to work for Polish Intelligence. Henryk Jasik, the chief of the Foreign Intelligence Department, called Zacharski. "Come to Magdalenka," he said.

"I think we know each other," Zacharski boomed, upon entering the room at Magdalenka and looking straight at Palevich. Palevich explained to Zacharski that he'd been under orders not to speak with him on the plane that brought them from the United States to

Germany in June 1985. "I wrote a report about you, John," Zacharski said. "This mysterious big guy always staring me in the eyes."

"You know," Palevich said, referring to Zacharski's activities in Los Angeles, "that operation you ran was very good."

"If you knew more about it," Zacharski smiled, "you'd say it was better than very good."

It was clear to Zacharski that Palevich was fishing for information about Polish penetration in the United States. The Americans still didn't know how much Zacharski had stolen. They wanted details of Americans who'd served as intelligence assets for Poland in the United States. Jasik ultimately supplied Palevich with a six-page list of technologies that Zacharski had obtained from his American sources. However, Jasik refused to disclose other operations. Zacharski supported him. "What was freedom for anyway?" Zacharski asked. "You cannot just exchange chiefs—from the Soviet Union to the United States."

At Magdalenka, Polish and American intelligence officers shared the conviction that they were reestablishing bonds that stretched back to the Revolutionary War. Everyone knew the story of Kazimierz Pułaski, a Polish cavalry officer, who saved George Washington's life in 1777, and that of Tadeusz Kościuszko, a skilled military engineer, who masterminded the game-changing British defeat at Saratoga that same year.

Pułaski and Kościuszko were more than mercenaries. The pair believed in democracy and in the young republic. Pułaski gave his life for the United States in 1779. Kościuszko served in the Continental Army longer than any other foreign officer and oversaw the building of military fortifications at West Point.

Kościuszko was a hit among his fellow officers and among the army's rank and file. As one American officer declared upon learning that Kościuszko had to skip a fireworks display to celebrate Britain's final defeat in 1783: "Liberty is nothing without a Pole!" On the outskirts of Warsaw in the early summer of 1990, Polish and American officers rediscovered that mutual enthusiasm; it would become a hall-mark of the relationship for years to come.

After the meetings wound up on July 2, things moved quickly. On July 6, Czesław Kiszczak stepped down as minister of interior and was replaced by Kozłowski. Prime Minister Mazowiecki then appointed a former jailed dissident, Andrzej Milczanowski, to take Kozłowski's place as deputy minister and chief of the UOP. This personnel move marked a watershed in the transformation of Poland's Communist-era intelligence operations. Now, the minister and vice minister of Poland's once-feared Ministry of Interior were both former dissidents. Poland's years as a police state were over.

Delegations of American and Polish intelligence officers began crisscrossing the Atlantic. American CIA officers, masquerading as employees of private contractors, came to Poland to lecture at Poland's Intelligence Training Center at Stare Kiejkuty, in the scenic Mazurian Lakes region northeast of Warsaw. Polish spies went to the United States for training in counterterrorism, counterintelligence, recruit-ment, and other skills. The US government began providing Polish Intelligence with millions of dollars in cash and equipment. Rozbicki and others helped Poland establish an analysis section in the UOP.

Combating counterterrorism also required armed operatives, and the CIA was there to support that, too. Early into his tenure as min-ister of interior, Kozłowski was approached by a formidably muscled lieutenant colonel from the spy service named Sławomir Petelicki. Born into a family of Communists, Petelicki was raised on his dad's stories of parachuting behind German lines to fight the Nazis in World War II. Petelicki was a so-so law student at the University of Warsaw in the early 1960s, and spent more time practicing judo than study-ing socialist jurisprudence. He joined Foreign Intelligence in 1969. By 1971, he was a military adviser in North Vietnam; two years later he was attached to the Polish mission to the United Nations in New York. Petelicki's responsibilities included shadowing prominent Polish

Americans, including Zbigniew Brzeziński, who in 1976 became Jimmy Carter's national security advisor. Petelicki gave Brzeziński a code name, "Ogiński," after a Polish prince.

Petelicki had interests beyond espionage. Inspired by the TV action series *Starsky & Hutch*, he bought a red Pontiac Firebird with white trim. He also liked street fighting. Sometimes, he'd head to Spanish Harlem for matches that could have come straight out of the 1999 film *Fight Club*. US counterintelligence officers learned about this pastime and decided not to recruit him. He was too volatile. His bone-crushing handshake was the stuff of legend. He only squeezed hard if he liked you.

By the early 1980s, as the battle between the People's Republic and Solidarity intensified, Petelicki was in Sweden, in charge of disrupting Solidarity's fund-raising efforts in Scandinavia. After the changes in 1989, Department I's legal adviser Wojciech Brochwicz got Petelicki rehired; he was just the type of tough guy needed by the new Poland, Brochwicz said.

In March 1990, after the Polish couple were shot on the street in Beirut, Petelicki was sent to Lebanon to secure the Polish embassy. Back in Warsaw in the halls of the ministry, Petelicki buttonholed Kozłowski and volunteered his services: "Mr. Minister, if you ever need a useful rascal to organize an anti-terrorist unit, that would be me." Kozłowski didn't take long to agree. On July 13, the Polish government commissioned GROM, which means "thunderclap" in Polish and stands for Grupa Reagowania Operacyjno-Manewrowego, or Group for Operational Maneuvering Response—a tongue-twisting way of saying a special operations unit. GROM wasn't put under the command of the Polish military, which was still riddled with Soviet-style thinking, and probably Soviet agents, too. Kozłowski asked Milczanowski at the Ministry of Interior to supervise GROM. Petelicki became its first commander.

Petelicki's next challenge was to scrounge up the money to fund the group. The Polish state was bankrupt. People were losing their jobs as state-owned firms failed. There were no funds in Poland for such luxuries as special forces.

During a US counterterrorism training course in the summer of 1990, Petelicki shared his dream with a group of CIA officers from the agency's Special Operations Group. "The phone rang in my office," Redmond recalled. "I had no idea there was this huge delegation of Poles in town with our paramilitary wing." Petelicki had been holding court in an inconspicuous office park in Maryland, outlining his vision for Polish special forces. A representative of the agency's Special Operations Group asked Redmond's opinion. Could Petelicki pull it off? Could he be trusted? "It's a wonderful idea," Redmond said. That single call led to millions more American dollars being committed, this time to build GROM. It was a testimony to the seat-of-the-pants nature of the emerging alliance. History was suddenly open between Warsaw and Washington and opportunities to rewrite it abounded everywhere.

During the morning he was set to return to Warsaw, Petelicki called Redmond, begging for help. He needed to buy Milczanowski a commando knife. It was a Sunday. "Where in the fuck am I going to find a big knife on a Sunday?" Redmond wondered. From his Capitol Hill home, he drove to meet Petelicki at the Ritz-Carlton in Tysons Corner, Virginia. They found a small gun shop on Route 123. It wasn't open yet and a line had formed outside. Petelicki's flight back to Poland was leaving in an hour. Redmond went to the front of the line with Petelicki in tow and banged on the window. "This guy is a professional killer and I'm from the CIA," Redmond barked. "He wants that Bowie knife over there." They were out of there in three minutes. "Petelicki was one of the great guys of all time," Redmond recalled. "He looked like an SS stormtrooper. But he had a heart of gold."

The CIA and other US military organizations along with the British Special Air Service subsidized GROM and provided instruction in Poland and at bases in the United States and Britain. One of the snipers training GROM's sharpshooters was Larry Freedman, a US

Army Special Forces sergeant major who would be killed by a mine during a deployment to Somalia in 1992. The Poles named a street for Freedman on GROM's main base.

Equipment and arms, such as the Heckler & Koch MP5 submachine gun, began flowing into GROM's armory from the United States, outside normal customs channels. "I knew about that and I was happy," Milczanowski said. "We were operating outside of political channels, too."

While the Americans were ready to train the Poles, they weren't exactly ready to trust them. US supervisors banned GROM members in the United States from taking pictures of training facilities and blacked out the windows of their buses and planes. "We were never told where we were," Jacek Kita, an early recruit, said. "But we could guess."

Like Derlatka, Petelicki was considered "crazy" by many of his colleagues. But it was the time for that kind of out-of-the-box thinking and action. "Everybody complained about Petelicki. 'Don't let him drink! If he drinks there'll be a fight!'" Milczanowski recounted. "But he had drive. He was a top-notch organizer. He was persuasive. He could bribe people with flattery. He was a real intelligence officer."

Andrzej Milczanowski was an enlightened choice to run the UOP. He liked to say he couldn't remember anything about the most important person in his life. "It may be grand rhetoric," he said, "but it's true." He loved his mother, his big sister, his wife, and their daughter, but it was the specter of his father—who'd vanished when he was four months old—that shaded his existence. Milczanowski's dad was a prosecutor in what was then the eastern Polish city of Równe. On September 26, 1939, a week after the Soviet Union invaded Poland, agents from the Soviet secret police, the NKVD, seized him and other leading Poles from the city administration. Other than a note smuggled from prison a few days later that read, "Take the kids and run," the family never heard from him again.

With "two children and her parents on her back," as Milczanowski put it, his mother kept the family together in territory occupied first by the Red Army and then by the Germans. First, she feared deportation to Siberia and then to a German labor camp. Thanks to her daring, the family remained intact.

With the end of World War II, Milczanowski's family became part of Poland's massive population reshuffle. Stalin turned Równe into Rivne and assigned it to Ukraine. Milczanowski's family was uprooted and moved four hundred miles westward to a Silesian town that hadn't been ruled by a Polish government in three hundred years.

The ghost of a missing father haunted Milczanowski, engendering a hatred of the Soviets and their client state, the People's Republic of Poland. "Let's just say, I wasn't predisposed to Communism," he observed. As a youth, despite being on the shorter side, Milczanowski loved to box. Well into his eighties, he retained the steely-eyed look and pit bull intensity of a man who could take, and give, a punch. A lopsided mouth added to this belligerent mien.

After graduating with a law degree in 1962, Milczanowski followed in his father's footsteps and became a prosecutor for the very system that had robbed him of his dad. Milczanowski married a law faculty classmate, Sławomira Ołtarzewska, and the couple moved to Szczecin on the Baltic Sea. Sławomira became a judge.

Milczanowski had a great boss at the prosecutor's office. He didn't pressure Milczanowski to join the Communists, i.e., the Polish United Workers' Party, or to take political cases. Milczanowski mainly prosecuted violent crimes—armed robberies and homicides. In 1968, Milczanowski discovered that working as a private lawyer offered three times the pay for one-fifth the workload. He quit his government job.

Andrzej and Sławomira settled into a comfortable existence as local worthies in Szczecin. Through their friends and contacts in the intellectual elite, they accessed banned books, like Aleksandr

Solzhenitsyn's *The Gulag Archipelago*, and anti-Communist magazines printed by Polish émigrés in Paris. Milczanowski nurtured a passion for American jazz, which came to him via Willis Conover's *Jazz Hour* on the Voice of America. Milczanowski even managed a serviceable version on the piano of the Louis Armstrong favorite "Muskrat Ramble."

In December 1970, demonstrations protesting food price rises erupted in industrial cities along the Baltic coast. In Szczecin, workers torched the Communist party's headquarters. Security forces killed sixteen striking workers. Milczanowski witnessed bloody clashes and took the case of a protester who was severely injured after she was run over by a police car.

A group of workers and intellectuals began gathering at the Milczanowskis' apartment to discuss politics. A strike committee was founded. In January 1971, representatives from that committee met with the Communist party chief, Edward Gierek, who acceded to some of their demands. A few years later, Milczanowski found himself leading a double life as a prominent attorney by day and a dissident working to unseat the People's Republic by night.

A liker of lists, Milczanowski credits three things with causing him to give up the "easy life" of a successful lawyer in Communist Poland: the intangible presence of his father pointing him toward righteousness; an instinctual hatred of Communism; and a character flaw. "I am an adventurer," he said.

Throughout the 1970s, Milczanowski provided legal advice to Poland's disparate worker and dissident groups as they organized strikes throughout the country. When martial law was declared on December 13, 1981, Milczanowski was sentenced to five years in jail. Amnesty International adopted him as a prisoner of conscience. Released early in April 1984, Milczanowski continued underground work for the next four years. During the Round Table talks in 1989, he counseled Solidarity leader Lech Wałęsa on legal matters.

Free Poland's first prime minister, Tadeusz Mazowiecki, initially offered Milczanowski the job of public prosecutor general, Poland's version of attorney general. Milczanowski turned it down; he'd already been a prosecutor. A few days later, Mazowiecki had another idea. Would Milczanowski consider directing the UOP, forming the first free intelligence service in the new Eastern Europe? "That's more like it," Milczanowski replied.

CHAPTER NINE

DON'T BLOW IT UP

Andrzej Milczanowski brought comrades from Solidarity's under-ground into the Polish spy agency. Dissidents like a twenty-eight-year-old with dreadlocks named Piotr Niemczyk. As a printer for Solidarity in Szczecin, Niemczyk operated in the shadows, hid from the security forces, and was imprisoned twice for publishing an illegal newsletter.

It turned out that undercover work as a Solidarity activist, setting up secret presses for samizdat publications, and maintaining surreptitious contacts with Western diplomats and labor union reps constituted good training for intelligence work. "It was a natural continuation of what we'd done before," Niemczyk recalled. Ex-Communist officers were initially unsure about the new recruits. But as one remarked, "Some [former] pacifists like guns, and some [former] anarchists love order and discipline."

Milczanowski understood that Poland needed seasoned spies. Given Poland's dangerous neighborhood, reinventing the wheel wasn't an option. He needed to merge fresh recruits in with the old. So, in

July 1990, the Poles began vetting officers in the Ministry of Interior in an effort to rid the service only of those who had seriously violated human rights during Communist times.

Milczanowski's boss, Krzysztof Kozłowski, led the Central Selection Committee, the main vetting organization. Milczanowski served as his deputy and brought Niemczyk and other Solidarity activists with him. Verification committees were established nationwide to deal with the vast number of security officers—some twenty-four thousand—who'd kept the Communists in power.

The Poles made up the verification process as they went along. "We had no example to follow," Kozłowski recalled. "Nobody had done this before. Nobody had exited from Communism." Vetted officers had to follow the "ethical principles of Solidarity," be willing to protect a democratic Poland, and possess an "immaculate moral and patriotic attitude." The committees were configured like courts, with one lawyer acting as a prosecutor and another acting for the defense. Wojciech Brochwicz, a legal adviser to the UOP, played the role of prosecutor at the central "court" in Warsaw. There were forty-eight more across Poland. Mistakes were made, some thugs got through, but those involved in the process were united by a belief that Poland couldn't afford to start afresh. "We knew this wasn't Sunday school," Brochwicz said. "We needed rough men and women to protect the new Poland."

Kozłowski was intent that Poland's democratic transition avoid a pitfall of past revolutions: the persecution of the losers. "We didn't want to perpetrate what we had fought against during Communism," Kozłowski told an interviewer in the documentary film *Polish Transformation*. "In other words, we didn't want revenge." Public opinion wasn't with the government. "The public wanted the 'zero hour.' The taking of the Bastille," Kozłowski recalled.

Kozłowski and Milczanowski debated with other former dissidents exactly who and how many to purge from the SB. Officials at the foreign ministry wanted to remove all Polish intelligence officers from diplomatic posts. Milczanowski pushed back. They were veteran spies, he argued, who could provide Poland with actionable intelligence about the Soviet Union, terrorism, narcotics smuggling, and, given Operation Bridge, the security of embassy staff and Jews transiting Poland to Israel.

Milczanowski also argued to keep the officers who knew Russia best. Even though Gorbachev was making nice, a fear of Russia was ingrained in the psyche of the Poles. Milczanowski wasn't the only one in the government who'd lost a parent to the NKVD. The Russians had a substantial network of agents inside Poland. "We needed to root them out or at least identify them," Milczanowski said. "We needed people in the service who knew them well."

There were other reasons for avoiding a total purge. "If we went for the zero option," Milczanowski noted, "we'd have an army of well-trained opponents." This became clear during one meeting between the vetting committee and a group of Communist-era officers. "Mr. Minister," one officer asked Milczanowski, "aren't you afraid if you sack us all, we'll go to the forests?" In a key move that won the loyalty of many officers, the government passed a law that counted their years of service during Communist rule toward their pensions. That commitment kept many of the best officers from leaving.

Out of an original group of twenty-four thousand officers in the security services, more than fourteen thousand signed up to be verified. Of those, more than ten thousand passed. Of that group, seven thousand were rehired.

Of the one thousand officers working in the far smaller Foreign Intelligence Department, only three failed verification. "The officers in Foreign Intelligence were the intellectual elite of the ministry and the party," Kozłowski said. "They were people sophisticated in the world, knowing languages, able to find their way in any situation."

As he managed this process, Milczanowski had a powerful ally: the CIA. The agency lobbied against a purge of the intelligence services. The reason was simple. Communist spies were often very good. The CIA just wanted them to work with America, not against it. Langley also worried that if too many officers were fired, they might succeed in derailing the revolution unfolding in the Eastern Bloc. "For sure," Milczanowski observed, "the CIA had its finger on the scale of history."

Some in Eastern Europe didn't listen to the remonstrations of the CIA. Czechoslovakia was one. Following the Velvet Revolution and the election of Václav Havel as president, the Czechs undid their intelligence agency, the StB. During the Cold War, the StB had gained notoriety for supporting the far-left Italian Red Brigades and supplying terrorist groups with the hard-to-detect, Czech-made plastic explosive Semtex. "Mostly playwrights, philosophers and actors," was how the CIA's Milton Bearden described Czechoslovakia's post-Communist leadership. "They basically put the lights out, locked the door, and walked away."

The CIA found other ways to support Havel. The agency bought the Czech president an armored car; Bearden test-drove it around the grounds at Langley. The CIA also provided the US ambassador to Prague, the former child film star Shirley Temple Black, with a list of names of high-ranking StB officers whom the CIA feared were plotting a revanchist coup. At a soiree in early 1990 at her Prague residence, a Gatsbyesque palace built in the 1920s by a Jewish coal baron, Black maneuvered Havel into a quiet corner. With dramatic flair, she pulled the list from her bodice. "These people could cause problems for you," she told the Czech president. Havel looked at the names, his eyes popped out, and, in short order, the spies on the list were retired with their pensions.

The Poles disagreed with Havel's decision to fire all of Czechoslovakia's spies. "This was not a time for experiments with tearing everything down," recalled Andrzej Derlatka, the brainy mastermind of Operation Unity. "It was a very hot time. We needed a group of professionals to keep watch. During communism Poland had three neighbors. Within two years, we had eight." When the Czechs dismantled the StB, "they were like a child in the fog," Derlatka said. "We ended up telling them a lot." Derlatka believed that Czechoslovakia's self-inflicted wound led directly to its fissure. On January 1, 1993, it split into two countries, the Czech Republic and Slovakia, in what was called the "Velvet Divorce."

The Polish service was a natural partner for the CIA. The agency didn't know the Czech service like it knew the SB. "We didn't have a Mr. Czechoslovakia," Milt Bearden observed. "Palevich really knew the Poles." And as for the Hungarians, Bearden noted, "they were pretty cerebral" and not incredibly interested in joint operations. After all, they'd backed out of the mission to transit Soviet Jewry. The Stasi in East Germany, Bearden added, "were capable but they were also an awful, un-deNazified lot." Besides, the West German intelligence service, the BND, was in the process of absorbing them. "The Poles were the only ones we had to work with," Bearden said. As Michael Sulick, another former CIA officer who ultimately ran the agency's clandestine service, assessed, "Of all the Eastern European countries, the Poles had the most capacity and were the most forward-leaning." Sulick was also aware of the connection between Americans and Poles. The camaraderie between them transcended national interest. "Poland was the only country," Sulick said, "where I continued relationships after I retired."

Another reason to cooperate with Poland involved how thoroughly Palevich and other US intelligence officers had penetrated the Polish government. As the relationship between the CIA and Poland deepened, Palevich found himself in meetings with Polish intelligence officers whom he'd once recruited to spy for the United States. He had to act as if they'd never met when, in fact, he knew intimate details of their lives. "That was strange," Palevich recalled. "But the times were changing." Palevich also knew most, if not all, of the bad apples. Ultimately, the CIA handed Kozłowski a list of security service officials with suspected links to Moscow; they were eased out.

This granular knowledge gave the agency the comfort to pursue collaboration as quickly as possible. Faced with fast-moving events in the USSR, the CIA didn't have the luxury of waiting for its new Eastern European partners to build intelligence agencies from scratch. The CIA was also eager to capitalize on Poland's enduring reputation as a Communist nation to cloak its espionage. Time was of the essence.

Some in the US government opposed the CIA's outreach to the ex-Communist spies. In March 1990, then deputy secretary of state Lawrence Eagleburger complained to Bush that the Poles were taking their time purging former Communist bureaucrats. But Bearden and Redmond, who didn't agree on much, agreed on the wisdom of cooperating with the UOP.

"How could you not benefit from dealing with the Poles who lived in the most dangerous piece of real estate in Europe?" Bearden asked. "They'd had forty-five years of liaison with the KGB. How was it possible that listening to them wouldn't be the smartest thing we could do?

"What's more, they sounded a lot like us. And they knew tons more about the Soviets. They'd had to live with them. And Moscow was still the A1 target."

Palevich was an important voice in pushing for cooperation with the ex-Communists in the Polish service. Sure, they had been Communist party members and some even seemed dedicated to the cause, but Palevich considered them intelligence professionals above all. That's why Palevich wanted to meet Zacharski in Warsaw in July. He wanted to demonstrate to the Polish dissidents now running Poland's government that the CIA respected good tradecraft. "I needed the cooperation of experienced officers," Palevich said. In numerous meetings with representatives from the Solidarity-led government, Palevich praised his former foes.

"The opinions of John Palevich were important to me," Milczanowski acknowledged. "He had great expertise in Polish Intelligence. Not only did he know us, he even knew how the desks were arranged inside the ministry and when one was out of place, he noticed."

"Andrzej took me seriously," Palevich recalled. "His first instinct when he took over was to get even with these guys. He associated them with the characters who'd sent him to jail. But friendly pressure steered him in the right direction. I convinced him that intelligence was a different thing." As he transformed the UOP, Milczanowski earned the respect of the ex-Communist officers who made up the bulk of the service. "We were worried that he would take a machete to the service but he didn't," Zacharski said. "He was a gold mine for the service and for Poland."

To realize his vision of an agency that pooled officers from Solidarity with officers from the old regime, Milczanowski needed partners among the Communist-era spies. One emerged: Colonel Gromosław "Gromek" Czempiński.

Hawk-nosed with piercing dark blue eyes, Gromek Czempiński was a dead ringer for the American actor Tom Selleck. Born just after the end of World War II in October 1945, Czempiński grew into a gregarious young man, gifted at striking up conversations with just about anyone. Like Zacharski, his engaging personality masked a titanic ego. In the field, he had a tendency to perform, one of his colleagues noted, like "a one-man orchestra."

Czempiński's father fought the German occupation and tried to get a job in the security services in the late 1950s but was rejected because he was considered too much of a Polish nationalist, which meant he didn't like the Soviets. Instead, he learned to fly and managed a flying club in Poznań, a city in western Poland one hundred miles from the East German border.

When Czempiński turned fourteen, his father brought him up in a plane. Flying became his passion. Czempiński dreamed of joining the Polish air force or flying for Poland's national carrier, LOT. Topping out at six-three, though, he grew too tall to become a professional pilot in Poland.

At university, Czempiński majored in economics but spent his early years there either playing sports or drinking. He risked flunking out, until he met a student named Barbara Malek. She got him off the bottle and back into books. "She told me I had charisma," Czempiński recalled. "She believed in me." They married soon after graduation.

Czempiński was weak at foreign languages but handy at strategy. After college, he joined the police and excelled in the field. He saved the lives of fellow recruits when a fire erupted during a training mission. Still, his superiors were wary of him. Czempiński was, his personnel reports said, "controversial," "unpredictable," "difficult to command," "stubborn." He had too many of his own ideas, officers complained.

In 1972, Department I invited Czempiński to Warsaw for interviews. He was lodged in an apartment with a fridge full of vodka and subjected to a battery of tests, psychological and otherwise. He didn't touch the alcohol. On the third day, he was summoned in front of a panel. He was told that he didn't read enough, that he was ignorant of many things, especially art, and that he'd passed.

In the fall, Czempiński was sent to a new school for spies established by the Polish government under the leadership of party boss Edward Gierek. The Intelligence Agency Training Center, in northeastern Poland, was something unique in the Eastern Bloc: a spy school with no Soviet officers and no Soviet instructors. In fact, at the opening ceremony, Stanisław Kania, the politburo member in charge of internal security at the time, didn't mention Communism, the USSR, or the Warsaw Pact: just Poland, patriotism, and the economy.

The eighty students in the first class, all male, had been chosen from a pool of one thousand candidates. They lived two to a room and were taught by fifty instructors, including one spy famed for penetrating US-funded Radio Free Europe. There was a lake on the grounds, along with an indoor swimming pool, a gym, Swedish fixtures in the bathroom, and a nuclear bunker. Poland also placed its signals intelligence unit on the campus, something that would benefit the US government later on.

A chef from Warsaw's Grand Hotel was hired to cook. The waitresses were pretty and there was an open bar after five in the afternoon.

Instructors drank with students, partly to determine who could hold their liquor. The curriculum mixed English-language classes, skydiving instruction, and firearms training with an important subject: how to make friends, a key competence for any spy. Czempiński's class contained some men who, like him, would mature into well-regarded intelligence officers, including a chess and crew champion named Bogdan Libera and Aleksander Makowski. John Palevich would also recruit several of Czempiński's classmates to work as agents for the CIA.

Czempiński almost got himself expelled after he cut school to take part in a glider competition in western Poland—when he was supposed to be on a field exercise trailing someone in Wrocław. School administrators discovered it after newspapers began writing about a dashing young pilot on track to win the event. Czempiński loved the limelight. Despite his battles with English, Czempiński graduated near the top of his class and was rewarded with a watch and a plum assignment in the American section of Department I.

In 1976, Czempiński was posted to Poland's consulate in Chicago as a vice consul in the scientific department. He was a quick study, memorizing the location of police cameras and other no-go zones in the city. He, Barbara, and their young daughter, Iwona, lived in a spacious apartment near the consulate on Lake Shore Drive. Even in his first posting, Gromek exhibited an independent streak. He advocated for closer ties with Chicago's Polish community, despite its tradition of zealously opposing Polish Communism. He suggested that the Polish government grant more visas to American Catholic priests of Polish descent. He wanted to give US churches money to offer Polish-language classes.

Czempiński's posting was cut short when a Polish defector who had been Czempiński's classmate gave Palevich the names of the whole class and where they'd been stationed. Czempiński returned to Warsaw and was assigned to counterintelligence, Poland's version of the FBI. From 1977 to 1980, he and his comrades unmasked five American spies. At the same time, the CIA was robbing Poland blind thanks to Colonel Kukliński and other sources. "It was a healthy competition," Czempiński recalled. In 1980, he returned to foreign intelligence work.

Gromek and Barbara were at the center of a big social circle in Warsaw. Young, beautiful, dynamic, and talented, they had a model marriage and were the life of the party. It was hard to imagine an event without them. In January 1982, Barbara gave birth to a son. Barbara knew immediately. Czempiński didn't want to believe there was anything wrong, yet he was haunted by his son's eyes. Piotr was diagnosed with Down syndrome.

To care for Piotr, Barbara ended a promising career in foreign trade. Czempiński turned to sports to expel his sorrow and frustration. He buried himself in work. At night, they cried alone. "We couldn't touch each other in bed," he recalled.

Foreign Intelligence offered Czempiński and his family a post in the West where care was better for children with disabilities. Czempiński and family were sent to Geneva; there he served undercover as a first secretary at Poland's mission to the United Nations. During the day, Piotr attended a Swiss institution. He learned to feed and bathe himself. Specialists predicted accurately that he'd start talking when he turned twenty.

Czempiński loved the job. He mingled with Americans, Arabs, Israelis, and Germans. He fraternized with British spies. At one point, the Americans even tried to recruit him and John Palevich was dispatched to reel him in. The operation was set to take place during a small dinner at the home of a CIA officer who worked at the US mission. But it was sloppily managed. Czempiński drove up to the house, realized what was about to happen, and rang the doorbell. When the American spy answered the door, Czempiński announced that he wouldn't be attending the dinner. "And by the way," he added, "I am going to use this as a negative example for my students in Warsaw." Years later after the fall of Communism, Palevich pulled Czempiński aside and acknowledged: "Gromek, you were a major defeat for me."

Still, Palevich comforted himself in the knowledge that he'd recruited one of Czempiński's closest associates, who, unbeknownst to Gromek, worked at the heart of Foreign Intelligence—and for the CIA—for years.

In Geneva, Czempiński basically pursued his own foreign policy. Poland was under martial law, but Czempiński, in cables back to Warsaw, advocated amnesty for political prisoners so Poland could convince the West, and particularly America, to lift economic sanctions. He traveled widely. He participated in a balloon race in the United States. (His team finished last.) He went again to the United States in 1983 for a UN conference on the future of Palestine and flew in a glider competition in California. He and Barbara were fixtures on the Geneva social circuit; Gromek caught the attention not only of the men but of the women. He was a constant flirt. At one point, a CIA officer griped that Gromek, with his ocean-blue eyes and killer mustache, seemed intent on compromising the careers of several CIA female intelligence officers. He was close with women the world over.

Czempiński's freelancing irritated the KGB station in Geneva, which complained that Czempiński was not being collegial with the rest of the Warsaw Pact spies. He missed meetings with Soviet counterparts; he fraternized with known Western intelligence officers; he'd never even been to the USSR. Gossip circulated that he was going to defect to the West. Czempiński got wind of a Polish operation to bundle him into the trunk of a car and drive him from Switzerland back to Poland. He told his bosses: "You don't understand me. I am a proud Pole. I love Poland." The operation was called off. Czempiński returned to Poland in 1987, this time as chief of counterintelligence.

Back in Warsaw, Czempiński led teams of officers into the homes of Western diplomats and suspected spies. He broke into the apartment belonging to CIA station chief Bill Norville and his wife, Maggi. He wanted to recruit Norville. "I knew Bill Norville better than he knew himself," Czempiński boasted. "He was my target. Unfortunately, I didn't find anything."

Following Poland's political revolution in 1989, Czempiński figured that everything was going to be blown up and that he was going to be out of a job. He prepared for a life in the private sector and laid plans to open an auto dealership, a safe bet as Poles lined up to buy cars. But the CIA lobbied Milczanowski and Kozłowski to positively vet as many intelligence officers as possible, especially those experienced in operations. Czempiński spent two days in a room alone with twelve interrogators, poring over his past. By that time, talks were already ongoing with the CIA and Norville had transitioned from an undercover CIA officer in a hostile nation to the announced station chief of an emerging friend. Norville even volunteered to testify on Czempiński's behalf at the hearing. It wasn't necessary. Czempiński passed.

Once vetted, Czempiński began defending Department I's other officers at their hearings in Warsaw. He won praise for backing his colleagues. Brochwicz, the chief "prosecutor" in the vetting process, faced off against him. "He was a chaotic man," Brochwicz recalled. "He was egocentric and annoying. Megalomaniacal and irritating. But I never caught him lying. He matured into a real leader."

Czempiński played a central role in Operation Unity. In November 1989, Foreign Intelligence chief Henryk Jasik directed him to contact an old friend from Geneva, Ian Penders Chalmers, a British intelligence officer who'd worked undercover as a diplomat for the British mission. By that time, Chalmers was serving as a deputy director of MI6. During four meetings in Vienna, a favorite locale for off-the-record gatherings among spies, Czempiński shared Poland's intelligence on the hush-hush talks between Germany and the USSR and Warsaw's opposition to any secret understanding between Moscow and Bonn. By the fourth get-together, in April 1990, the pair agreed to formally establish contacts between the UOP and MI6—a few weeks in advance of the Lisbon meeting with the CIA.

In 1990, Kozłowski promoted Czempiński to deputy operations chief of the UOP. Czempiński backed Sławomir Petelicki's idea to form a special operations unit inside the ministry. In fact, its acronym, GROM, was a double entendre. In addition to "thunderclap," it was the root of Gromosław, Czempiński's first name.

Czempiński was an enthusiastic chief of the UOP's clandestine services. "I wanted to do things," he said. "I didn't want to be an administrator." He was a fan of the Americans and had forgiven the CIA for its bungled attempt to turn him into an asset. "Sometimes you don't need to recruit someone to keep him on your side," he said.

Inside Warsaw's Intelligence Command, Czempiński proved adept at mixing the cultures of the Communist-era officers with those from Solidarity. "He brought the old guard in with the new recruits. He got people to work together," said Piotr Pytlakowski, a Polish investigative journalist, who wrote a book on the first class at the Intelligence Training Center. "He married fire and water."

There are only a few examples of pendulums not swinging radically once a revolution occurs. Poland's experiment was a case in point. Rather than throwing out the old system to ring in the new, Poland's leaders made the epochal decision to preserve much of the Communist infrastructure as they transitioned to democracy. The Intelligence Command, backed by the CIA, played a key role in the drama. So did Poland's not-so-Communist Communists. Josef Stalin had been right. Turning the Poles into revolutionaries was as hard as saddling a cow.

PART THREE

PERILOUS PARTNERSHIP

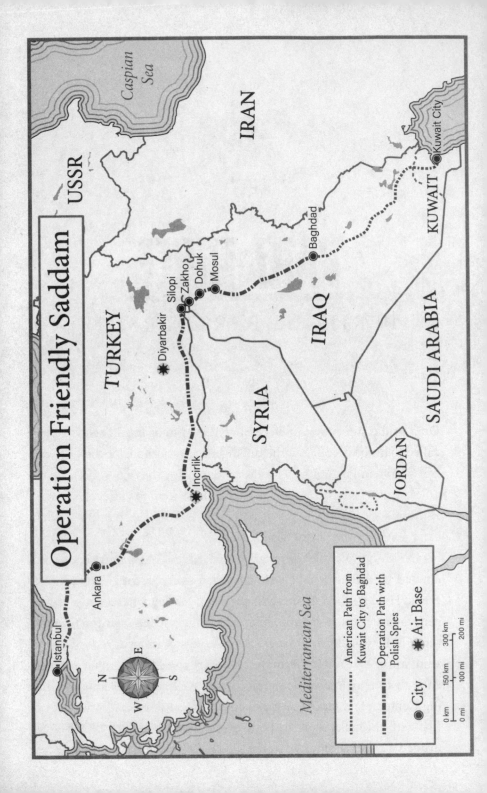

CHAPTER TEN

BAGHDAD SURPRISE

On a Friday afternoon in December 1989, Major John Feeley Jr. was called to his boss's office at the Intelligence Directorate for the US Central Command in Tampa, Florida. "Schwarzkopf has a question," Brigadier General Henry Drewfs announced, referring to General Norman Schwarzkopf, CENTCOM's commander. "What's the worst thing that can happen in the Middle East?"

At thirty-nine, Feeley had been around the army since he'd entered West Point in 1969. He'd learned strategy from Vietnam veterans. He'd studied Chinese history at Berkeley where, thanks to a generous army scholarship, he had so much spare cash that people thought he was dealing drugs. He'd served as an armored officer in an infantry division in Germany and had grasped Russian tactics well enough to play a Soviet commander at the army's National Training Center. He'd taught world history at West Point and understood that with the collapse of the Berlin Wall a month earlier, CENTCOM needed a new mission. With the Cold War ending and an expected peace dividend, "everybody and his brother," he observed, "was look-ing for something to do."

A competitive sailor since his days growing up in Southern Cal-ifornia, Feeley had a regatta the next day. He raced on Saturday and on Sunday he went into the office to write his report. On Monday, he turned it in. The worst thing that could happen in the Middle East, he concluded, would be for Iraq's dictator—Saddam Hussein—to invade Kuwait and then head south and grab Saudi Arabia's oil fields. On the following Friday, Feeley found himself briefing Schwarzkopf and the rest of CENTCOM's command.

Feeley's report was out of left field. Ever since the ousting of the Shah of Iran and the American hostage crisis of 1979–1981, Iran—not Iraq—had been America's foe. During the Iran–Iraq War from 1980 to 1988, the United States had provided Saddam with intelligence and arms. Now a US army officer was singling out Saddam, a de facto US ally, as the biggest threat to stability in the Middle East. Still, Feeley's report tracked with intelligence that US forces in the Middle East had picked up. Iran had been weakened by the war, but Saddam's army remained huge and, with Soviet help, he was rebuilding. Even Ameri-can military sales to Iraq continued until 1989.

Schwarzkopf directed Feeley to head to Washington and brief the Pentagon, the CIA, and the Defense Intelligence Agency. When Fee-ley returned to Tampa, Schwarzkopf asked him to work with the staff and draw up plans to counter a possible invasion. Schwarzkopf then ordered his staff and Feeley to organize war games at an air force base on the Florida panhandle to test those plans.

By this time, it was July 1990. Since the spring Saddam had been accusing Kuwait and other members of the OPEC oil cartel of pur-posely depressing oil prices as part of a plot to sabotage Iraq's war-torn economy. Saddam began to threaten Kuwait and Saudi Arabia. Feeley found himself in the disorienting position of war-gaming a scenario that was simultaneously unfolding in real life. Each day, he'd brief twice: once to the war gamers and then to CENTCOM's command. The war game and reality began to merge.

On July 23, Schwarzkopf ordered Feeley to travel to Kuwait with a stack of satellite photographs to show members of the ruling Al Sabah clan what was transpiring on Kuwait's border with Iraq. Saddam was massing troops. Schwarzkopf told Feeley to report back only to him and to CENTCOM, not to the State Department or the CIA.

The State and Defense departments differed fundamentally in their reading of Saddam's playbook. US embassy officials had told the emir that the Iraqi dictator was bluffing. They predicted that the Kuwaitis and Saudis would pay Saddam off and the kerfuffle would subside. The US Army was ginning up a crisis, they said. General Schwarzkopf thought Saddam was serious and that Kuwait's rulers needed a wake-up call.

In Kuwait City, Feeley briefed royal family members on July 27 and 28. Feeley's message: this was no bluff and the crisis was real. He pointed out something in satellite images that others had missed: the presence of water trucks among the military equipment. That indicated an army on the move.

On the night of August 1, Feeley attended a reception at the US embassy, then returned to his room at the International Hotel Kuwait across the street. At 2:30 A.M., he was awakened by explosions. Weapons fire lit the nighttime sky. Blasts shook the hotel. Feeley ran to the embassy to call CENTCOM in Tampa on a secure line. "Hey, it's on," he told his comrades in Florida. Feeley, the man who'd predicted the invasion and helped draw up plans to counter it, was stuck in Kuwait.

Over the next few days, hundreds of Americans flocked to the US embassy, including stranded American passengers from a British Airways flight that had landed hours before the attack. Iraqi soldiers entered Kuwait City and began rounding up Westerners at Kuwaiti hotels. Among those taken away from the Sheraton was Martin

Stanton, a US Army major and military adviser stationed in Saudi Arabia. In violation of a CENTCOM travel ban, Stanton had come to Kuwait City for the weekend to sightsee.

Iraqi secret police seized two British officers and beat, tortured, then interned them. These actions sent a chill through all US military assigned to the US embassy. In response, US military personnel in Kuwait destroyed their ID cards, uniforms, and anything else that linked them to the armed forces. Using Motorola radios, US Army officers and other Americans living in Kuwait City set up a radio net to report on the occupation. Many of the American officers wanted to escape south across the Saudi border, which remained open. However, the US ambassador to Kuwait, W. Nathaniel Howell, was worried about someone getting killed. He prohibited anyone with a diplomatic passport from leaving—a deeply unpopular ruling. Still, a few Americans, including the daughter of CIA station chief Hunter Downs, trickled out before August 11, when the Iraqis shut the crossing and killed a British citizen to show they were serious. Hundreds more Americans, oil workers, teachers, and businessmen and -women hid in their homes.

On August 6, reports that Iraqi soldiers were arresting Westerners prompted Ambassador Howell to allow members of the US military who held diplomatic passports and their families into the embassy. One of them was Fred Hart, a forty-two-year-old army major. Hart belonged to the US Liaison Office in Kuwait, which managed US weapons sales to the Kuwaiti army. A father of two, Hart was born in Georgia, where his mother, a white Russian from Shanghai, had taught Russian to air force pilots.

In army vernacular, Hart was known affectionately as a "gun runner." The job was considered good duty. The Kuwaitis were easygoing and the post was supposed to be a cushy ticket to a promotion. Instead, Hart found himself and his family—wife Chris, six-year-old Natasha, and two-year-old Mary—living through an invasion.

A night before Saddam invaded, Hart had been up on Kuwait's

border with Iraq and had seen the Iraqi army mustering for the attack. He tried to warn the Northern Kuwaiti Brigade, which was supposed to be manning the defenses, but its commanding officers had fled. On the night of the invasion, Hart climbed onto the roof of his villa and watched flares explode like fireworks. Along the border, Westinghouse technicians at a radar installation told the embassy that the invading Iraqi army looked like an enormous iron pipe rolling downhill. By morning light, Bayan Palace, the emir's main residence, and the international airport were under air assault. Hart fielded calls from Kuwaiti colonels pleading with him to send in the Eighty-Second Airborne Division. Kuwait's military had done nothing to prepare.

On August 8, heavy weapons fire erupted outside the embassy, with tracer rounds coming over the compound. All those inside the compound were ordered to squeeze into the embassy's vault. After a few minutes, the firing stopped. At that point, Howell, not wanting to see the mission turned into a modern-day Alamo, ordered the marines to disarm and that communications links with CENTCOM be severed. The marine detachment had no choice but to follow Howell's orders. They dismantled their weapons in full view of the surrounding Iraqis. Communications links, however, were maintained. "We couldn't follow all the orders," Feeley noted. "We had to keep lines open to the outside world." Howell was petrified that the Iraqi army would invade the compound.

One hundred and seventy-five people crowded inside the embassy. Hart and Chief Warrant Officer Dave Forties, who'd been in Kuwait for two years and spoke passable Arabic, inventoried the snack bar stocks and discovered they had just a few days of food. Thanks to a home-brewed beer operation he'd run in a country that technically banned alcohol, Forties was plugged in with Kuwaitis and expats. Forties and Hart took over the job of scrounging up provisions. Daily, the pair skulked out of the embassy on scavenging runs in a late-model Chevy Blazer to tap Forties's contacts. One of Forties's

Indian sources had access to an underground warehouse in a suburb of Kuwait City. One morning, as they bartered for stocks of canned tuna and frozen turkeys, a platoon of Iraqi soldiers showed up. Hart and Forties ducked behind bags of flour until the Iraqis, bribed with cases of Pepsi-Cola, left. The pair added a dozen fifty-pound sacks of rice and a shipment of frozen beef to their tuna-and-turkey stash. The Americans paid for the food with IOUs, promising US government reimbursement once the conflict ended. Their biggest IOU was for $20,000. It's unclear whether the US government ever honored those chits.

At the embassy, American women, the majority of them military spouses, took up cooking duties and organized the living quarters. Adults were rationed one meal a day; children, two. After two weeks, the adults inside the compound had lost an average of fifteen pounds.

The food runs served another purpose. CIA station chief Hunter Downs had asked for intelligence on Iraqi troop movements and on chemical or Scud missile units. Hart and Forties never saw any signs of either but witnessed looting and pillaging on a grand scale. The entire Kuwait Gold Souk had been stripped bare. At the apartment of one American diplomat they discovered that Iraqi soldiers had fired up some Gaines-Burgers dog food on the grill.

In Kuwait since 1989, Hart had moonlighted for the CIA. Station chief Downs was a renowned Cold Warrior, laser-focused on countering the Soviet threat. Downs had asked Hart to develop a relationship with Russian military officers based in Kuwait. Downs tasked Hart with collecting the serial numbers of Russian equipment purchased by the Kuwaitis to determine whether the equipment was newly manufactured or surplus. US–Soviet arms control agreements limited the sales of some conventional weapons to surplus. Hart discovered, much to Downs's glee, that the Russians were cheating.

A few days after the invasion, the Russians flew in a Soviet Il-76 transport plane. Within hours Hart received a call from a Russian colonel offering him and his family seats to fly out. Hart politely declined.

As the United States and Britain patched together a coalition to liberate Kuwait, negotiations proceeded over the fate of diplomats there. Saddam's government announced that its forces would shut all of Kuwait's embassies on August 23. It ordered those holding diplomatic passports and their family members to leave Kuwait for Baghdad. All other foreigners in Kuwait were directed to surrender to Kuwait's Iraqi occupiers.

Feeley had traveled to Kuwait on an official US passport and didn't have diplomatic status. But he'd need it if he was going to slip out of Kuwait for Baghdad with the rest of the embassy's staff. An embassy official discovered a diplomatic passport, left behind by a mustachioed American who'd gone on vacation. "You could pass as this guy," the official remarked, handing Feeley the document. Feeley stopped shaving.

Hart and other members of the liaison team put together a convoy of fifty-seven American diplomats, their families, some of their belongings, more than one hundred gallons of water, and the remaining tuna fish. At six in the morning of August 23, the convoy left Kuwait City, bound for Baghdad, 415 miles away. Ambassador Howell's big black Cadillac, with American flags flying, was in the lead. Hart and Forties had collected a small supply of glint and duct tape to stick on the vehicles' roofs so US satellites could track the convoy's progress.

Leaving Kuwait City, the Americans encountered a landscape of utter devastation: corpses, burned-out vehicles, gutted buildings, and swarms of Iraqi soldiers. Some of the drivers were so astounded by the carnage that they took their eyes off the road and rear-ended cars in front of them. One American was gravely injured and had to be rushed back to Kuwait for surgery.

At the Safwan crossing into Iraq, thousands of refugees massed on both sides of the border. Iraqi soldiers marching past the convoy banged their rifle butts on the roofs of the Americans' cars. Border guards held the convoy for four hours in 120 degree heat under the sun. Pets, including Ambassador Howell's dog, died. The Americans kept their children alive by sprinkling them with precious drinking water. The Harts used almost a whole case on Mary, who was suffering from heatstroke. Finally, the Iraqis waved the convoy through. Halfway to Baghdad, Hart was close to collapse. He'd been up organizing the caravan since before dawn and was drained by the heat and stress. Hart's wife, Chris, took the wheel.

At one thirty in the morning on August 24, the convoy reached the US embassy in Baghdad. Everyone had been up for twenty-four hours with no food and no rest. Deputy Chief of Mission Joe Wilson greeted the beleaguered travelers with cold drinks and canapés and put them up in vacant diplomat homes around the embassy compound.

The Iraqis agreed to let the women and children leave Iraq and on August 26, they set out for the Turkish border. Only two of the women could handle a stick shift. Chris was one of them. She drove out in an armored embassy vehicle with Natasha and two-year-old Mary, who vomited throughout the journey. With mom driving, Natasha spent the long trip caring for her little sister.

Stopped at every Iraqi checkpoint north of Baghdad, the convoy of women and children took twenty hours to travel the 320 miles to the Ibrahim Khalil border crossing into Turkey. At the border, the Iraqis forced the Americans to abandon their vehicles and walk across to waiting passenger buses for the ride to the NATO base at Diyarbakir and flights home. It was a memorable day, not least because it was the Harts' twelfth wedding anniversary. "I was devastated," Hart would later write, "but had a sense of well-being, knowing they would make it home safely." Once in America, the wives were told not to talk to the media; it might endanger their husbands.

Saddam's government demanded that the US embassy in Baghdad turn over all eleven of the US military personnel who'd been serving in Kuwait. The embassy declined and did its best to shield the officers, including Feeley, under the protection of diplomatic passports. Western journalists, who attended briefings at the embassy, withheld the officers' names in reports they filed from Baghdad.

Feeley felt that there was an unstated agreement among the Americans who knew his story that he could not get caught. "They didn't want me to have my feet in a barrel of acid. They didn't want me telling Saddam everything that was going to happen," Feeley said. He even began to imagine that "some Jason Bourne–type character would blow my brains out" if it became evident that the Iraqis were going to capture him. Deputy Chief of Mission Joe Wilson recalled that he was told early on that Feeley possessed "critical military intelligence that would be of strategic importance to the Iraqis." Feeley needed to be kept safe.

Five others from Kuwait also knew US government secrets. There was Hart, who'd assisted the CIA. There was Downs, the CIA station chief. And there were three more: cryptanalysts employed by the CIA and the National Security Agency whose intimate knowledge of US signals tradecraft would be a gold mine for any American foe.

One of those "communicators" was Nick Lahoda, a forty-one-year-old Pennsylvanian, whose teenage daughter, Nicole, and wife, Mary, had driven out of Iraq in the same convoy as Chris Hart.

Lahoda was built like a fireplug. Five foot nine and about two hundred pounds with what his brother-in-law described as an "interesting" mustache, Lahoda favored beer over other spirits. He wouldn't come at you but, if riled, he wouldn't back down. A hard rock, blue-collar character, Lahoda could've passed as a Pennsylvanian miner although he'd never worked underground. After high school in Forest City, an old coal and lumber town near Scranton, Nick took a job in communications with Western Union. That led to the US Army, then to the Bureau of Alcohol, Tobacco and Firearms, and then in 1985 to the CIA as a communicator and cryptographer. Before Kuwait, Lahoda had been posted to Burma.

The year 1988 was a tumultuous one in Burma. A nationwide uprising forced the military dictatorship that had ruled the country since the 1960s to agree to elections. In September, the military overturned the results, locking up the winners and killing protesters. Lahoda worked twenty-hour days in a room filled with clangorous machines monitoring radio traffic and encrypting the embassy's reports. His nerves and hearing were shot; he drank to excess. In letters home, he described seeing the heads of executed demonstrators dangling in open-air markets. More than five hundred protesters were gunned down in front of the US embassy alone. Lahoda's family was evacuated to Thailand. Lahoda left Burma in late 1989.

After a few months in America to settle his nerves and deal with his drinking, Lahoda and his family were transferred to Kuwait in February 1990. Like Fred Hart's billet, Lahoda's was supposed to be an uneventful posting, his reward for living through a bloody coup. Suddenly, he and his family were refugees. Lahoda was the lowest-ranked and highest-strung of the six Americans who needed special protection.

At the US embassy, Joe Wilson and the security detail weighed a few plans to get the men out of Iraq. One idea was to send the group to the Jordanian border and hope, amid the chaos of thousands of people clamoring to leave, they'd be able to sneak out. Another was to conduct a military operation to punch out through the Syrian border. One evening, Feeley was told that they were going to attempt to escape via Syria. Weapons were cleaned and readied but at the last minute the operation was called off.

On the morning of Sunday, August 5, three days after the invasion of Kuwait, Krzysztof Smoleński had just finished breakfast at home in Warsaw when he received a call from the duty officer at the UOP. "There's an urgent message for you, Major," the clerk said. After a career spying on the United States, Smoleński was now at the center of the emerging relationship with the CIA as the chief of the UOP's American section.

Smoleński went to the ministry and read the cable. "What a bomb!" he recalled. A Polish worker in Iraq had discovered that Saddam had placed Americans, Japanese, French, and Germans in a chemical factory in the desert outside Kirkuk, 160 miles north of Baghdad. The worker had given their names to the Polish embassy in Baghdad.

Smoleński reached out to Bill Norville, the CIA's station chief in Warsaw. Smoleński's report to Norville was confirmation of what came to be known as Saddam's "human shield" policy. In all, Iraqi forces placed more than one hundred Americans and seven hundred British, European, Australian, Japanese, and Kuwaiti men at scores of strategic sites in Iraq and Kuwait as a hedge against military action. Smoleński considered that intelligence to be humanitarian in nature. "People worried about their loved ones," he recalled. "It was the least we could do."

But Smoleński had more. Among the group at the chemical plant, he told Norville, was Martin Stanton, the army major who'd disappeared while on a weekend holiday in Kuwait. Stanton had entrusted letters to the Polish worker who'd brought them to the Baghdad embassy, which had transmitted them to Warsaw. Smoleński handed the packet to Norville. In code, Stanton described in detail several of the strategic sites he'd visited courtesy of Saddam's forces. Stanton spent four months in Iraq as a "special guest" of Saddam Hussein.

On August 20, Norville asked Smoleński whether, given all the construction Polish firms did around Baghdad, the Poles might have a detailed map of the Iraqi capital. The answer was yes. Polish firms had been working in Baghdad since 1965 and cartographers had been drawing such a map for years. The map, which had already been presented to the Iraqis, was a treasure trove of strategic military intelligence. It showed Baghdad's sewage system, its electrical grid, the locations of Saddam's palaces, the headquarters of the army and secret services, other ministries, factories, and sensitive facilities. The cartographers had retained their notes, early mock-ups, and drafts, which filled three large bags and weighed more than 120 pounds. The challenge was to get the materials out of Iraq.

Poland's *rezydent* in Baghdad was Colonel Andrzej Maronde, a veteran spy, fluent in Arabic and English, with postings in Cairo and New York. Since February, Maronde had been serving undercover as the head of the consular section. Because Poland was between ambassadors, Maronde was the highest-ranking official in the embassy. Maronde was one of the first foreigners to learn of Saddam's "human shield" policy during a dinner with a high-ranking member of Saddam's Baath Party shortly after the invasion of Kuwait.

In an attempt to get the map materials to Warsaw, Maronde reached out to his contacts in the Baath Party and requested that LOT Airlines be permitted to fly into Baghdad to evacuate several Polish workers. He claimed they were deathly ill and needed immediate medical attention. The Iraqis turned him down. Then in early September, a deputy minister of foreign affairs approached Maronde and said Iraq would let a plane land if it could take an extra passenger out of Baghdad. A relative of Iraq's deputy prime minister, Tariq Aziz, had been a medical student in Kraków and was desperate to get back to Poland. As the chief consular officer, Maronde issued him a visa; Maronde's wife stamped his passport herself. In passing, Maronde informed the Iraqi official that the embassy would be sending its "archives" to Warsaw in three large sacks. The official agreed.

A few days later, the sacks arrived in Warsaw with a few Poles and one relieved Iraqi. The map brought cooperation between the United States and Poland to a new level. The Poles presented the three sacks with full knowledge that US Air Force and Navy pilots would be using the intelligence to target Baghdad once Desert Storm began. As Minister of Interior Krzysztof Kozłowski told friends later: "The Americans would've traded Florida for those bags." Just a few months earlier, cooperation between the CIA and Polish Intelligence had been nice in theory. Here it was in practice.

On September 20, shortly after noon, Norville called Smoleński again and requested an urgent meeting. The pair had been talking almost every day following the invasion. Smoleński was on an ad hoc committee put together by the Polish government to manage the evacuation of thousands of Polish workers from Kuwait and Iraq. He had access to information that the Americans could use.

Norville invited Smoleński for a stroll in Ujazdów Park, a stone's throw from the US embassy. The skies were clear and temperatures hovered in the seventies. Smoleński walked from the ministry, arriving at the southeast entrance of the park at two P.M. Norville was waiting. Krzysztof took Bill's promptness as a sign that something was up. The pair, both dressed in blue suits, subdued ties, and white shirts, walked down a row of chestnut trees. Norville checked for a tail and suggested a bench.

Norville said he'd been instructed by CIA headquarters to ask Poland to sneak—the technical term was "exfiltrate"—six US officers out of Iraq. He said the officers were in bad psychological condition and were in danger of being arrested by Iraqi forces at any time.

"Why are you asking us?" Smoleński inquired.

"Because you can do it," Norville replied. Years of working with Polish officers such as Kukliński, and against Polish officers such as Zacharski, had convinced Norville, Palevich, and others at the CIA of the excellence of Polish tradecraft. When CIA headquarters had asked Norville if the Poles could handle the operation, he'd agreed without reservation. Norville made it clear to Smoleński that the CIA would reward Poland handsomely for its service.

The CIA had already approached allied intelligence agencies, including the British and the Germans, for help, but they were busy trying to extract their own people. The Americans couldn't pull off the operation themselves. The US embassy in Baghdad was surrounded by Iraqi troops. Unspoken was the fact that no one in Washington wanted a repeat of the calamitous Operation Eagle Claw, when, on April 24, 1980, eight US servicemen died trying to free the US hostages in Iran.

The Poles had good cover in Iraq and Kuwait. More than five

thousand Polish workers, engineers, cartographers, and administrators had been working there, building dams, roads, and factories. Thirty Polish firms operated in both countries. A Polish spy or spies could vanish inside this cocoon. Still, Smoleński was taken aback. He told Norville that he'd meet immediately with Foreign Intelligence chief Henryk Jasik to consider the request. "Give me twenty-four hours," Smoleński said.

Bespectacled, bookish, and circumspect, Henryk Jasik had been a compromise candidate to run the foreign intelligence service under Andrzej Milczanowski. During Communism, his forte had been industrial espionage, so he was considered less controversial than some comrades who'd specialized in political work. He was more diplomatic and slightly older than the brash Gromosław Czempiński, who became his deputy and head of operations. In the files of the Ministry of Interior, Jasik's evaluations chart the transformation of an introverted officer who had difficulty cultivating sources to an "exceptionally discreet" administrator, known for organizational skills and tact.

Smoleński met Jasik at three that afternoon. Jasik and Smoleński drew up a one-page report asking Milczanowski to let them "study" Norville's proposal. "Typical word play" was how Smoleński termed that formulation; everyone knew they weren't asking for approval to *study*, they wanted permission to *do* the mission. Jasik brought the document to Milczanowski.

Jasik, the Communist-era spy, and Milczanowski, Solidarity's ex-jailbird, made an odd couple. Jasik came from a family of farmers; Milczanowski's father had disappeared into the maw of the Soviet secret service. Jasik was cautious; Milczanowski was a self-described adventurer. They'd bonded over a shared love of boxing. Twice a month they'd attend matches at the Gwardia Warszawa Sports Society, where they got an early look at the Ukrainian heavyweight sensations Wladimir and Vitali Klitschko. Together they underwrote promising Polish fighters.

After a short conversation, Milczanowski gave Jasik a thumbs-up. And why not? This was Poland in 1990. There were "shock therapy" measures being taken to salvage Poland's economy. There were the negotiations on the withdrawal of Soviet troops. A whole new generation of entrepreneurs was diving into the sea of private business. The Communists had lost control of the old world but the new world had yet to take hold. The stakes were high everywhere and everyone was making big bets.

Decades later, analyzing his decision with lawyerly exactitude, Milczanowski listed three reasons. First, he'd been under a lot of pressure from purists within the Solidarity camp who'd demanded a complete cleansing of the security services. He wanted to prove the wisdom of the decision to keep Communist-era officers around. "We needed a spectacular success to quiet these attacks," he said.

Second, Milczanowski knew firsthand how much the CIA had helped the Solidarity movement, with cash, printing presses, and intelligence during the struggle in the 1980s. In Szczecin, his own work had directly benefited from CIA support. "The Cold War was won by the Americans," Milczanowski said. "We owed them." Finally, Milczanowski believed that the new Poland needed to show the United States that it was worthy not only of American handouts but of American respect. Saving American officers would provide a solid foundation for future cooperation between the UOP and the CIA.

As they pondered the mission from various angles, everybody had something to prove. As Jasik saw it, the operation would give the Communists a chance to show they were loyal to Poland. As Milczanowski saw it, it'd give Poland the opportunity to show that it was loyal to the United States. And as Norville saw it, it'd give the CIA the opportunity to confirm the wisdom of its decision to collaborate with its former foes.

Milczanowski decided to keep the decision at his level and forgo consulting his boss, Minister Krzysztof Kozłowski, or the boss of all of them, Prime Minister Tadeusz Mazowiecki. Milczanowski worried that either might nix the mission. The presence of thousands of Polish workers in Iraq coupled with Saddam's apparent willingness to take revenge on civilians raised the risk of negative consequences in case of failure. Among those consequences, Milczanowski considered, was the collapse of the new Polish government. "Can you imagine what would've happened if we'd gotten caught?" he asked. "Saddam could've executed some Poles. The Solidarity government could've fallen. Who knows what would've replaced it?"

Politics also induced Milczanowski to go it alone. In 1989, Solidarity's leader Lech Wałęsa had opted to take no formal office in the democratically elected government he'd helped create. Now, he wanted to become Poland's next president. Wałęsa began lobbying for a new, directly elected presidential election. He argued that having Wojciech Jaruzelski, an ex-Communist military officer, at Poland's helm was an embarrassment as Communist regimes crumbled across Eastern Europe. Prime Minister Mazowiecki also wanted to run. Milczanowski worried that if he asked, Mazowiecki wouldn't approve the operation because failure would kill his chances to beat Wałęsa. "I made the decision so I could take all of the blame if we flopped," Milczanowski said. "The downside was so huge that only a deputy minister like me was stupid enough to try."

By five that afternoon Jasik was back in Smoleński's office with a signed document. Smoleński then sketched out a draft plan. He code-named the operation The Great Evacuation. A bit later, thinking that the appellation was somewhat bombastic, never mind the scatological overtones, he changed it to Friendly Saddam. At seven, Smoleński called Norville. "We've got the green light," he said. The following day, parliament set presidential elections for November 25. Wałęsa would beat Mazowiecki and several other candidates in a run-off.

The next issue was who would lead the mission. Jasik initially wanted Operation Friendly Saddam carried out by officers from the Baghdad station. So began intensive communication between Warsaw and Baghdad over the operation's feasibility. Warsaw thought that *rezydent* Maronde could handle it. Maronde wasn't so sure.

Smoleński began interviewing Poles returning from Iraq to get a sense of the challenges. One involved Iraq's shifting rules and their haphazard implementation. On September 4, for example, Iraq announced that foreign airlines were barred from landing at Baghdad. Then it allowed a few planes to come through, including the LOT flight that flew the Baghdad map material to Warsaw. When Iraq issued a new requirement for exit visas to leave the country, some foreigners succeeded in departing without them.

Norville and Smoleński met daily. At headquarters in Langley the CIA formed a team—including Palevich and Ren Miller, the chief of operations for the Middle East. Scenarios were built. The two sides determined that the best plan would be to disguise the Americans as Polish workers and somehow sneak them out of Iraq.

Lag time emerged as another challenge. Replies from Baghdad sometimes took three days. Langley could be slow as well. After two weeks, Norville observed that Maronde was "not pulling it together."

Maronde was pushing sixty and, after thirty-six years in the service, was looking forward to retirement. He fretted openly about the fate of Polish citizens if the operation failed. As Smoleński put it, Maronde was "too mature to handle this type of surgery." On October 10, Maronde formally acknowledged that he wouldn't be able to lead Friendly Saddam. Warsaw needed to send someone else.

Jasik first considered Smoleński as he'd been on the project since the beginning. But Norville and the CIA team at Langley wanted Smoleński to stay put. He'd quickly evolved from an excellent spy into an indispensable liaison officer.

The same day Maronde backed out, Gromosław Czempiński returned to Warsaw from a seven-week counterterrorism training course in the United States. Jasik called Gromek to his office and asked him to volunteer. Sending the director of Poland's clandestine service to do the operation himself definitely increased the risk if things went belly-up. But Jasik didn't have too many other operatives with the experience and English-language skills to pull it off. "The new recruits from the ranks of Solidarity were too green to do something like Iraq," recalled Piotr Niemczyk, who himself was a new recruit at the time. "Jasik needed a pro." Gromek made sense to the Americans as well. He was known to Polish-speaking members of the CIA as a *kombinator*, Polish slang for an operator or a hustler. "He could wheel and deal with the best of 'em," Norville said. "He was the right man for the job."

Czempiński agreed to limit his activities to organizing the escape. He'd let others actually move the men. Milczanowski invited Norville to his office and told him the news. Gromosław Czempiński was going to Baghdad.

CHAPTER ELEVEN

NO EXIT

On October 12, 1990, a LOT Airlines plane with 180 seats took off from Warsaw, bound for Baghdad. Only two passengers were on board: Krzysztof Płomiński, the newly appointed ambassador to Iraq, and a second secretary assigned to the embassy named Andrzej Nowak.

The Poles used the appointment of the two diplomats as cover to launch Operation Friendly Saddam. In Baghdad, parties were thrown, meetings were held, and the embassy, which had been asleep, woke up to introduce Płomiński and Nowak to Baghdad. In reality, Nowak was Gromosław Czempiński.

In his carry-on, Czempiński had the passports of six Polish workers. CIA and Polish counterfeit artists had fabricated fake documents for the group. At Langley, Palevich had come up with names—Marek Anders, for one—that the Americans could pronounce. Another alias—Jerzy Tomaszewski—honored Ricardo, the Lisbon *rezydent*. Packed in Czempiński's suitcase were six pairs of workers' uniforms, sized correctly and stitched out of suitably threadbare cloth.

At the embassy, Czempiński met with *rezydent* Maronde, who expressed reservations about the chances for a successful mission. For one, there was no freedom of movement. Diplomats weren't allowed to travel without asking for permission a week in advance, and they were required to announce their destinations, their routes, and their intentions.

The exit visa situation was another headache. To get one, foreigners were obliged to report in person to the police and have a police file on record. Those whose passports indicated that they had been in Kuwait needed to inform the Iraqi authorities of their activities there.

Maronde and others at the embassy told Czempiński that Friendly Saddam was a fool's errand. You're finished, they told him. The risk is too high. The rules change every day. There's no chance of success. "This is it," Czempiński remembered thinking. "I have no ideas."

Czempiński tried to move around Baghdad with more freedom than the average diplomat. He discovered that Polish workers were not as restricted. Maronde's wife dug up the papers of an executive of a Polish state-owned company who'd left Iraq before the invasion. She gave them to Czempiński. Now Gromek had two covers: diplomat and business executive.

Czempiński tested the executive's documents at checkpoints, driving a banged-up Russian-made Lada through the Iraqi capital, probing to see if he'd be turned back or detained. He sailed through. Czempiński didn't inform Warsaw that he was now also masquerading as a businessman. After all, his orders were not to carry out the operation; he was to supervise others. He swore Maronde to secrecy.

In Warsaw, Smoleński directed his team to count the checkpoints around Baghdad and on the major routes leading out of the city. Four possible routes were considered: by air, and by land to Jordan, Syria, or Turkey. Early on, Czempiński suggested making a run for the Syrian border. Jasik rejected the idea as too risky. "He was right," Czempiński recalled. Smoleński also began tracking those Iraqis who worked for the police and had visited Poland. Thousands of Iraqis had studied in

Poland during the 1970s and 1980s. It turned out that at least three Polish-speaking Iraqis were serving in the border guards. Smoleński directed the station in Iraq to find out where they were. They needed to be avoided at all costs.

On October 4, eight days before Czempiński landed in Baghdad, Fred Hart and the other five men met with the US Army colonel in charge of security. He informed them that, as Hart wrote in his diary, "creative ways" were being explored to get them out of Iraq. The colonel didn't elaborate but asked them to pack a small bag in case they needed to leave quickly. The men were paired off; Hart was teamed with Nick Lahoda. Hart quickly discovered that Nick was very nervous about the future. "We're going to get killed," Nick declared as they packed together. "I've got a bad feeling about this." Hart tried his best to calm Lahoda down. Hart poured on the charm to loosen him up. Nick was wound tight.

Joe Wilson put the six men on watch duty. They went into and out of the chancery at all hours. The idea was to get the Iraqis who monitored the embassy accustomed to seeing them move around.

On October 11, the Iraqis threatened to stop all evacuation flights after Israeli security forces shot Palestinian demonstrators in the Gaza Strip. "We're fucked," Hart told his diary. "It's been 40 days in Baghdad and 70 days since the invasion." He noted that the Iraqis had intensified their demands for all embassies to turn over those who had worked in Kuwait. Joe Wilson had steadfastly refused. Hart overheard Wilson on the phone with the Iraqi Ministry of Foreign Affairs warning the Iraqis to stop harassing the embassy or he'd call President Bush and tell him to start bombing.

When Saddam sent Wilson a letter threatening to execute anyone caught sheltering foreigners, Wilson appeared at a press conference wearing a handmade noose around his neck. "If the choice is to allow American citizens to be taken hostage or to be executed, I will bring my own fucking rope," he declared. The Iraqis then cut off all food deliveries to the embassy. Wilson issued a new rule that Western reporters in

Baghdad needed to bring a bag of flour, rice, sugar, or other groceries if they wanted to attend embassy backgrounders. Wilson briefed the six men again on the mounting pressure from the Iraqi side. "I'd rather not know this stuff," Hart wrote. "Things are still fucked up."

Joe Wilson worried openly that he wouldn't be able to help the six leave. At one point, an Iraqi troop truck showed up in front of the embassy at two in the morning. US Marines locked and loaded their weapons and girded for an onslaught. After an hour, the truck drove off.

On October 14, John Mooneyham, the colonel managing security at the embassy, went over the prisoner-of-war code of conduct with the six men. Two days later they huddled again and Hart taught the other five the tap-code for imprisoned soldiers that had been developed by American POWs during the Vietnam War. The six also learned the technique of using their fingers to pass a message if they were photographed in captivity. It was based on the word HOSTAGE. H meant you were being held as a Hostage, O meant out of town, S stood for safe, T for tortured, A for armed guards, G for guarded 24/7, and E for no escape. "Worried that the Iraqis are planning to incarcerate us," Hart wrote. Lahoda seemed to be breaking under the pressure. He woke up from nightmares in a cold sweat.

Hart and Lahoda were told to explore the neighborhood outside the embassy to familiarize themselves with the surroundings. Feeley, paired with an NSA communicator, Dan Hale, did the same. So, too, Downs and his partner, Lance, a twenty-one-year-old cryptanalyst whose real name is being withheld because he continues to serve in the US government.

On October 18, the men were briefed on a new plan to get them out. They were going to pretend that they were Polish engineers. They were given names, fake bios, and a Polish phrase book and were ordered to start memorizing. They were told they'd be provided with Polish passports and that they'd leave Iraq with some other Poles. Feeley was, as he remembered, "gobsmacked" that he was going to pretend to be an Eastern European, but he didn't think about it much. He focused on the mission. "I had a Polish family, a Polish name. I had to learn some Polish and the Poles were going to be the ones who were going to help us 'e and e,'" he said, using military slang for "evasion and escape." Downs, the inveterate Cold Warrior, groused that the United States shouldn't be relying on a nation that was still technically part of the Warsaw Pact. "For all I know maybe they're working with the Iraqis, too," he grumbled.

Hart buried himself in the tasks at hand, familiarizing himself with his Polish "roots" while struggling to remember his new name, Jacek Rucin. "It was a hopeless cause, I couldn't even pronounce it!" he recalled. On October 21, his diary notes that the Iraqis announced gasoline rationing, which meant more logistical hurdles if they were driving out. "Things again placed on hold," Hart wrote. "I hope the big day will come," he added. "I'm ready for it but it's looking doubtful." Hart observed that on November 3 there'd be no moon, a perfect night for an escape.

Czempiński was moving along but he couldn't carry off the operation alone. He'd heard of a Polish engineer who'd been around the Middle East since the late 1960s and spoke Arabic. Born in 1933, Eugeniusz, who has asked that only his first name be used, was the youngest of ten children. Several of his elder brothers had been highly decorated for fighting the Nazis during World War II. "I used to play with my brothers' medals when I was a child," he recalled. "I wondered, when will I get my chance to be a hero?" His chance came in Iraq.

Following the invasion of Kuwait, Eugeniusz had shuttled convoys of Poles from Baghdad to the Jordanian border. On one day alone, he arranged for 350 Polish workers to walk out of Iraq. He moved hundreds more on subsequent trips. Czempiński invited him to the roof of the ambassador's residence for a bottle of water and a chat. "We have some unfortunate foreigners," Czempiński told Eugeniusz. "They need to get out of Iraq."

"Well," Eugeniusz replied, "I believe in helping people who need help." Eugeniusz had no idea who they were. He thought they might be Europeans. "I would rather not have known," he recalled.

Smoleński, Norville, Czempiński, and the other members of the two teams in Washington and Warsaw determined that an escape by road had the best chance of succeeding. The route would depend on the location of the Polish-speaking Iraqi border guards. All indications were that they'd been deployed south to Jordan. So the team planned to head north through Mosul, on to Zakho, and the Ibrahim Khalil border crossing to Turkey. Two Polish officers were dispatched to Turkey to arrange for transportation from that side. Eugeniusz and officers from Maronde's station would be responsible for getting the Americans to the border. Once there, the Americans would have to cross it alone.

After Polish-speaking border guards, the exit visa problem was the next hurdle. Iraq's internal security computer system ran on French technology. It was considered one of the most advanced in the Middle East. Almost every highway checkpoint had a link into the system and could check Iraqi or foreign documents. There was no sense trying to trick the system or forge the visas. They had to be genuine. But how to get them? "I was ready to give up," Czempiński recalled.

One evening, an opportunity surfaced at a function on the campus of a Polish engineering firm. An Iraqi woman was there. The wife of a high-ranking official in the Ministry of Transportation, she'd been a longtime source for Polish Intelligence. She stood out because she was dressed, Czempiński remembered, like a European.

Apparently, Czempiński had met her previously. Perhaps Geneva or an earlier operation in the Middle East, he's never revealed exactly where. But access to Transportation Ministry officials had always been important to the Polish government. Thousands of Poles worked on highways and other infrastructure projects in Iraq. Transportation Ministry officials negotiated contracts and arranged visas to get workers into and out of the country.

Czempiński said that he believed the woman was linked to Iraqi counterintelligence. He'd first encountered her years ago when he was posing as a representative of a Polish state-owned company. Luckily, that was one of his covers this time, too.

He renewed their acquaintance. "I feel trapped," she told Czempiński. "War is coming." She said that she still liked his mustache. The pair saw each other regularly.

Polish intelligence officers were well acquainted with "sexpionage." At the Intelligence Training Center, Czempiński and his classmates had been trained in the art of seduction. They were also aware of the history of such operations. In the late 1950s, a contingent of Polish honeypots charmed four American diplomats and ten marine guards at the Warsaw embassy. While the Americans dallied with their sweethearts, Polish and Soviet KGB officers rifled through embassy documents and safes.

Czempiński pursued the Iraqi woman, his charm cooking on all burners. He bemoaned their fate in Baghdad, alone together, with war looming on the horizon. If there was a little bit of *Casablanca*'s Humphrey Bogart in Gromek, there was a little bit of Ingrid Bergman in her.

Czempiński disclosed that he was responsible for a group of six Polish engineers who, since the invasion, had devolved into animals, drinking and whoring as if the world was about to end. They'd worked in Kuwait, he said, and so their names weren't in the Iraqi database. He knew they needed to register with the police but they'd been on a binge for weeks and were completely incapacitated. "They are afraid and drunk constantly," he said. "Can you help me?"

The woman agreed to register the men and arrange for exit visas. Czempiński gave her the passports and a day or so later she returned with the exit visas in place. "You're going to stay though, aren't you?" she asked.

The CIA needed the blessing of President George H. W. Bush to launch the operation. There was so much going on—building a coalition to reverse Saddam's invasion—that it seemed almost impossible to get on the president's calendar. Finally, the CIA briefed Bush and he signed off.

A twist precipitated commotion in Warsaw. Originally, the Americans had requested that once in Turkey, the six should be taken to a

NATO airbase near the Iraqi border and handed over to US forces there. But on October 23, Norville told Smoleński that the CIA now wanted the Poles to bring the men back to Warsaw. The agency didn't want to risk involving another government, in this case the Turks, in the subterfuge. The six would need to stay in character until they were out of Turkish airspace. This wrinkle necessitated a whole new layer of planning for the two Polish officers who'd been sent to Turkey to collect the would-be escapees.

Fred Hart's journal entry on October 24 noted unusually gray skies with a hint of rain. On the BBC broadcast that morning he'd heard a report that fourteen Americans had made it out of Iraq through Jordan. Word came down that they would be moving that night. "I'm concerned about Nick," Hart wrote. Lahoda had become increasingly skittish and talked openly about getting shot or tortured by the Iraqi police. At least, he seemed resigned to the mission. "This way is better than no way," Nick said. Still, he was sure that it would fail. Hart worried that Lahoda would crack if something went wrong. Hart's last journal entry read: "Hope this isn't my last. Better get Nick squared away and hit the bricks." He made a final call to Chris and told her via a prearranged code that something was up and that she might not hear from him for a few days.

That evening, Hart and Lahoda dined on lasagna and an unidentified green vegetable rustled up by Dave Forties. At nine P.M., the pair left the embassy compound from a backroom without telling their roommates. They avoided the Iraqi guards on the mission's perimeter and headed toward an intersection where they'd been told to wait. Piles of garbage smoked on the sidewalk. True to the forecast, it began to drizzle. Fred and Nick lingered in front of a jewelry store window. Hart bought a "Welcome to Baghdad!" postcard from a street vendor. A white hatchback, driven by a member of Poland's Baghdad station, pulled up. "That's us," Hart said to Lahoda. The pair got in. The car sped off.

Feeley and Hale followed at their assigned time. Five Iraqi officers were standing on the spot where they were supposed to meet their ride. "Oh shit," Feeley groaned. The pair crossed the street and walked away from the officers. After wandering aimlessly for fifteen minutes, they circled back to the pickup spot. The Iraqis were gone. They were a few minutes late. As if on cue, Czempiński pulled up.

Czempiński zipped through Baghdad's back streets. Slow enough to avoid suspicion, but fast enough to shake a tail, he traced an itinerary laboriously drawn up to skirt checkpoints. "It was Mr. Toad's wild ride," Feeley recalled. Maronde drove behind them to ensure they weren't being followed. Soon all six were reunited at an abandoned camp for Polish workers on the outskirts of Baghdad.

There, as they were handed their Polish workers' uniforms and shown their passports, Czempiński addressed the group. He introduced himself as Andrew. "I'm going to be leading you out," he said. "You must follow my instructions. You must follow my lead."

Feeley turned to Hunter Downs. "Who is this guy?" he asked. "Polish Intelligence," Downs replied. "That makes sense," Feeley said. Downs wasn't happy. He began to talk over Czempiński. It was unheard of, Downs said, for the United States to turn over its men to officers of another country. Even the Canadians who helped save a group of American hostages from Iran in 1980 didn't have control over them once the CIA got involved, he declared. "This is unprecedented," Downs told the group. "It's never been done before." Downs was doubly miffed that a former Eastern Bloc spy was leading the mission. Hart thought that Downs was going to try to assume control.

Czempiński let Downs finish. "If you want to make it out of Iraq, you'd be advised to follow my instructions," he cautioned. "Getting out of Baghdad will be the easy part. The hard part is making sure we don't run into the Iraqi officers who speak Polish.

"If they discover who you really are you will be detained," Czempiński continued. "I can't speak for what may happen after that."

Downs fell silent. No one spoke in his defense. Hart was relieved that Downs had been put in his place. Downs's single-minded obsession with the Soviet Union complicated his ability to understand changes that were happening in the world around him. Besides, two commanders don't make for a good mission. After seeing Gromek in action, Fred had more faith in Czempiński than he had in Downs. To Hart, Downs exemplified a certain type of CIA station chief, who sat in the embassy's vault all day reading classified reports. Perhaps some of them were good field guys. Not Downs. "He didn't even have a map or a compass," Hart observed.

The Poles, however, seemed to be energized, professional, dedicated, and smart. Again, there was an unguarded quality in the way Americans and Poles interacted. As Hart put, "It was all about trust and ironically I trusted the Poles more so than Hunter. Something about them just clicked." At the end of Czempiński's presentation, they were served tea off a hot plate and some dried fruit. They bunked down in the room together for the night.

That evening, Maronde received a cable from Intelligence Command expressing reservations about Czempiński taking part in the operation. Warsaw was worried about failure. Warsaw hadn't known about Czempiński's plans to leave his diplomatic passport behind and travel on the papers of the Polish engineer. That was the sole way to get out of Baghdad. But it also meant that Czempiński, if unmasked by the Iraqis, wouldn't have the luxury of diplomatic immunity. He'd be tried as a civilian in a nation where the penalty for espionage was death. Czempiński was putting his life on the line. The telegram reiterated that Czempiński was supposed to oversee the operation, not participate in it.

Maronde brought the cable to Czempiński at the work camp. "What would you do if you were me?" Czempiński asked him. Maronde believed that if Czempiński had someone else lead the convoy, the operation would collapse. There really was no one at the Polish station in Baghdad who could match Gromek's mixture of tradecraft and nerve. To complicate matters, the CIA assumed that Czempiński would be in charge. At Langley, a team of officers had been assembled and was monitoring the operation in real time. "It's up to you," Maronde said. "But if it was me, I'd go." Czempiński crumpled the cable into a ball and set it on fire. "Let's pretend we never saw this," he said.

Over the course of the evening, the Poles lost track of one of the Polish-speaking Iraqi security officers. Before dawn the next day, Czempiński decided to head north anyway, betting that the officer had remained in the south.

At five A.M., two vehicles rolled out of the Polish workers' camp. Hale, Feeley, Lahoda, and Hart squeezed on top of one another in the backseat of a hatchback with Eugeniusz at the wheel. Another Pole drove the second vehicle, a pickup, with Czempiński in the front passenger seat and Downs and Lance in the pickup's cab. The pickup led the way.

No sooner had it hit the road than the little convoy ran into checkpoints. In all, there were five along the way, with a sixth at the border. Czempiński spoke a little Arabic, but if that didn't smooth their passage, he had a front seat full of cartons of Marlboro cigarettes and fifths of Johnnie Walker Black. Those got a lot of attention. After the first checkpoints, Feeley and Hart began to relax. It seemed that their exit visas, which had been checked at each roadblock, were working.

Feeley and Hart started taking notes on what they saw: tanks and armored personnel carriers with unit numbers stenciled on their sides. Passing through Saddam's hometown of Tikrit, one hundred miles north of Baghdad, the convoy came upon a huge buildup of troops and weaponry. At a pee stop, Czempiński discovered the two had been gathering intelligence. "Are you hiding anything else from me?" he asked. The six revealed that they'd kept their American passports. "What are you guys doing?" he asked. "How are you going to explain all this if we get caught? Are you crazy?" He shook his head like an exasperated schoolmarm and confiscated the documents.

At the approach to Mosul, 250 miles north of Baghdad, Czempiński pulled over for a refueling stop. Another Polish team had prepositioned a fifty-five-gallon drum full of gas by the side of the road. As Czempiński and Eugeniusz filled their vehicles, a Bedouin appeared as if out of a desert mirage, yelling in Arabic and flailing his arms. Czempiński moved over and in broken Arabic addressed the man. A carton of Marlboros didn't seem to calm him. Neither did a fifth of Johnnie Walker Black. Czempiński blocked him from getting closer to the cars. Inside the hatchback, Lahoda's eyes bugged out of their sockets. "He's going to get the Iraqi army and they're going to shoot us," he said. "In the fields. I've seen this in movies. We're going to die with goats and sheep."

Eugeniusz sidled over to the Bedouin, smiled ingratiatingly, and steered him away from the convoy. Finally, Czempiński disappeared with the man over a berm on the highway. Looking out from the confines of the cramped hatchback, Hart figured that Czempiński had killed him. That wasn't the case. Czempiński had given him a wad of cash. Still, Czempiński worried that the Bedouin would report them to the local militia. They needed to get through Mosul fast.

Czempiński left Downs and Lance at the refueling stop and headed into Mosul by himself. It was the biggest city in northern Iraq and he figured the checkpoints would be tighter than the ones they'd already crossed. He was right. Then Czempiński made a disturbing discovery. The missing Polish-speaking Iraqi had surfaced. He was manning the barricade leading into town.

CHAPTER TWELVE

DIDN'T GET THE MEMO

Czempiński returned to the group with the bad news. They had two options: head back to Baghdad or risk the checkpoint. He had the Americans try to pronounce their names one more time. They mangled every syllable and even flipped the names. "Andy Mark" was how the American who'd been given the name Marek Anders introduced himself. "My stomach went through my nose," Eugeniusz recalled. "They couldn't even speak English with foreign accents. They sounded like Americans right out of the movies."

A return trip could actually end up being more dangerous than continuing north. Every checkpoint would want to know why they'd turned around. Czempiński decided to proceed but he tweaked the plan. Given that his six charges had flunked their language test, he decided that the only way they'd pass would be as drunk Poles, happy to be going home and so blotto that they could barely speak.

"Drink," he commanded as he handed each of them a fifth of whiskey. And they drank. Feeley looked over at Lahoda, who was guzzling with enthusiasm. "You're not supposed to *get* drunk," he cautioned. "You're supposed to *pretend* to get drunk."

With a flourish, Czempiński took another bottle and poured it on the men. "This is Polish style," he declared. The whiskey didn't calm Lahoda's nerves. "I'm too old for this," he mumbled. The convoy began moving north.

At the checkpoint into Mosul, the Polish-speaking Iraqi was sitting on a chair by the side of the road with an AK-47 on his lap. Iraqi militiamen, toting automatic weapons, motioned the two vehicles to stop. Czempiński shouted a greeting in Polish and the Iraqi jumped from his seat with a big smile on his face. "It's so nice to hear Polish again," he yelled, striding over to Czempiński's pickup. Eugeniusz leapt from the sedan, embraced the guard, and planted a Slavic triple kiss on his cheeks, nudging him away from the cars. "How great it is to see some Poles!" the Iraqi exclaimed.

It was afternoon. The sky was gray. Traffic had petered off after lunch. Everything suddenly seemed to get very quiet and time slowed. The attention of the Iraqi border detachment fixed on Gromek, Eugeniusz, the other driver, and their six passengers. "Stay for dinner," the Iraqi said. "Come on. What's the hurry?"

Czempiński and Eugeniusz politely declined. "You bastard, may hell swallow you," Eugeniusz thought. "Who wants to eat with you?" Inside the car, Hart felt Lahoda trembling underneath his whiskey-soaked clothes.

Czempiński brought out more cigarettes and two bottles of Johnnie Walker. The Iraqi smiled. "You're sure you're not going to stay?" he asked. Then he looked into the vehicles and saw the Americans. Hart and Feeley had closed their eyes, pretending to sleep. "I hope we look Polish," Hart remembered thinking.

"Go," the Iraqi officer said to Czempiński, smiling. "But don't drink and drive."

North of Mosul the road zigzagged through fields of bloodred poppies before it dropped down to the regional capital, Dohuk. After a checkpoint there, the route rose north until it spilled out at Zakho, a mostly

Kurdish enclave on the banks of the Little Khabur River. At an intersection, Czempiński and Eugeniusz turned left, bound for the border.

It was a little after four in the afternoon. There was no line at the crossing. Czempiński parked the pickup, walked to a booth, and presented a guard with the six passports. Hart imagined this next step would be easy; the Iraqis would stamp the documents and they'd be over the bridge in no time. No such luck. The Iraqi border guard took the passports into a back office. After about half an hour, Czempiński directed the men to sit inside the border station on a bench facing a big clock.

Hart, Feeley, Downs, Lahoda, Hale, and Lance each carried a small bag of cigarettes, whiskey, and a change of underwear. In their worn workers' uniforms with a sack on each lap, the men looked more like convicts awaiting sentencing than the pride of the United States.

Through a window, they could see the border guard on the phone, taking a tea break, and back on the phone again. A few stray cars crossed the border, as did a pedestrian or two. This was nothing like the scene down in Jordan where thousands were clamoring to get out. The Turks weren't accepting refugees.

Czempiński entered the offices and came out quickly. "Don't say anything," he said under his breath. "Don't make eye contact. Act tired and not interested. Take a bathroom break." Hart sat there thinking, "They're going to call us by name and I don't even remember what mine is." Another fifteen minutes passed, then another. Pretty soon, an hour. The big hand on the big clock moved at a glacial pace. The sky darkened. They could see the Iraqi border guard slapping the stack of passports against his thigh as he talked on the phone again and entered data into a computer. Even Czempiński, who'd been so unflappable from the get-go, was stretched tighter than a drum.

The Iraqis had been known to issue exit visas and then revoke them for no reason at the last minute. "Had the Iraqis decided to interrogate us we would have been exposed and imprisoned," Hart later wrote. "Traveling under this cover would probably have gotten us all a death sentence." He wasn't exaggerating.

"Are you cold?" Eugeniusz asked Lahoda, who was shivering. "Yes," he replied. Eugeniusz saw Lance wiping sweat off his forehead. "When I'm free, I'm going to confess all my sins to a priest," Lance announced.

At a few minutes before six, after almost two hours, the guard opened the window. Hart could hear the comforting sound—*kachunk, kachunk, kachunk, kachunk, kachunk, kachunk*—of him stamping six documents. Gromek walked over, collected the passports, and then handed them to the men. "You're going to have to walk across. The Iraqis will check your bags. Give them whatever they want. Whatever you do, don't run." Czempiński paused and smiled. "Adios, amigos."

The Americans, still grim-faced, stood up and made for the crossing. At a final checkpoint, an Iraqi pointed his weapon at Lahoda's bag. "*Shinu hatha, shinu hatha*," he asked. "What is this? What is this?" Nick froze. Downs had walked ahead without the rest of them. The tight formation was elongating as Lahoda stood paralyzed facing the guard and Downs strode ever closer to Turkey. Hart worried that Downs would leave everyone behind. Hart reached into Lahoda's bag, pulled out a carton of Marlboros, and handed it to the guard. The guard noticed a bottle of Johnnie Walker and grabbed it, too. "*Min fadlika*," Hart said. "If you please." Hart put his hand on Lahoda's elbow and steered him toward the border. In the gloaming under some streetlights on the Turkish side, Hart could see two men, a plume of cigarette smoke rising above their heads. Then, suddenly, Hale and Lance began running. Hart remembered thinking, "We're not supposed to do this." On the Iraqi side, Eugeniusz watched three of the six men sprint toward Turkey. He promptly fainted.

As Hart and Lahoda approached the bridge leading into Turkey, another Iraqi guard started toward them. "Here we go again," Hart thought. The Iraqi made hand gestures like smoking a cigarette. The pair had already surrendered their last cartons. But Hart had a pack in his shirt pocket. "*Min fadlika*," Hart said again, and they passed the cigarettes to the Iraqi. Hart and Lahoda then picked up the pace. Against overwhelming odds, all six made it over.

Passing through Turkish customs, the Americans stayed subdued. There was no celebrating. Hart remembers being leery of what was to come. One of the two waiting men, a burly character in a tan suit, approached them with his hand out. "Welcome to freedom," he said under his breath. "Call me Richard." He'd been a Polish Intelligence officer for twenty years, some of them in Chicago, where he'd become a baseball fan. In remote southeastern Turkey, just hearing Richard say "Wrigley Field" broke the ice; everyone relaxed.

It was six twenty in the evening on October 25, 1990. The group, along with Richard and another Polish officer, squeezed into Richard's VW Passat station wagon. First stop was Silopi, a muddy one-horse town twenty miles up the road. Richard had cased it and found the only two functioning coin-operated phone booths: one next to a police station and one at a truck stop on the edge of town. He pulled into the truck stop. The Polish embassy in Ankara had provided Richard with a one-pound sack of Turkish lira to feed the phone. He called international long distance to Warsaw. Spy chief Henryk Jasik was at his desk. "Just received the package in good shape," Richard reported. "No damages. I am shipping it further up the road."

"You've made my day," Jasik responded. "See you soon." That was at seven in Turkey and six in Warsaw. Almost immediately, a cable winged its way from the US embassy to Langley, Virginia, where it was noon. There, the roomful of CIA officers who'd been monitoring Operation Friendly Saddam erupted in cheers. Milczanowski told Prime Minister Mazowiecki a day later. After hearing the story, Mazowiecki paused to let the news sink in. A look of relief spread over his face. "He had to think a little," Milczanowski recalled.

In Turkey, Richard's partner drove like Mario Andretti through the nighttime countryside. The going was slowed by a massive deployment of Turkish tanks due to tensions with Turkey's Kurdish minority. At a dinner in the city of Diyarbakir, the men clinked glasses of Turkish beer but otherwise stayed low-key.

Hart and Feeley figured that the Poles would drop them off at one of two NATO bases near the border, but Richard informed them otherwise. "We're taking you to Warsaw," he told them. "You'll love it."

Later that night, after a pit stop at a hotel for a shower, they set off for Ankara, 750 miles away. With Richard's partner at the wheel, they arrived a little after dawn. Richard found seats on a long-haul bus to Istanbul. Passengers chain-smoked throughout the seven-hour ride, sending Lahoda into spasmodic fits of coughing. Richard told the men to stay in character. Arriving in Istanbul on October 26, Richard brought the group directly to the airport.

In Warsaw, Smoleński visited LOT's deputy director. The airline's daily Istanbul–Warsaw flight was sold out. Arrangements were made, passengers were bumped, and eight tickets surfaced for the evening flight. As the plane took off, Richard gave them a sign. "You can become Americans again," he said. Five of the six whooped and hollered. Lahoda cracked a wan smile.

In Warsaw, as the men deplaned, Lahoda knelt and kissed the ground. Polish intelligence officers took them to a dacha where Soviet leader Mikhail Gorbachev had stayed during a state visit in 1988. Bill Norville was there to meet them. "He seemed very happy to see us," Feeley said. "That's when things started to make sense."

Norville observed that the men smelled like camel dung and suggested a shower and some fresh clothes. The Poles took the Americans to a spa on the dacha's grounds with a steam bath and a heated pool. After a meal and a night at the dacha, the men woke up to Warsaw. Norville handed them $300 each and took them downtown to the Pewex department store to buy souvenirs. Marian Zacharski, who by this time had become the firm's director, was there to greet them with his easy smile. Feeley bought a black leather jacket. That night they partied with the Poles, drank copious quantities of vodka, and told their stories. Nick was especially happy that he'd made it out of Iraq with a fake Rolex with Saddam's face on the dial. "My buddy Saddam," he called it. "You know," Nick said to Hart, "when this is over and we're all home, it will be like it never happened and I'll probably never see you again." He was right.

The next day, a CIA delegation of four men arrived from Washington. Led by Palevich, it included Ren Miller, the director of the CIA's Middle East division, and a psychologist (for the six men). The fourth man was a mysterious individual with a black suitcase handcuffed to his wrist. He was introduced to the Poles as "Pablo, the money man." Norville told Smoleński that Pablo's attache case was full of cash. The US government wanted to reimburse Poland for its expenses conducting the operation. Smoleński relayed this to Milczanowski, who refused payment outright. Poland did the operation, Milczanowski told the Americans, "NOT for money, but because US officers were in danger. That's what partners are for." There would be plenty of time for US financial support later on.

In the United States, the families of the six had been awaiting word. Chris had even called one of Hunter Downs's colleagues in the CIA to plead for information. "All I want you to tell me is, if I don't hear from Fred again, where can I go look for him?" she asked, worried. "Go north," the officer replied.

Within hours of the escape, a major from the US Army's Casualty and Mortuary Affairs Branch contacted Chris, who was staying with her mother in Columbus, Georgia. "Casualty Affairs?" Chris thought when the major identified himself at the door. She almost passed out. Then he told her Fred was alive and coming home.

Back on the Iraqi side of the border, Czempiński picked Eugeniusz up off the ground and walked with him to the vehicles. The plan was for them to spend the night in Mosul, but after downing a greasy sausage and checking out a fleabag hotel, they decided to head back to Baghdad. Eugeniusz only drove the sedan into a ditch once. For the rest of the trip, he kept his eyes fixed on Czempiński's taillights until they arrived. Maronde was livid that they'd returned early. "You were supposed to spend the night in Mosul!" he screamed. He wasn't used to Czempiński's incorrigible freelancing. At work the next day, Eugeniusz's driver asked him where he'd been. "When an old man goes to a brothel," Eugeniusz proclaimed, "he doesn't tell the kids."

The Poles did their best to make sure that no one knew about the operation. Word of the mission didn't leak to the Western media until 1995. But there were indications that Saddam's secret police had picked up clues. And here is where the real-life Polish mission veered from the cinematic *Casablanca* version. In the movie, Bogart's character, Rick, ensures that Bergman's character, Ilsa, makes it to safety. But Czempiński didn't follow the script. He flew out of Baghdad alone.

The Iraqi computer system was advanced enough that any officer could trace who'd issued the exit visas for the Americans. That would naturally lead to the official from the Ministry of Transport and to his wife. Many worried that in their eagerness to fashion an alliance with the United States, the Poles had sacrificed the woman upon whom the success of the entire operation had depended. Was she executed? It's unknown. But after Friendly Saddam, no Pole saw her again.

On October 29, an unmarked Gulfstream II, flown by US Air Force pilots and generally used by First Lady Barbara Bush, landed in Warsaw to pick up the six Americans. After an obligatory touchdown for a customs check at Andrews Air Force Base, the six were flown to the CIA's Farm at Camp Peary outside Williamsburg, Virginia. Their families were waiting. It was Fred Hart's younger brother's birthday. "What a present," he told Fred.

The next morning Hart and Feeley met with special operations officers, who questioned them about the embassy compound, obstacles, and Iraqi deployments around the embassy. Hart and Feeley were then brought to the Pentagon to brief officers further. Hart was still sporting long hair and a beard. A major general pulled him aside and suggested he shave. Pentagon officials ordered the pair not to speak with reporters or tell anyone else about their ordeal.

Two days later, Feeley was fast asleep in his hotel room in northern Virginia when the phone rang. "Is this Major Feeley?" asked a voice. "Yes," John replied.

"Stand by for General Schwarzkopf."

"John, you've been on vacation too long. I need you here in Riyadh," Schwarzkopf growled. "Yes sir," Feeley replied. After a short break, Feeley found himself in Saudi Arabia at the general's side as Desert Storm unfolded. He'd later be awarded the Army Legion of Merit for his service in Kuwait.

A statue of Revolutionary War hero Tadeusz Kościuszko over-looks the Hudson River and the Highlands at West Point. Whenever Feeley visits his old alma mater, he walks out to the monument, says a prayer, and leaves a red rose in honor of America's, and now his, enduring connection to the Poles.

Fred Hart remained on pins and needles, worrying about those in the embassy whom he'd left behind. Under intense international pressure, Saddam released them just before Christmas 1990. After some downtime in the United States, Hart was also called back to the Gulf to help reconstitute the Kuwaiti land forces. He also received a Legion of Merit, and a Bronze Star for protecting Nick Lahoda. He was promoted to colonel in 1998.

The experience in Iraq haunted Lahoda. He was convinced that Saddam had put a contract on his head. "You don't want to be around me too much because they still can get me," he'd repeat to friends and family. As time passed, Lahoda's fear of assassination grew into an obsession. He drank; his first wife divorced him. In 1992, the CIA let him go. Lahoda moved back to Pennsylvania from northern Virginia. To make ends meet, he worked on the line at a coffin manufacturer for minimum wage, then in the maintenance department of a local high school. Still, he couldn't kill the feeling that somewhere out there, Saddam's agents were waiting to pounce.

Why Lahoda had been included in the group of six always befuddled his family. He never discussed his work; it was classified. On September 2, 2008, Lahoda suffered a heart attack and died in the Veterans Affairs Medical Center in Plains Township, Pennsylvania. He was sixty. His family filed Freedom of Information requests with a variety of US agencies about Lahoda's service. They've never received a response.

On November 17, 1990, three weeks after the successful conclusion of Operation Friendly Saddam, CIA director William Webster boarded an unmarked United States Air Force jet outside Washington and flew to Warsaw. Webster's trip marked the first visit of a CIA director to Eastern Europe. Air traffic controllers in Warsaw directed the airplane to an isolated corner of the airport to avoid notice. Webster had brought along a team of high-ranking CIA officers including Dick Stolz, the deputy director for operations, Milt Bearden, and John Palevich.

Prime Minister Mazowiecki was in the midst of campaigning for president, so arranging a time for him to meet Webster proved a challenge. Smoleński found a thirty-minute window at eight thirty in the evening on November 17 after Mazowiecki had returned to Warsaw from an event outside the capital. Webster presented Mazowiecki with a letter from President Bush. "America will never forget what Polish officers did to save American citizens," the president wrote. Bush pledged that the United States would not abandon Poland and promised that the United States would convince Western nations to forgive a substantial portion of Poland's $33 billion in foreign debt. To this day, more than thirty years after the event, the full text of Bush's letter remains classified.

After meeting with Webster to discuss future cooperation, Warsaw's Intelligence Command took the CIA delegation sightseeing to a castle outside Warsaw and then, in the helicopter that used to belong to Communist leader Wojciech Jaruzelski, to the historic city of Kraków. On a cold November evening in a restaurant in the Old Town, Webster and Henryk Jasik exchanged toasts. Then Czempiński rose to speak. The room quieted.

"Here's to John Palevich," he declared. "He spent his career picking us off one by one and concluded it by bringing us all over altogether."

To have his life's work given such confirmation by his former foes moved Palevich deeply. Coming from Czempiński, a heralded Warsaw Pact officer who'd refused the opportunity to become an American agent and had crowned his career by saving six Americans, made it all the sweeter. "It was just absolutely delightful to have something like that said in front of Webster and the others," Palevich recalled. "Mr. Poland" had been honored by the Poles.

CHAPTER THIRTEEN

THE FLOODGATES OPEN

After Iraq, the CIA invited Milczanowski, Czempiński, Smoleński, and others to tour the United States and discuss in more detail plans for their emerging partnership. The delegation visited the CIA, the National Security Council, and Congress. Milt Bearden arranged for them to tour NASA's headquarters in Houston and to meet an astronaut. At the beginning of the trip, Czempiński was held up for a few hours at Kennedy Airport courtesy of the FBI. For some, the Cold War hadn't quite ended.

For others it had. Operation Friendly Saddam opened the floodgates for cooperation between Poland and the United States. "It quickly became a kind of blood bond between the two services," recalled Bill Norville, who became the manager of a growing number of joint operations. Before the Gulf War, the relationship had been friendly but narrow. After Desert Storm, the door flew open.

Intelligence cooperation was strengthened and formalized by the visit of the next CIA director, Robert Gates, to Poland in October 1992.

This time it wasn't secret. Gates's trip inaugurated permanent top-level contacts between the CIA, the FBI, the UOP, and Poland's military intelligence service. Subsequent CIA directors were eager to put Poland on their itineraries: the Poles didn't criticize the CIA (or the FBI) like some other allied services did.

Czempiński took the helm of the UOP in 1993 after Henryk Jasik was promoted to deputy minister of interior under Milczanowski. The CIA found itself working with Polish spies across a wide range of activities, spanning the globe. "There was literally nothing they wouldn't do to support us," Norville said. And, he added, given US trust in Poland's espionage capabilities, "there was very little we wouldn't ask them to do."

Poland was in an unusual position. It had embassies in countries that Americans couldn't access. Many of those embassies sat on large plots of land, a legacy of the Cold War, where, as a socialist brother, Poland had been offered choice swaths of real estate in central locations. This was true in Beijing; it was also true in Pyongyang, where Poland's embassy occupied a veritable campus near the much smaller British mission.

During the Cold War, Poland had fostered close ties to North Korea. As far back as the end of the Korean War in 1953, Poland, along with Czechoslovakia, represented North Korea on the Neutral Nations Supervisory Commission, the organization established to monitor the armistice. Sweden and Switzerland stood in for the West. Starting in the 1950s, Polish military officers detailed to the commission's offices in South Korea spied on behalf of the Warsaw Pact.

In the 1980s, Poland's Communist party chief Wojciech Jaruzelski pursued closer ties with North Korea. In September 1986, he visited Pyongyang, accompanied by then spy chief Czesław Kiszczak. There they concluded agreements with North Korea's security services. In 1986–1987, 280 Polish delegations, including military officers, pianists, scientists, and businessmen, visited North Korea.

Once Poland came in from the cold, its connections, access, and insight into North Korea constituted a treasure trove of information for the United States. And instead of spying on South Korea for the Warsaw Pact, Poland's representatives to the Neutral Nations Supervisory Commission began spying on North Korea for the United States.

For a while, Poland considered selling its embassy campuses in Pyongyang and in other cities around the world so it could downsize to cheaper diplomatic digs. Washington opposed this plan and the Poles didn't sell. Pretty soon, Polish diplomatic couriers began bringing American-made intelligence equipment to the embassy in North Korea to fill up the otherwise empty space. Even as trade evaporated between North Korea and Poland, the traffic between Warsaw and Pyongyang picked up. So did CIA financial contributions to the coffers of the UOP.

After a while, the North Koreans caught on to Poland's changes. But in Pyongyang's case, as with other countries, it took far longer than one would expect, allowing Polish intelligence officers time to maneuver. In November 1989, months after ex-dissident Tadeusz Mazowiecki had become Poland's prime minister, North Korean officials were still confidently predicting that Poland's changes would be short-lived and that the Polish United Workers' Party would soon defeat the "agents of imperialism." As for the Neutral Nations Supervisory Commission, Polish military officers served on it until 1995, when Pyongyang turned off the water and the power to the mission. That was *six* years after Poland began collaborating with America.

North Korea was just one place where Poland had access and the United States did not. Cuba was another. Poland's first post-Communist *rezydent* in Washington was a veteran officer, Ryszard Uniwersal. CIA heavyweight Burton Gerber said he knew the Cold War had ended when Uniwersal surfaced next to him at a pool party at John Palevich's Bethesda split-level. Uniwersal came to Washington with a long list of contacts in Havana. In the late 1970s, he'd been stationed there, had met Fidel Castro, and had established intelligence links to Cuba's spy agency. Uniwersal and other Poles renewed those connections to spy *on*, not *with*, the Cubans. Poles provided intelligence from other places: Nigeria, Iran, Angola, and the Palestinian settlements in the West Bank and Gaza Strip. Poland placed intelligence officers inside UN missions around the world. In Mogadishu in 1993, a senior Polish operative worked for the UN during the US military operation that was chronicled in the book and movie *Black Hawk Down*. Officers based in Lebanon cultivated sources in Iranian-backed terrorist organizations, such as Hezbollah. They met with Hassan Nasrallah, Hezbollah's chief, to help secure the release of Westerners taken hostage in Iraq.

The Poles were well versed in recruiting agents, what insiders called "humint," or human intelligence. That was a weak point of the CIA in the 1990s, when the number of agents the CIA recruited fell to an all-time low—down 25 percent from the height of the Cold War. Under a series of directors, the CIA had deemphasized such painstaking labor and relied on "sigint," signals intelligence (basically high-tech eavesdropping) instead.

The strengths and the reach of Polish intelligence made it an ideal partner for the agency. As the CIA's Gerber said matter-of-factly: "We saw clearly that we could exploit them in ways very important to national security issues."

The Poles had a naive trust in the CIA and treated its officers in Poland as if they were all members of the same service. "I could walk around the ministry unescorted," recalled one senior CIA officer. "'Leave on your own,' they'd say. 'Just don't take anything off the desks.'"

Among those traipsing through Poland's Ministry of Interior were officials from the National Security Agency who established listening posts along Poland's border with the collapsing USSR. The CIA also paid to build a facility at the Intelligence Training Center in Stare Kiejkuty, something not even the Soviets had done. That installation, intelligence officer Piotr Niemcyk noted, "was a very secret place." Spies from both sides of the Atlantic, Norville said, began to characterize their bond as "a special relationship."

The UOP also worked with the Defense Intelligence Agency. One of the biggest operations, which would span more than a decade, was a joint UOP–DIA endeavor in Eurasia, according to Andrzej Derlatka, the brainy Polish analyst who'd cooked up Operation Unity. "We worked in nations which supported terrorism where Americans couldn't go. We still had the access from Communist times. It was a great cooperation for both sides," Derlatka said.

When US military forces began using cruise missiles and, later, drones for strikes against targets in Sudan, Afghanistan, and elsewhere, Polish operatives were often there on the ground to guide the missiles to the intended target. Derlatka noted that the US global positioning system wasn't always accurate enough to conduct a "surgical strike" in a crowded neighborhood.

Derlatka insisted that those operations saved civilian lives, avoided collateral damage, and were a "fantastic example of our common work and common interests." He declined to go into further details. "We cooperated with the American services very closely starting from 1990," Derlatka recalled. "We did what was possible. Some of the operations were risky but we knew the consequences." For his work on the operation with the DIA, Derlatka and three other officers were awarded the Legion of Merit, the US military's most prestigious award for foreigners, in 2004.

Poland's spies did some of their best work in the former Soviet Union. They identified and tracked down Ukrainian physicists who'd received job offers from Iran and Iraq. Both Tehran and Baghdad were interested in building nuclear bombs. The Poles found a Ukrainian woman with a PhD in nuclear physics who was working as a nightclub hostess. They recruited her and passed her on to the CIA. In Moscow, Zdzisław Sarewicz stayed on as the UOP's *rezydent* for six years. During the August coup attempt in 1991 against Mikhail Gorbachev, Sarewicz was generally credited with collecting the best information. "His friends from the Russian services treated him like a comrade," said Jan Olborski, a longtime Polish spy. "They told him everything."

Sarewicz's successes suggested that even during the Cold War, Polish Intelligence had maintained assets in the USSR that it'd kept secret from its purported comrades in the KGB.

Farther afield, in the former Yugoslavia, which constituted one of Europe's biggest foreign policy crises since World War II, Polish spies dug up critical intelligence on the various factions that were tearing that country apart. In North Africa, the Poles provided information on the Libyan chemical weapons plant that Redmond had asked about in 1990. Polish specialists had aided the regime of Muammar Gaddafi for years. In the 1980s, they'd worked on Gaddafi's "Al Fatah" missile project and were employed at two Libyan chemical weapons plants. Officially, they were listed as engineers involved in the production of spare parts for agricultural machinery. In reality, they were engaged in the development of missiles that could target Israel with chemical weapons or nuclear warheads. From them, the UOP gleaned details of Gaddafi's plans to develop weapons of mass destruction. That intelligence was shared with the CIA and used by the United States in its ultimately successful effort to force Gaddafi to disarm in 2003.

Soviet, and later Russian, penetration in Poland remained an issue. According to Derlatka, the Defense Intelligence Agency partnered with the UOP out of concern that Poland's military intelligence service, known as WSI, was riddled with Soviet spies. During the 1990s, Derlatka noted, Polish counterintelligence succeeded in unmasking five Soviet spies inside the WSI. In 2000, the Poles shut down a Russian spy ring, laying waste to the Warsaw station and expelling nine Russian officers.

Warsaw used to be the place where the KGB sent older officers for light duty before they retired. "Nice city, good salary, access to Pewex. You didn't have to make an effort, everything was open. You just needed to reach for the government phone and you knew it all," was how Minister of Interior Krzysztof Kozłowski described the life of a Soviet spy. But as Poland moved closer to the West, and the USSR was no more, the Russians began sending younger, more aggressive spies to Warsaw. To Kozłowski, there was a certain irony to this. "At a time when the Americans and the Germans watched us with reserve, disbelief, distrust," he observed, "the Soviets classified us as belonging to the Western camp. They were the first."

Senior CIA officers came to Poland to advise Milczanowski on how to reform the agency to cope with the challenges of the new world. Maurice "Mo" Sovern, a veteran operations officer who'd managed the CIA's liaison with the rest of the US intelligence community, spent hours with Milczanowski helping him understand how the CIA fit into the US system. Karen Rozbicki, who'd participated in the first meeting in Warsaw, returned to Poland several times to work on terrorism-related issues and to help establish an analysis division inside the UOP. The Poles weren't accustomed to working with senior female intelligence officers; their service had been almost completely male. But they got used to it. "It was a special time," Henryk Jasik recalled. "The whole society was open to new ways of thinking. The service was no exception."

The CIA also provided money, lots of it. In addition to GROM, the CIA bankrolled numerous joint operations and also provided the UOP with millions of dollars in what basically were donations. The CIA felt that it was getting its money's worth—so much so that it played a behind-the-scenes role in the biggest debt-reduction package ever.

In March 1991, following the Iraq operation, the Paris Club, an informal grouping of Western governments, agreed to forgive about half of the $33 billion that Poland owed them. Obviously, it was in the West's interests to support Poland's transition toward a market economy and away from the Soviet bloc. And the "shock therapy" transition was already showing some results. But no nation before Poland had ever had *half* of its debt wiped clean. And for that, the Poles gave some credit to the CIA. For freeing the six Americans, the Poles were effectively paid $3 billion a head.

There were frustrations, of course. Every time Washington *rezydent* Ryszard Uniwersal met with his counterparts at the FBI, they'd ask for a list of Communist Poland's old sources in the United States.

"My response was always the same," Uniwersal said. "It's not my business. It's in the past." The FBI harped on the issue. "The next meeting always began the same way," Uniwersal said. "I got used to it."

In April 1990, the Soviet Union acknowledged that Soviet forces had perpetrated the Katyn Massacre, murdering twenty-two thousand Polish military officers, government officials, and intellectuals from April to May 1940.

From the moment he'd started his service with the new Polish government, UOP director Milczanowski had tried to determine the fate of his dad—through official channels and informal contacts. In November 1992, a Polish consul in Moscow was summoned to KGB archives in Lubyanka Square where he was handed a list. "This will be of interest to Minister Milczanowski," a Russian said. On it was a name, Stanisław Józéfowicz Milczanowski, and those of forty additional Poles. All of them had been executed by the NKVD in Kiev in April 1940. Milczanowski had never entertained fantasies that his father was alive somewhere in the Soviet gulag. But seeing his father's name on a list brought a grim finality to the story of a man who, in Milczanowski's estimation, had watched over him all his life. It also underscored the otherworldly compassion evinced by Milczanowski and other comrades in the Solidarity movement who refrained from exacting revenge on the Communists in their midst.

However, not everyone in Poland concurred with the idea that a "thick line" should be drawn between Poland's Communist past and its democratic present. In October 1991, Poland held its first fully free parliamentary election. More than one hundred political parties participated and no single party received more than 13 percent of the vote. Right-wing candidates performed best, and Poland got a new prime minister, Jan Olszewski, a conservative lawyer and a former member of Solidarity's legal team.

Olszewski appointed Antoni Macierewicz, a famed dissident and political prisoner, as minister of interior. During his student days in the 1960s, Macierewicz was a fierce anti-Communist with a weak spot for Latin American revolutionaries. A portrait of Che Guevara and a Cuban flag hung above his bed. His unruly facial hair recalled Fidel Castro's beard.

In 1976, Macierewicz joined one of the first groups to support striking Polish workers. The Workers' Defense Committee became an important forerunner of the Solidarity trade union. But Macierewicz's sharp tongue and uncompromising manner alienated the committee's cofounders, Jacek Kuroń and Adam Michnik, who went on to become the intellectual mentors of Poland's transformation.

Macierewicz was jailed during martial law. He escaped from prison and, in hiding, continued battling Communism. For a time he reportedly toyed with the idea of advocating a violent urban-guerrilla campaign to overthrow the Polish state. His militancy disturbed his comrades in Solidarity who favored nonviolence. In the winter and spring of 1989, Macierewicz was excluded from the Round Table talks. He resented this. And he changed his public persona. From an in-your-face, brassy revolutionary wannabe, Macierewicz metamorphosed into a European gentleman with over-the-top, old-school manners. He became a hyper-devout Roman Catholic. His fuzzy sideburns gave way to a neatly trimmed goatee.

Olszewski and Macierewicz represented a zealously anti-Communist faction of the Solidarity movement. They believed deeply that Poland's transition to democracy was being hijacked by a shadowy cabal of ex-Communists who controlled the financial and banking spheres. Disinvited, Macierewicz labeled the Round Table agreement "a Soviet plot."

As minister of interior, Macierewicz made it clear that the new government was not satisfied with the decommunization efforts carried out by Mazowiecki and Milczanowski. He styled himself a "Communist hunter" and promised to purge all ex-party members from the intelligence agencies. Gone were Mazowiecki's conciliatory approach and pragmatic compromises, replaced by the politics of vendetta and retribution.

The tenor of the relationship between the CIA and Polish Intelligence changed as well. Norville and the rest of the CIA had been cooperating with ex-Communists. Norville and Czempiński played tennis together. Norville's wife, Maggi, and Czempiński's wife, Barbara, went shopping and did lunch. Maggi tutored Czempiński's daughter, Iwona, who was studying for the SATs. Norville dined with Zacharski, who lived in the same neighborhood. Zacharski clearly had money to burn. His home sported Cypriot marble in the kitchen and a high-end German water filtration system years before they became all the rage in Warsaw.

With Macierewicz at the helm of the ministry, Norville discovered that Polish security officers had resumed monitoring his movements. Polish security service types began showing up again in a small booth behind the embassy that had been used to track the comings and goings of Americans during the Cold War. It hadn't been manned since 1989. Electronic surveillance resumed as well. "This thing was a vestige of the past," Norville recalled. "We just could not believe that they would do this." Norville told Macierewicz to knock it off. Macierewicz complied.

In early 1992, Macierewicz announced that he wanted to re-check the ex-Communist intelligence officers who'd already passed the vetting process. Many saw this move more as a way to go after his enemies than as a legitimate exercise in decommunization. As a cable from the US embassy observed, "Macierewicz's 'crusade' against former communists was actually a pretext for attacking rivals in the Solidarity camp."

In June, Macierewicz declared that he and his allies had drawn up a list of sixty-four major politicians who, he alleged, had collaborated with the Communist secret police. A second document directly accused President Wałęsa, Solidarity's leader, of passing information to Poland's Communist-era security services. Macierewicz demanded that the UOP turn over the names of the agents who worked for Intelligence Command. UOP chief Gromosław Czempiński ignored the request.

Macierewicz allowed the lists to leak to the Polish media, precipitating a political crisis. The tactic backfired. Macierewicz's lists had been drawn up shoddily. High school students had been on his team and they'd made mistakes. Many on the list hadn't collaborated with Communists at all. And in attacking Wałęsa, the hero of Poland's democratic transition, Macierewicz had gone too far. There's little doubt that Wałęsa had been a source for the SB in the early 1970s, but it's also clear that his collaboration was half-hearted and that it ended in 1976—before he cofounded Solidarity. Poles in general didn't support Macierewicz's obsessive score settling. "There is a crazy political paranoia in the air now that has its roots in the idea that you can somehow have a totally clean, pure state," observed Jan Lityński, a former anti-Communist dissident, at the time.

Poland's lower house of parliament, the Sejm, established a committee to investigate Macierewicz for misusing secret police archives. That panel determined that his actions "could have led to the destabilization of the highest organs of the state." As a result of Macierewicz's machinations, Prime Minister Olszewski lost a vote of no confidence in the parliament and he and Macierewicz were forced to resign. Worse, the crisis occurred just as Poland was deep in negotiations with Russia over the final terms for the withdrawal of Russian forces. Russian officials were delighted with the political chaos.

Macierewicz and his followers suffered a serious defeat. Their targets in the UOP, including Czempiński, and the CIA station in Warsaw breathed a sigh of relief. But the conviction among the more uncompromising members of the Solidarity coalition—that Poland's revolution needed finishing, that ex-Communists were pulling the strings behind the scenes, and that old scores had to be settled—lingered as a powerful undercurrent in Polish politics. It would resurface again.

CHAPTER FOURTEEN

SLOUCHING TOWARD NATO

While Polish Intelligence and the CIA cooperated around the world and UOP officers like Andrzej Derlatka argued that an alliance with America was the only way to secure Poland's future, politicians in Washington and Warsaw were more cautious. In Washington, fears about Russia's reaction, for example, undermined America's resolve to add to its alliances in Europe.

In fact, when the world changed in the summer and winter of 1989, the first instinct of the Bush administration was not to expand NATO; it was to alleviate Moscow's concerns. In December, after thousands had breached the Berlin Wall, President George H. W. Bush met Soviet leader Mikhail Gorbachev for a summit in Malta. Bush assured Gorbachev that the United States wasn't interested in taking advantage of the tumult in Eastern Europe to challenge Soviet interests. As Bush reminded the Soviet leader: "I have not jumped up and down on the Berlin Wall."

In meetings with their Soviet counterparts, American officials let it be known that the United States would not support the expansion of

NATO to include Poland or any of its neighbors. On February 9, 1990, Secretary of State James Baker told Gorbachev that "there would be no extension of NATO's jurisdiction . . . one inch to the east." German, French, and British leaders followed with similar denials, all part of a coordinated cascade of guarantees that Soviet security concerns would be addressed in the new world dawning along its borders.

The political leadership that emerged from Poland's Solidarity trade union movement was equally unsure what direction Poland should take. Polish statesmen and intellectuals had explored various approaches to unscramble Poland's historical conundrum: how to attain security while living on an invasion route. Free Poland's first prime minister, Tadeucz Mazowiecki, envisaged a mini-alliance between the countries of Eastern Europe. Other intellectuals contemplated the prospect that Poland could embrace a "third way" somewhere between Russia and the United States.

Inside the Intelligence Bureau, however, ex-Communists Czempiński, Jasik, Smoleński, and Derlatka believed that an alliance with the United States, achieved via membership in NATO, was the only way. These same men had once been integral cogs in a system that viewed America as public enemy number one. Now they'd concluded that only the United States could serve as the principal custodian of Poland's security. They were pragmatists, with few illusions, schooled in the politics of power. They'd gone from serving as the guardians of socialism to believing in the necessity of protecting the Polish state. "We thought the idea of a third way between Moscow and Washington was a fantasy cooked up by an intellectual," Derlatka recalled. "Once we no longer leaned toward Moscow, our only choice was to lean toward Washington."

Ironically, this view didn't have much traction with Poland's liberals, at least not in the beginning. It did, however, resonate among those on the right of Poland's political spectrum. That made for some odd bedfellows. Politicians like Prime Minister Jan Olszewski and his minister of interior, Antoni Macierewicz, who'd advocated a complete purge of all ex-Communists from the service, fundamentally agreed with some of those same ex-Communists on the strategic direction that Poland should take. Along with the ex-Communists, they began to raise the possibility with their counterparts in the West.

In the spring of 1992, Radosław Sikorski, Olszewski's deputy minister of defense, invited all the ambassadors from NATO members to a gathering at the Ministry of Defense. As a brash, Oxford University–educated twenty-nine-year-old journalist, Sikorski had reported for Britain's *Spectator* magazine from the front lines of the Soviet occupation of Afghanistan. Witnessing Soviet power firsthand gave Sikorski a deep appreciation of the perils, and what he believed to be the inevitability, of resurgent Russian nationalism. In his upper-crust British accent, Sikorski kicked off the meeting with an announcement: "We're here to talk about NATO enlargement." It marked the first time a senior Polish official had aired Poland's intentions in public. US ambassador Thomas Simons promptly stood up and walked out. A few weeks later, as Prime Minister Olszewski was preparing to visit Washington in April, Olszewski told Simons that he planned to raise NATO membership with Secretary of Defense Dick Cheney. Simons convinced him to bite his tongue. Washington wasn't ready for such talk.

Events soon conspired to push the notion of Poland's membership in NATO from the extremes of Poland's political spectrum toward the middle. The August 1991 aborted coup in Moscow gave the Poles a renewed sense of vulnerability by underscoring the opposition to Gorbachev's reforms that bubbled beneath the surface in Russia. 1991 had also witnessed the rise of Russia's hard-right Liberal Democratic Party, led by ultranationalist Vladimir Zhirinovsky. He railed against the collapse of the Soviet Union and threatened to "wipe Poland off the map" if it tried to stop Moscow from reestablishing its sphere of influence.

In August 1993, Russia's new leader, Boris Yeltsin, came to Poland for a thirty-six-hour visit as the last Soviet troops were withdrawing from Polish soil.

On the evening of August 25, Wałęsa told Yeltsin that Poland wanted to enter NATO. Yeltsin nodded, which the Poles interpreted as an indication that he was sympathetic to the idea. During the night, lower-level officials from both sides worked on a communiqué. The Russians refused to insert any understanding of Poland's desire to find its own security arrangements. In the early morning hours of August 26, after apparently enough vodka, Wałęsa bated the Russian president. "Who's the boss, Boris? You or your people," he asked. "I'm the boss!" Yeltsin bellowed. Immediately, the communiqué was revised. It didn't mention NATO by name, but the implication—that Russia recognized Poland's right to forge new alliances—was clear. A press conference followed as did a huge sensation.

Russian officials went into damage control. Two weeks after Yeltsin returned to Moscow, he fired off a confidential letter to the leaders of key NATO members putting them on notice that Russia opposed NATO's expansion. Poland obtained the document from friends in the CIA.

Regardless, Polish envoys used the communiqué to push even harder to convince the United States that NATO should welcome Poland and other nations of Eastern Europe into the fold. Poland began to draw a distinction between it, Hungary and the newly formed Czech Republic, and less-advanced nations, such as Ukraine and Belarus, to its east.

In the United States, the election of a new president, Bill Clinton, in November 1992, brought the idea of NATO expansion into the mainstream of US politics as well. *Foreign Affairs*, the house magazine of the influential Council on Foreign Relations, published the first serious article advocating NATO enlargement in September 1993. Written by three analysts from the RAND Corporation, the article warned that unless the boundaries of NATO moved east, a security vacuum would open in Central Europe that could derail its democratic and economic transformation. Other leading Americans began to sidle over to the cause. Zbigniew Brzeziński supported the idea. There was opposition, and it was not without merit. *New York Times* columnist Tom Friedman and Clinton's close friend and adviser, Russophile Strobe Talbott, fought expansion for fear that it would antagonize Moscow. Jack Matlock, the former US ambassador to the Soviet Union, argued that NATO expansion violated America's implied promise not to take advantage of the Soviet retreat from Eastern Europe.

Secretary of Defense William Perry opposed enlargement out of concern that it would dilute the alliance. Perry proposed a NATO-lite, which he called Partnership for Peace: a loose relationship between NATO and Eastern Europe. Raised in the traditions of Middle European literature, Eastern Europe's leaders saw that partnership for what it was: a Kafkaesque antechamber, where the vast Eastern European region would wait in futile perpetuity to enter NATO.

On January 6, 1994, Vice President Al Gore addressed an audience dominated by Polish Americans in Milwaukee and returned to the White House with a message for Clinton: the NATO issue was becoming a big one for voters in the Midwest. The twenty million Americans of Central European descent in the United States were heavily concentrated in battleground states that accounted for almost two hundred electoral votes—more than two-thirds the amount needed to win the White House. NATO's potential enlargement to include Poland, Hungary, and the Czech Republic had become a domestic political issue in the United States.

A day after Gore's speech, three Eastern European–born American officials, UN ambassador Madeleine Albright (Prague), chairman of the Joint Chiefs of Staff General John Shalikashvili (Warsaw), and State Department official Charles Gati (Budapest), visited Warsaw to sell the Partnership for Peace to Poland's president Lech Wałęsa. Wałęsa—who wasn't well read in history but had a talent for straight talk—accused them of plotting another Yalta. They returned to Washington and warned Clinton: a backlash was coming if the United States did not offer full membership.

The ground was beginning to shift. On January 10, Clinton made his first trip to Europe as president. His first stop was a NATO summit in Brussels. The next day in Prague, in a joint press conference with the leaders of four Central European nations, Clinton made the historic announcement that it was "no longer a question of whether, but when and how" NATO would expand.

At the CIA station in Warsaw, the torch had passed in July 1992. Bill Norville was replaced as station chief by Michael Sulick, a Vietnam vet who'd joined the CIA in 1978 after completing a doctorate in comparative literature at Fordham University. Raised in the Bronx, Sulick had learned Russian from a Russian émigré and had translated absurdist Polish poets into English. Sulick compared the French and Russian versions of Shakespeare's *Hamlet* in his dissertation. Sulick had been interested in a position on the analysis side of the CIA. But when he got downtown to the federal complex in Manhattan for his interview, he was told there were no openings. Staff there suggested he try for operations. Sulick agreed, was hired, and evolved into, as *Newsweek* wrote in 2006, one "of the agency's most skilled field operatives and espionage managers." From his base in Warsaw, Sulick liaised with the nascent intelligence agencies of the newly independent Baltic States. He'd already visited Lithuania—on a secret mission in August 1991—soon after it had declared independence from Moscow.

As politicians on both sides mulled the future of the relationship, the pace of joint operations between Poland and the United States quickened. Soviet hardware—weapons systems, computers, satellite arrays—that interested American experts flowed back to the United States in the embassy's diplomatic pouch. Polish Intelligence was also willing to share information on its own government to help American policymakers. After the NATO summit in January 1994, Clinton had scheduled a meeting with the presidents of Poland, Hungary, the Czech Republic, and Slovakia. Spooked by the tongue-lashing Wałęsa had given the US delegation a week earlier, Clinton wanted to know what the Polish president was going to say. Wałęsa was mercurial. The Americans were worried that he'd sandbag Clinton and insist on a strict timetable for NATO enlargement. Sulick called a senior Polish intelligence officer. The officer called back and gave him Wałęsa's position point by point. "I could not have done that in any other country," Sulick said. In very few places did the American special services enjoy such an easy relationship as in Poland.

Marian Zacharski had always itched to be back in the intelligence game. While at Pewex, Zacharski had been the subject of snarky stories in the Western press. His career path made him a curiosity, a sign of the times as Poland transitioned to a free-market economy. "The Spy Who Went into Retailing," tittered one *New York Times* headline. "Epitaph for a Spy," went another, in the business magazine *Forbes*. But Zacharski, a successful lathe salesman in America, fumbled when it came to managing a business in the new Poland. Once Pewex lost the monopoly it had on selling imported goods, it couldn't compete with Poland's private retailers. Its fortunes faded. In 1993, Pewex declared bankruptcy.

Zacharski became an adviser to Andrzej Milczanowski, who'd been appointed minister of interior in 1992 after the arch anti-Communist, Antoni Macierewicz, resigned in disgrace. Zacharski undertook intelligence operations on the Korean peninsula, establishing good relations with his South Korean counterparts. But Zacharski's conviction in the United States followed him like a curse. Unwilling to do business with a convicted spy, France, Germany, and Switzerland denied him visas.

Milczanowski complained about Zacharski's treatment every time he met with an American. FBI director Louis Freeh went to Warsaw on July 1, 1994, to open the FBI's first office in Eastern Europe. Milczanowski spent the better part of their meeting badgering him about Zacharski. "Pardon Zacharski," Milczanowski insisted. "We're your allies now." Inside the CIA, John Palevich also sang Zacharski's praises. In fact, Palevich became such an advocate for Zacharski within the CIA and with the Poles that fellow CIA officers advised him to cool it. Palevich had always been fond of repeating the first rule of a CIA case officer: never fall in love with your agent. Many of his colleagues felt that Palevich had broken that very rule.

Palevich's advocacy on Zacharski's behalf contributed to a crisis. On August 15, 1994, Milczanowski appointed Zacharski head of the foreign intelligence bureau of the UOP. Like Palevich, Milczanowski had always been taken by what he called Zacharski's "dynamism" and his ideas for reforming the service. Palevich's praise of Zacharski factored into his decision, too. "I always paid attention to everything John Palevich said," Milczanowski recalled. Zacharski's promotion meant that a felon convicted in a US federal court and sentenced to life in a US prison would now be running foreign intelligence operations for a nation seeking admission into NATO.

Nicholas Rey, a Polish-born investment banker, had replaced Thomas Simons in December 1993 as US ambassador to Poland. Rey had just celebrated the wedding of his daughter and was on a short summer holiday in the Tatra Mountains in southern Poland when news of Zacharski's promotion broke. "I mean the phones were ringing off the hook," Rey later recalled. "What are they doing? . . . They still want to get into NATO?" Opponents of Poland's entry into NATO had already been asserting that Poland couldn't be trusted with NATO's secrets. And now Poland had appointed as its intelligence chief a man who'd made his career spying on the United States.

Rey cut his holiday short, returned to Warsaw, and met with President Wałęsa and Minister Milczanowski. The promotion had to be rescinded, he announced. A démarche from the US embassy on August 17 made it official. "I gave Rey a cold response," Milczanowski recalled. "We are who we are," Milczanowski told him. To which Rey replied, "If Poland was Russia, we'd tolerate it. But Poland is not Russia, so we object."

On the evening of August 17, Zacharski visited Sulick. The two were neighbors. Sulick's house was full of boxes. He was packing up to move his family to Moscow, where he'd been named station chief. Sulick felt for the Polish spy and was a little embarrassed by America's overbearing behavior. The CIA was looking like the KGB, pushing Poland around. In Sulick's view, Zacharski was a professional and had excelled at his craft. "I'm going to resign tomorrow," Zacharski announced.

"I'd talked him up so favorably that they appointed Zacharski as head of the service and the US government went bananas," John Palevich recalled with a laugh. "They had to take it away from him, but Zacharski was very, very sharp." Zacharski stayed at the UOP but stepped down as its foreign intelligence chief. The crisis passed, but it left some Poles with the sense that the United States had assumed the role of judge and jury over what it meant to be a Polish patriot. The US government, and the FBI in particular, had never forgiven Zacharski for refusing to defect to the United States. This would not be the last time that the United States sought to school the Poles on the proper way to manage alliances.

Milczanowski turned to Bogdan Libera, a soft-spoken, well-respected engineer, to lead foreign intelligence for the UOP. Libera was free of Zacharski's bombast and ego. He and Milczanowski also shared a history. Libera's family had been terrorized by Communists, too. In 1948 when he was four, Polish secret police detained Libera's father, Stefan, because he'd been part of the anti-Communist resistance to the Nazi occupation. During Stefan's six-month absence, Libera's mother, with no job and no income, kept her three small sons alive by begging. Neighbors lent the family a goat. "The milk from that goat saved our lives," Libera recalled.

Libera had entered the intelligence service in the 1970s, when Poland's Communist leadership was less interested in the ideological purity of its recruits. He was an excellent student; he'd studied petroleum engineering and had worked in the mines during the summer to earn extra cash. "I could've been a Texan," he quipped.

He was also his school's chess champion and rowed stroke on the crew team.

Libera was part of the first class at the Intelligence Training Center in Stare Kiejkuty, along with Gromek Czempiński. He'd focused on German affairs and, as an undercover officer detailed to the Ministry of Mines, sought to steal West German know-how.

As spy chief, Libera actively pursued opportunities for the UOP to work with the CIA. He figured, like other members of the Foreign Intelligence Bureau, that the more Poland contributed, the better Poland's chances would be to join NATO. Operation Unity was something all of them had gotten behind. Libera sent teams into Libya to look for chemical weapons and plotted missions to fight illegal arms smuggling and nuclear proliferation. His office helped the United States collect intelligence on North Korea, Cuba, and Iran.

"We worked in different places where the Americans had no access," Libera recalled. "I had many sleepless nights." He comforted himself with the knowledge that, during his tenure, no Polish agent was outed, arrested, or died in service to Poland—and by extension, the United States.

CIA directors valued Libera's contributions. A few months after Libera retired in 2001, then CIA director George Tenet wrote a long letter praising him as "a trailblazer, a man who presciently saw the opportunities of the future beyond the old paradigms and political bonds that defined most of the past century."

Tenet paid tribute to Libera for helping to create what he described as "one of the two foremost intelligence relationships that the United States has ever had." Given America's longtime intelligence partnerships with Britain, Australia, Canada, Israel, and other democracies, that was truly extraordinary praise. Bill Norville was spot-on: the Poles *had* succeeded in fashioning a special relationship with the United States.

Poland, however, was still waiting for this special relationship to lead it into NATO. In April 1994, the Polish government appointed a new ambassador to the United States. Jerzy Koźmiński, who'd played a key role managing Poland's shock-therapy economic transformation in the early 1990s, was given one objective: NATO. For the next five years, a throng of officials—four prime ministers, five defense ministers, four foreign ministers, four intelligence chiefs, and two presidents—shuttled into and out of office in Warsaw. All the while, Koźmiński stayed put in Washington, trying to turn Poland's political untidiness into a strength. No matter which political party was in power at home, and there were many, all of them wanted NATO membership. Koźmiński was the diplomatic version of Polish Intelligence. Both maintained a similar focus on the singular goal: forging an alliance with the United States.

Koźmiński had partners in Washington. The Republican Party, for one, became a backer of NATO enlargement, seeing it as a cudgel to bash Clinton. Koźmiński lobbied his Republican friends to include NATO enlargement in the GOP's Contract with America, the 1994 manifesto that helped usher in the first Republican majority in the House of Representatives and the Senate in decades.

Prominent Polish Americans provided help, as well. Koźmiński collaborated closely with Brzeziński and Zdzisław Jeziorański, a World War II freedom fighter known by his nom de guerre, Jan Nowak. Small in stature, Nowak was a giant in Poland; he'd parachuted behind enemy lines to resist the Nazi occupation and after the war he ran the Polish service of Radio Free Europe. Through his daily broadcasts, he'd become the most revered radio personality in Communist Poland and in Polish-speaking communities around the world.

Within the Clinton administration, too, Koźmiński found supporters. Daniel Fried, a longtime US diplomat and expert on Soviet affairs, had worked in the embassy in Warsaw. He'd returned to take a job on Clinton's National Security Council to advise the president on Central Europe. Fried and Koźmiński could've passed for brothers. Both had slight builds, boyish features, and nasal voices. Koźmiński kept trim by combining scores of push-ups, yoga, and endless pacing in his office. Fried was an obsessive runner.

The son of Polish-speaking Jews who had fled the Holocaust, Fried viewed NATO expansion as a way to expunge America's choice to isolate itself from the rise of Fascism in the 1930s. He'd always maintained that woeful decision had led directly to the historical wrong of Yalta.

The return of another diplomatic powerhouse to the United States further bolstered Poland's cause. In the fall of 1994, Richard Holbrooke left his post as US ambassador to Germany to become assistant secretary of state for European affairs. While the larger-than-life Holbrooke is most famous for his work ending the war in former Yugoslavia, arguably his most impactful contribution was pushing the Department of Defense and some reluctant American allies, particularly France, to accept NATO's expansion. The Poles called Dick Holbrooke "the tank."

Holbrooke championed NATO enlargement for a different reason than Fried. For him, an expanded alliance would clinch Germany in the warm embrace of its friends and prevent it from roaming around Central Europe on its own.

Koźmiński did his lobbying on a tight budget. Poland's Ministry of Foreign Affairs had only authorized $30,000 for the embassy's outreach, a pittance compared with much larger funds at the Hungarian, Romanian, and Czech embassies, which were also being considered for NATO admission at the time.

Koźmiński and his team befriended all the key staffers at the White House, all the key staffers at the Pentagon, and all the key staffers in the Senate—the chamber that would in the end have to approve any change in the NATO treaty. Embassy staffers played soccer with Pentagon officials and hosted them at the embassy for beers. In a small room in the embassy, Koźmiński's team put a diagram on the wall. It depicted all the senators, split into five columns in terms of their support of NATO's enlargement. When the poster first went up, only four were openly in favor. Sixty-seven were needed to vote yes.

Despite Clinton's vague promise of NATO enlargement, opposition to growing the alliance remained strong. Koźmiński understood that Poland needed to perform like a NATO member, in fact, to outperform other NATO members, if it wanted into the club. Poland had to create a situation where the Americans tangibly felt the value of the alliance. In Warsaw, US ambassador Rey postulated that "people from various parties . . . must have gotten all together in a smoke filled room and decided, 'What do we need to do? We want to get into NATO, what do we need to do to embarrass the bloody hell out of the West, particularly the Americans to force us to join it?'"

Polish Intelligence was crucial to this process. The service was Warsaw's strong suit. "Espionage cooperation was important. It showed everybody that we were different," said Bogusław Winid, who ran congressional affairs for the embassy under Koźmiński. "During those days on Capitol Hill, everybody was looking for something to distinguish themselves from the others. Intelligence cooperation was a trump card we could play." Successful operations turned Poland "into the most popular kid in class," Winid recalled. "Everybody loved us."

Daniel Fried noted that classified reports on these missions changed the minds of several key senators. "These operations showed a lot of skeptics in the United States that Poland could actually be an ally," Fried said. "Like, these guys were good." This didn't surprise Fried. "Countries like Poland tend to develop good intelligence services," he observed, "otherwise they cease to exist."

CHAPTER FIFTEEN

THE PRIME MINISTER IS A SPY!

While to many, NATO membership may have seemed inevitable, a conflict was still playing itself out within Poland. Political infighting, the quest for power, issues of identity, and allegiances threatened to scuttle Poland's chances. Would Poland lose this precious opportunity or keep its eyes on the prize?

One Sunday in the late spring of 1994, the chairman of the US Joint Chiefs of Staff, General John Shalikashvili, called Ambassador Jerzy Koźmiński at his residence in Washington, DC. Warsaw-born, Shalikashvili had a warm spot in his heart for Poland and its new ambassador. He explained that the United States wanted to restore democracy on the Caribbean island nation of Haiti. Three years earlier, Haiti's military had ousted President Jean-Bertrand Aristide, who'd won office in the first free and fair democratic election in that island's history. A general, Raoul Cédras, had seized control in the coup. The Clinton administration had demanded that Cédras step down and make way for Aristide's return. One of the few at the top of the US military who was sympathetic to Poland's security concerns, Shalikashvili told the Polish ambassador that the United States was looking for partners. "Why doesn't Poland volunteer?" he suggested. "It'd help with your NATO aspirations."

Koźmiński contacted Warsaw. Soon after, President Lech Wałęsa convened the Council of Ministers and asked how long it would take the Ministry of Defense to muster a unit for Haiti. "Six months," came the reply. Andrzej Milczanowski interrupted. "It'll take me six hours. I've got GROM."

The CIA had been training GROM since it was founded in 1990. Piotr Gastał was one of the first members. After flunking a law school entrance examination in 1988, Gastał joined the Polish army. He completed two years of service when a friend told him about a new unit being formed inside the Ministry of Interior. A black belt in karate who spoke decent English, Gastał interviewed with GROM's commander, Sławomir Petelicki, who recognized in Gastał a kindred spirit. At one training exercise Petelicki had sharpshooters fire at targets on either side of his head. "Petelicki was truly crazy," Gastał remembered with a wistful smile. "Crazy enough to make something completely new."

Gastał and the rest of the recruits trained with American intelligence operatives, FBI agents, Delta force commandos, and Navy SEALs. By the spring of 1993, Gastał and his comrades were ready for action. Shalikashvili had learned of the unit from a senior US Special Forces officer who'd watched them in joint special operations exercises.

It was unclear what the deployment in Haiti would be. As Cédras dug in his heels, US military planners readied an invasion. Gastał and fifty other GROM members went to Puerto Rico to await orders. They were incorporated into a unit of the US Army's Green Berets that had planned to land in Haiti in advance of the bulk of the invading force, the US Army's Eighty-Second Airborne Division.

On September 18, 1994, with elements of the Eighty-Second in the air and the Green Berets mobilizing for an assault, diplomacy averted a war. Former president Jimmy Carter convinced Cédras to step down and restore Aristide to office. For Gastał and the rest of GROM, that meant a change of mission. GROM pulled guard duty as part of a military occupation of the island, providing security for the commander of the Tenth Mountain Division, Major General David Meade, and other dignitaries. GROM's men were vastly overqualified for the job. Clinton's national security adviser, Tony Lake, told stories of visiting Haiti and being surrounded by menacing Poles in black uniforms with lightning bolt patches on their shoulders.

In Poland, skeptics worried that history would repeat itself. In 1802, Polish officers, seeking an alliance with a great power, in this case Napoleonic France, dispatched more than five thousand troops to Haiti to quell a slave rebellion. Back then, the hope was that, in exchange, France might save Poland from being carved up by Russia, Prussia, and Austria. Instead, in 1815, at the Congress of Vienna, Poland effectively vanished.

This time around in Haiti, Poles congratulated themselves on the deployment. Some griped about serving as bodyguards. "Never send a Ferrari to dig coal," quipped one GROM vet. But GROM, a child of the CIA, had acquitted itself well, garnering plaudits from the Department of Defense and the rest of the US national security structure. It would be called on again.

The specter of Russia continued to shadow Poland's dream of forging an alliance with the United States. Within the Clinton administration, many officials still argued that maintaining good relations with Moscow outweighed guaranteeing the security of Eastern Europe. Another problem troubled US policy makers: a persistent suspicion that Russian spies still penetrated the governments, security services, and militaries of the young democracies in the region.

Against that backdrop, the rise in Poland of former Communists, who'd renamed their party the Democratic Left Alliance (or the SLD), concerned Washington. In September 1993, in the third parliamentary election since 1989, the SLD won the most seats. Although it publicly embraced the same foreign policy plank as the right-wing government it replaced, in Washington doubts remained.

Then, in 1995, the leader of the SLD, Aleksander Kwaśniewski, a mediagenic former Communist student activist, announced he was running for president against the incumbent Lech Wałęsa. With his walrus mustache and man-of-the-people demeanor, Wałęsa had been an inspiring revolutionary. But he'd proven to be a shambolic manager as Solidarity's coalition of workers and intellectuals fractured into political parties. As one observer put it, "Heroes do not make good politicians." Wałęsa stumbled badly in the campaign, losing the sole debate to the younger, smoother Kwaśniewski. On November 19, Polish voters chose Kwaśniewski, who became the first ex-Communist to be directly elected president, not only in Poland but in all of Eastern Europe.

Wałęsa couldn't accept the defeat. He searched for something to reverse it and bring down the ex-Communist SLD. Milczanowski announced he was in possession of some intelligence that could do the trick.

Over the summer, Milczanowski had sent his prized officer, Marian Zacharski, to the Spanish resort island of Majorca. Zacharski met a Russian intelligence officer, Colonel Vladimir Alganov, who'd served in Poland both for the KGB and for its Russian successor, the FSB. Zacharski claimed that he maneuvered Alganov into admitting that the Russians had been running an agent at the heart of Poland's political establishment for a decade. That agent was none other than Józef Oleksy, Poland's prime minister and one of the leaders of the SLD. If true, this allegation could cripple the ex-Communists.

In early December, the CIA station in Warsaw got wind that Wałęsa and his associates were conspiring to kneecap the ex-Communists by charging that the prime minister was a spy. Ambassador Rey reported it to Washington. From the National Security Council, Daniel Fried invited Ambassador Koźmiński for a stroll in Lafayette Square Park, a stone's throw from Fried's office. "What do you know about this?" Fried asked.

Koźmiński's contacts in Warsaw confirmed Fried's fear. Koźmiński reached out to Zbigniew Brzeziński for help. Brzeziński was already planning to travel to Warsaw in the middle of December to receive the Order of the White Eagle, Poland's highest honor. In a meeting with Wałęsa on December 19, Brzeziński urged the defeated Polish president to keep the allegations quiet. He proposed establishing a panel to investigate the charges behind closed doors. Any public airing of dirty laundry involving Russian espionage, Brzeziński warned, could block the path to NATO.

Wałęsa wouldn't budge. He ordered Milczanowski to make the allegations public. On December 21, on the floor of the Sejm, Milczanowski branded Oleksy a Russian spy. In Washington, Koźmiński went into damage control. He had to answer two questions: If the allegations were true, how could Poland sincerely aspire to NATO membership? If they were false, how could a Polish president have his minister of interior level such an incendiary charge?

Koźmiński had friends everywhere, including in the CIA. The agency's first reaction was that Oleksy was not a spy. He was, its analysts posited, a pretty competent prime minister, gifted in retail politics, backslapping, and drinking. With a bald pate that suggested a well-polished cue ball, Oleksy was seen often glowing in the middle of a noisy circle of people, cigarette smoke billowing from its center. Among those around him, there'd be a priest, a colonel from the intelligence services, students, writers. "He loved meeting people, schmoozing, and debating," Koźmiński said, "but that didn't make him a Russian asset."

Further investigation focused on the role that Zacharski had played in the affair. For years, his detractors inside the UOP had argued that Zacharski was, at best, an incomplete spy. In the United States in the 1970s, he'd stumbled on Bill Bell and had proved to be a creative risk-taker. Some Americans had been taken with his tradecraft, John Palevich for one. But Zacharski's colleagues in the UOP saw him as a blowhard who lacked the necessary precision of a good case officer. There was always concern about how Zacharski would handle himself should he go up against a pro like Vladimir Alganov.

Russia opposed NATO enlargement. All its officials and military officers railed publicly against it. Behind the scenes, Moscow tried to sow political divisions throughout Eastern Europe and schemed to split Warsaw from Washington. When Zacharski found Alganov in Majorca, many inside Polish Intelligence concluded that Zacharski had blundered into a trap. Asked to reveal his assets in Warsaw, Alganov naturally fingered Oleksy. Even if Oleksy was just Alganov's drinking buddy, what better way to give Washington pause about accepting Poland into the NATO family than to claim that Poland's prime minister was an asset of the FSB? Zacharski was so sure of himself, his colleagues in Warsaw believed, that he couldn't contemplate the possibility that he was being played.

At the embassy, Ambassador Rey felt he was writing his own "dime-store novel" as he fired off cable after cable on the affair. With the CIA's help, he'd determined that the attack on the ex-Communists was "a political ruse" and "not something which clearly damages the Polish desire to get into NATO." Rey observed that Wałęsa "strutted around feeling that he had screwed the commies." Instead, Wałęsa's gambit, which he ended up regretting, damaged his political career.

On January 25, a little more than a month after Wałęsa had precipitated the crisis, Oleksy quit. But his resignation didn't spell the end of the SLD. Instead, it opened the field for President Kwaśniewski to dominate the party *and* Poland's political landscape for a decade to come.

Still, the Oleksy affair had repercussions for Kwaśniewski, too. Allegations of KGB penetration left a lingering sense that, as ex-Communists, Kwaśniewski and his team would need to constantly prove how committed they were to an alliance with America. It was a weakness that the CIA would exploit later on.

The Oleksy affair ended the eventful career of dissident-turned-spymaster Andrzej Milczanowski. Soon after he'd labeled Oleksy a spy on the floor of Poland's parliament, he retired to his row house in

Szczecin, where he became a patent lawyer and passed his time listening to American jazz.

As for Marian Zacharski, he departed Warsaw as well, decamping in 1996 to Switzerland, chased by accusations of flagrant mismanagement at his former employer, Pewex. Zacharski thought Geneva made sense for his family. He'd already enrolled his daughters in Swiss boarding schools. But Basia refused to leave her aging mother's side. The couple divorced. Zacharski went to live by the shores of Lake Geneva, where he penned memoirs and histories of intelligence operations during World War II. He remarried. His daughters headed back to America to study, Małgosia to Cornell and Karolina to Pepperdine University, near the city of her birth. Zacharski was always grateful that the US authorities never let the sins of the father prevent his daughters from pursuing an American education. He had a little help from John Palevich, who kept tabs on them both.

It seemed like the end of an era, yet the question of what it meant to be a Polish patriot remained a battlefield—in Poland and in the United States. Espionage lay at its heart. The climax and swift termination of Zacharski's storied spy career became entangled in the tale of yet another American spy.

For years, American officials had called for the exoneration of the CIA's greatest Polish asset, Colonel Ryszard Kukliński, and for Poland to formally recognize that he was not a traitor but a patriot. In an interview with Polish television in 1992, Zbigniew Brzeziński credited Kukliński's espionage with helping the United States counter the USSR. "Such things should not be considered treason," Brzeziński said. "I believe it is high time to acknowledge that Kukliński served Poland well." David Forden, who'd been Kukliński's case officer at the CIA, had developed a deep bond with the man. After Forden retired in 1988, he devoted himself to clearing Kukliński's name. He and others worked to make a pardon for Kukliński a condition for Poland's entry into NATO.

Poland's supreme court, acting under a December 1989 amnesty law, had already commuted Kukliński's death sentence, issued in absentia, to twenty-five years in prison. But Polish society was split about a total pardon. The right-wing factions that had emerged from the Solidarity movement idolized Kukliński, but other former dissidents were outraged that Kukliński had known about the imminent imposition of martial law in Poland in 1981 and had done nothing to alert the movement to the coming crackdown. In a survey in September 1994, more Poles (17 percent) thought Zacharski had served Poland better than Kukliński (7 percent).

When Zacharski was named intelligence chief, in 1994, some Poles saw an opportunity to exchange an American acceptance of Zacharski's appointment for a Polish pardon for Kukliński. But the United States wasn't interested and Poland didn't push the case. "This was an opportunity to confront painful things in our past and to compromise," said Piotr Pacewicz, the deputy executive editor of *Gazeta Wyborcza*, Poland's leading daily at the time. "It didn't happen."

In Washington, Koźmiński sensed the pressure mounting. At an embassy function, a CIA officer approached him and volunteered that "if Poland ever needed some fuel, the agency could brief senators on the Intelligence Committee" about Poland's exploits on behalf of the United States. In the same breath, the officer suggested that Poland come to grips with Kukliński. "Those two messages came at the same time," Koźmiński recalled. The Clinton administration also felt some heat. Former ambassador to Poland John Davis wrote that it was ironic for Poland to be lobbying for NATO membership when it refused to recognize the crucial contributions of one of its officers to NATO's security. Daniel Fried told Koźmiński that unless the issue was dealt with, Poland's entry into NATO would "be a real problem." Finally, the White House asked Zbigniew Brzeziński to get involved. Brzeziński and Koźmiński had grown close. In 1996, they began working on the issue together. Then a deadline emerged. NATO was planning a summit in Madrid in July 1997. Poland, the Czech Republic, and Hungary hoped to be invited to join the alliance there.

The one ex-Communist who stridently opposed any reconsideration of the verdict against Kukliński was Poland's former president, General Wojciech Jaruzelski, the dictator in dark sunglasses who'd led the crackdown on Solidarity. Jaruzelski had justified imposing martial law on Poland in 1981 as the lesser of two evils. He claimed that he'd faced a Hobson's choice between martial law and a Soviet intervention. Jaruzelski cast himself as Poland's savior. But Kukliński's espionage contradicted Jaruzelski's narrative (as did a subsequent release of classified material from Soviet archives). There was no imminent Soviet threat. Jaruzelski was further outraged that an officer whom he'd trusted had been cooperating with a foreign power behind his back. Koźmiński feared that military officers still loyal to the old general might try to scupper the project to clear Kukliński, thus derailing Poland's NATO dream.

But it wasn't just an old general and his wounded pride that united Poland's military against a pardon. How, officers asked, are we going to educate our young soldiers to be loyal to the state if we lionize a spy?

Koźmiński met Kukliński in the United States. In Kukliński, the Polish ambassador found echoes of Poland's grand romantic tradition of the lone fighter against the world. Koźmiński was taken, too, by the tragedy that had befallen Kukliński's family after he'd defected to America. His two sons had died in the United States.

Koźmiński began searching for a trustworthy interlocutor in the new government of ex-Communists in Warsaw. He found one in Leszek Miller, whom he'd gotten to know during the summer of 1996 when Miller visited three cities in the United States, including Atlanta for the Summer Olympics. Back in Poland, Miller was known as "Comrade Shaggy," the embodiment of a hard-boiled Communist apparatchik, used to lording it over his small provincial town, a grimy textile hub some thirty miles outside Warsaw. Nonetheless, Miller was a powerhouse in the SLD; he played the role of the earthy hayseed in contrast to the urbane charm of President Kwaśniewski. Koźmiński saw Miller for what he was: a politician who could deliver.

While Koźmiński was taken with Kukliński's story, Miller viewed it unemotionally. "I knew it was a problem because American politicians wouldn't stop banging on about it," he recalled. "Personally, I didn't care whether he was a traitor or a hero. His case was an obstacle to our accession to NATO and it had to be removed." Miller was the ideal candidate for the job; for him it was a Nixon-goes-to-China moment. Only a wily ex-Communist functionary like Miller could make Kukliński's case in Poland, where ex-Communists remained a force in the security services and the army.

In January 1997, Miller was appointed minister of interior. The next month, he came to the United States for meetings with, among others, the CIA. Koźmiński arranged for Miller and Brzeziński to meet for a drink. Miller informed the two that he'd come to America with a mandate from President Kwaśniewski to find a solution to the Kukliński affair. His only condition was that in order to exonerate Kukliński, Polish prosecutors needed to be involved and Kukliński would have to testify.

At the meeting, Brzeziński pressed Miller to promise that if Kukliński did testify, the results would be, as Brzeziński put it, "productively handled." Miller gave what Koźmiński called "an almost guarantee" that Kukliński would be cleared. Brzeziński called Kukliński at his home in Florida and convinced him to come to Washington to speak to Polish prosecutors.

On Saturday evening, April 19, two Polish military prosecutors flew into Dulles International Airport. Koźmiński went to the airport alone to meet them. In the waiting area, Koźmiński bumped into a major from the Polish defense attaché's office, also awaiting the men. It was supposed to be a hush-hush mission, kept from the defense attaché for fear that it would get back to Jaruzelski's loyalists in the army, who'd leak it to the press. But secretaries at the Ministry of Defense handling the prosecutors' travel arrangements had naturally informed the defense attaché that two military officers were heading his way. Top secret bumped up against standard operating procedures and standard operating procedures won.

Koźmiński concocted a story. One of the visiting officers was his friend, he told the major. He was there to surprise him. "You'll spoil it if you stay," Koźmiński told the major. Koźminski's ruse succeeded; the major left.

Starting the following Monday and continuing until Friday, the two officers met secretly with Kukliński at Brzeziński's K Street offices at the Center for Strategic and International Studies. Brzeziński and Koźmiński served as witnesses. Under the rules, the officers addressed Kukliński as "colonel." David Forden, another CIA officer, and a husky former FBI agent, formed an ad hoc security detail, shuttling Kukliński each day from Forden's home in Northern Virginia to downtown DC. Koźmiński and Brzeziński steered the conversation toward elements in Polish law that could be used to pardon Kukliński; specifically, something called "a state of higher necessity"—under which a crime is justified if it serves a greater good. The argument that they helped construct was that Kukliński committed treason because he wanted to save Poland. Koźmiński kept Miller informed via phone calls from the embassy; he never put anything in writing. Everyone had a code name: Kukliński was "our friend." The prosecutors were "the travelers." Brzeziński, "the professor."

As this tussle over the past played out, the future was happening. GROM commandos undertook their second deployment, this time to former Yugoslavia. The war in ex-Yugoslavia had left hundreds of thousands dead. It'd ended in late 1995 and the United Nations and NATO had been called in to enforce an uneasy peace. GROM was given responsibility for security at a UN mission in Croatia, near the border with Serbia.

The GROM team was led by Major Jacek Kita. Like Andrzej Milczanowski back in 1990, Kita had something to prove. Pressure was rising in Poland to disband the outfit; Kita wanted to show that his men could match up with the special forces of any nation and do something worthy of a NATO ally. In Haiti, GROM had played a bit part. Kita knew that GROM was capable of more.

In March 1996, the International Criminal Tribunal for the former Yugoslavia at The Hague had secretly indicted Slavko Dokmanović, a Serb leader who was charged with genocide for participating in one of the conflict's worst crimes: the November 1991 massacre of 260 wounded Croat soldiers and civilians. Serb irregulars operating in the city of Vukovar took them from their hospital beds, drove them to a field, and gunned them down. Dokmanović had holed up in a Serbian town just across the border with Croatia. UN officials, led by Jacques Paul Klein, a cigar-chomping Texan with a French name, began working with Kita on a plan—called "Operation Little Flower"—to have GROM operatives arrest Dokmanović. As Milczanowski had done before him in Iraq, Kita kept his commanding officer in Warsaw in the dark.

On June 27, 1997, a sultry Balkan summer day, UN officials lured Dokmanović into Croatia with the promise of a meeting to discuss compensation for property that he and other Serbs owned in the region. At the border, Dokmanović transferred into an armored UN Chevrolet. A GROM commando was at the wheel, while Kita rode shotgun. The GROM base was on the way to the UN office. As the Chevy neared GROM's facility, a truck, driven by another GROM operative, pulled out in front of it. Pretending to avoid a collision, the Chevy veered into the base.

Black-clad GROM commandos leapt out of nowhere, pulled open the rear doors, yanked Dokmanović from the car, and hustled him in front of a representative of the Hague Tribunal, who read him the indictment. A GROM member threw a hood over Dokmanović's head and bundled him back into the Chevy. It sped to a local airport. There a Belgian Air Force plane was waiting to fly Dokmanović and tribunal investigators to The Hague. Upon arrival in the Netherlands, investigators discovered that GROM's operatives had overlooked a handgun in Dokmanović's handbag. GROM had shown it was ready for prime time, but there was always room for improvement.

Dokmanović's capture was big news. It marked the first time since the Nuremberg trials after World War II that an accused war criminal had been detained on orders of an international tribunal. At the White House, President Clinton was impressed. In a statement that day, Clinton congratulated the tribunal. Clinton's statement didn't say it, but implicit in the praise was a question to the tens of thousands of American forces who were concurrently deployed in Bosnia: Why haven't you arrested any war crimes suspects?

Klein wrote a glowing report about GROM's contributions that landed on Clinton's desk. Kita's commanding officer back home only learned of GROM's participation in the mission when a US Army officer congratulated him at a US embassy function in Warsaw. The Serbs were told that Russian mercenaries had been hired to capture Dokmanović. He hanged himself in his cell in 1998.

Barely two weeks after Dokmanović was arrested, Poland, the Czech Republic, and Hungary were formally invited to join NATO during the fifteenth summit of the treaty alliance in Madrid. American patience was running thin. It was time to clear Kukliński.

The terrible twins, Daniel Fried and Jerzy Koźmiński, worked out a deal. Following the Madrid summit, Clinton would fly to Warsaw on July 10 and meet with President Kwaśniewski. At the meeting, Clinton would thank Kwaśniewski for all the work he'd done on the Kukliński case and inform him that the United States looked forward to a "timely conclusion." There'd be no criticism or blatant pressure. A mention would be good enough.

Clinton flew into Warsaw as scheduled. Before landing, the American president had asked to review a special set of troops. He wanted GROM. Walking down the receiving line, the American president shook all of their hands. The Poles didn't tell Clinton that it wasn't the unit that had apprehended Dokmanović.

Later that day, Clinton was treated to a tumultuous welcome. With Yalta on his mind, Clinton told a cheering crowd in Warsaw's Old Town that Poland's acceptance by NATO was "a promise redeemed." A banner reading THANK YOU, BILL fluttered above the crowd. Declared Clinton: "Never again will your birthright of freedom be denied."

In September 1997, things began to shift for Kukliński. The prosecutors returned to the United States with sixteen pages of testimony for Kukliński to review and sign. They told him they'd concluded that he'd broken the law but was acting in "a state of higher necessity." Back in Warsaw, Kwaśniewski, never one to embrace tough jobs, directed Miller to break the news to Jaruzelski. Miller recalled it as the most difficult conversation of his life. "I had stage fright; my legs went weak," he told friends.

On September 20, Poland announced that Kukliński had been cleared of the charges against him. Thirty former generals, led by Jaruzelski, signed a letter of protest. "He was made a hero, have we been traitors?" it asked. The issue of what it meant to be a Polish patriot would remain contested ground.

Even though Poland had formally been invited to join NATO, Koźmiński's work wasn't done. He still needed sixty-seven US senators to vote in favor of revising the treaty. Ferocious lobbying continued. In the diagram on the wall of the Polish embassy's NATO command center, senators were shifted from the "no," to the "maybe no," to the "maybe yes," to the "unenthusiastic yes," and finally to the "definitively yes" column. On the night of April 30, 1998, by a vote of 80 to 19, the Senate approved the enlargement of NATO to include Poland, the Czech Republic, and Hungary.

Kukliński was on his first full day back in Poland since late 1981—when CIA officers had bundled him out of his homeland, covered in blankets and Christmas presents. Soon after the final vote was tallied at 10:41 P.M. in Washington, Koźmiński called Kukliński with the news. Dawn was breaking in the southern Polish city of Kraków. Kukliński was going to be named an honorary citizen of the city that day. Koźmiński told him the news and Kukliński broke down in tears. "It was Kukliński's grand finale," Koźmiński said. "A screenwriter couldn't have done it better."

CHAPTER SIXTEEN

MISSING BIN LADEN

The camaraderie between American and Polish spies extended beyond the agencies. The sense of a shared mission ran so deep that even those who'd been purged from the UOP kept their eyes peeled for opportunities to assist the United States. Aleksander Makowski was a case in point.

During Communist times, Makowski was one of the preeminent intelligence officers in Department I. Raised in the United States and the UK, where his father had also served as a Polish spy, Alex spoke fluent English, Italian, French, and Russian. Both he and Gromek Czempiński were in the elite first class at the Intelligence Training Center in 1972.

With the face of an altar boy, Makowski matured into a smooth operator. His small frame masked an athlete's body, honed by long runs and hard-style karate. In 1975, while working undercover at the Institute of Legal Sciences in the Polish Academy of Sciences, Makowski charmed several visiting American professors, who, after meeting him in Warsaw, arranged for a scholarship for a year at Harvard Law School. Makowski, the Warsaw Pact spy, chose to study constitutional law.

After Harvard, Makowski was posted to New York, where he was the subject of a botched recruitment effort by the FBI. There he conducted operations with the likes of Sławomir Petelicki. By the mid-1980s Makowski had moved on to Rome, where, as *rezydent*, he led a team tracking Western material support for the Solidarity movement. Because of his labors against Solidarity, he was one of only three Foreign Intelligence officers who failed the vetting process. Makowski went into private business as a security consultant. That didn't stop him, however, from moonlighting as a spy.

In 1993, Makowski was hired by the UOP as a freelance agent. He ended up working for an intelligence officer who'd been his underling during Communist times. That officer was Włodzimierz Sokołowski, who took the name Vincent as one of his aliases.

Tall, bald, and goateed, with a husky voice and hawk nose, Vincent struck an imposing figure, mixing cool bonhomie, black turtlenecks, and a dash of controlled aggression. During the Communist era, Vincent had been part of Alex's team. Along with Petelicki, Vincent operated out of the embassy in Stockholm, posing as a press attaché.

In 1990, Vincent passed the vetting process but decided to stay in Sweden to try his hand as an entrepreneur. "I was thirty-three," he recalled. "I thought there was a chance in business for me." But as with several other former spies, like one who worked as an advertising director for a Polish FM radio station that went belly up, Vincent discovered that making it in the free market wasn't so easy. When the UOP came knocking again, Vincent rejoined the service.

Returning to Warsaw, Vincent was surprised by the changes within the agency. A mix of officers—from Solidarity and the Communist era—worked together. A new ethos was being born. "We were very tough, very open minded, and very active," Vincent recalled. What struck Vincent most was the women. In the old days, Department I was a purely male affair. Many floors of the intelligence HQ didn't even have a women's restroom. All that had changed.

"When I came to the office, I saw a woman there and I said, 'Hey, girl, what are you doing?'" Vincent said. "She turned and said, 'I'm your new boss.'" The woman had been in the Solidarity underground; she and Vincent would cooperate closely in the new Poland. CIA officers witnessed the cultural shift as well. "Had there been any misogyny or condescension," said one female CIA analyst who collaborated with the UOP on counterterrorism, "I would've remembered that."

After rejoining the service, Vincent was sent to the United States for training. Upon his return to Warsaw, he was detailed to the division responsible for monitoring arms trafficking and the proliferation of weapons of mass destruction. Vincent partnered closely with the CIA and Israeli intelligence, participating in 140 missions in 50 countries, until he retired in 2007. These jobs, he said, "remain highly classified. Hopefully, forever." (Later, Vincent found success in the capitalist world, not as a businessman, but as a bestselling author of thrillers, earning the sobriquet "Poland's John le Carré.")

Makowski's first operation as an agent, not an officer, of the UOP was a joint mission with the British spy agency MI6, the fruit of the cooperative agreement hashed out in 1990 in Vienna by his spy-school classmate Gromek Czempiński. The operation involved a controlled sale of weapons to the Ulster Volunteer Force, a loyalist group in Northern Ireland that was locked in a war with the Irish Republican Army. Masquerading as a Polish arms dealer, Makowski met two Northern Irish terrorists—hard types, both suspected murderers—in a pub in Geneva in the spring of 1993. Under a bar table, they cracked open a briefcase stuffed with the equivalent of $200,000 in British pounds. Makowski walked away with the money and in exchange filled a shipping container with three hundred AK-47 automatic rifles and Polish-made Glauberyt submachine guns, thousands of bullets, two tons of explosives, and detonators. On November 24, British customs officers at a port in northern England seized the shipment as it arrived from Poland. The Ulster Volunteer Force called it a "logistical setback," but it was a serious blow. In appreciation, British spies gave Makowski a personally autographed copy of Margaret Thatcher's memoirs.

In March 1997, the CEO of Polish trading house InterCommerce asked Makowski whether he'd be interested in traveling to Afghanistan. The internationally recognized government of that country was looking for three things: weapons, a secure place to print its national currency, and a channel through which to export its emeralds, some of the most desirable in the world. The next month, Makowski found himself in northern Afghanistan, meeting with Ahmad Shah Massoud, the fabled mujahideen commander known as the "Lion of the Panjshir." So began Makowski's involvement in Afghanistan and his work for Vincent and the CIA.

Massoud's forces belonged to a loose collection of guerrilla groups called the Northern Alliance, which was fighting the Pakistan-backed Taliban for control of the country. Massoud wanted Polish weapons because his fighters were familiar with Soviet-style hardware. Makowski estimated the worth of a potential arms contract at $150 million.

Massoud also had information on Stinger missiles that the US government wanted retrieved. To fight the nine-year Soviet occupation of Afghanistan that'd ended in 1989, the CIA had supplied the mujahideen with more than two thousand Stingers, which the rebels deployed with deadly effect against Soviet helicopter units. Several hundred Stingers remained unaccounted for and were much coveted by terrorist organizations due to their ease of use. The CIA was willing to pay hundreds of thousands of dollars per missile. Massoud bet that by offering Poland that information, he could deepen relations with the CIA. He gave Makowski the serial numbers of four in his possession.

When Makowski returned to Warsaw, he passed the numbers to Vincent along with a proposal that Poland sell weapons to the Northern Alliance. A meeting had already been scheduled for May between senior Polish intelligence officials and the CIA's deputy

MISSING BIN LADEN   195

director, George Tenet. The Stingers and the arms sales were put on the agenda.

Tenet vetoed the Polish request to sell weapons. CIA officers told the Poles that Massoud was too close to the Russians. Besides, he seemed too weak to take on the Taliban, which was winning battles against various tribes and factions across Afghanistan. The CIA did, however, want the Stingers. In early 1998, J.N., a Warsaw-based CIA officer who won't be identified because he continues to serve, met with Alex, told him that the Americans had confirmed the serial numbers, and praised him for his work. "A few years back I would have never dreamed of hearing a CIA operative thanking me for something," Alex mused. "Times change."

Soon after, Alex got word from his sources in Afghanistan that a CIA delegation had visited Massoud in February with the serial numbers in hand and had purchased the four Stingers for $600,000. Makowski and his minders at the UOP were miffed at the agency for going behind Makowski's back.

In a stormy meeting with Vincent and J.N. in the spring, Makowski blasted the agency for trying to muscle in on his contacts. The CIA's gambit had harmed his status as an intelligence asset in an active war zone. "If you guys keep on going like this, big trouble is around the corner," he warned J.N. "People who are sympathetic to your cause will stop talking to you."

Makowski continued doing business in Afghanistan. At one point, he ferried into northern Afghanistan thirty-seven tons of Polish mining equipment for the emeralds and several tons of Afghani currency that he'd succeeded in getting printed in Poland.

Whenever he returned from a trip, he briefed Vincent. The CIA sent interminably long questionnaires with detailed requests for information, but it was clear to Makowski and to Vincent that the agency's attention was elsewhere. Afghanistan, Massoud, and the Taliban had become a sideshow.

On August 7, bombs went off nearly simultaneously in front of the

US embassies in Kenya and Tanzania. Two hundred and twenty-four people, including twelve Americans, died in the blasts. The attacks, carried out by al-Qaeda and masterminded by the Saudi terrorist Osama bin Laden, thrust Afghanistan back into the limelight. Bin Laden and al-Qaeda were based along Afghanistan's border with Pakistan. On August 20, President Clinton ordered the launch of seventy-five cruise missiles from US warships at bin Laden's Afghan training camps. A few days later a federal grand jury in New York indicted bin Laden on terrorism charges. The hunt for the Saudi began and the CIA became interested in Makowski again.

In November, a few months after the embassy attacks, Makowski returned to Afghanistan. In July 1999, he met with Afghan intelligence officials in London, and in August he went back to Afghanistan. In these meetings, Massoud's intelligence officers claimed that their sources could track bin Laden almost in real time. They told Makowski they knew not only bin Laden's whereabouts but also had information on his dealings with the Taliban regime, Pakistan's Inter-Services Intelligence agency, and other organizations.

There is no shortage of braggadocio among spies. Makowski knew this. So he returned to Poland with a recent timeline of bin Laden's movements for the CIA to confirm. The timeline included information that bin Laden had holed up in the old Cuban embassy in Kabul. Alex passed it to Vincent, who gave it to the agency. The CIA later told Vincent that Makowski's information had checked out.

In September, Massoud's men provided Makowski with a tip that bin Laden was planning to spend two weeks, from November 15 to December 1, in a house in the southern Afghan city of Kandahar. They provided the house's location and details on the surrounding neighborhood.

Makowski's sources in Afghanistan also told him that bin Laden was planning to attack US warships in the Middle East. A second source in Dubai informed Makowski that al-Qaeda had already assembled a team of twenty-seven men to carry out those strikes, led by an experienced terrorist. Bin Laden "adores spectacular fireworks," Makowski's Dubai source said. The cruise missiles that fell on bin Laden's camps had been fired from US warships. It'd be bin Laden's way of getting even. Makowski shared the material with his case officers at the UOP, who passed it to the CIA. Makowski was asked again to fill out multiple questionnaires by the agency.

On October 14, Makowski met with CIA officers at UOP headquarters. Among those in attendance was a Warsaw-based CIA officer named Ksawery Wyrożemski. In addition, a member of the CIA's Counterterrorism Center had flown in from Washington.

Makowski argued that the best way to deal with bin Laden would be to assassinate him. An operation to snatch him would be too risky. American operatives might be caught or killed. The Americans should pay someone else or launch a drone strike, Makowski suggested. The CIA officer from Washington responded that the agency didn't have, as he put it, "a license to kill." The United States, he stressed, "must have him alive and kicking to stand trial before a court of law. . . . No other solutions can be considered."

In the meeting, Makowski noted, as he had in numerous CIA questionnaires, that the African embassy bombings had only whetted bin Laden's appetite for deadlier attacks against American targets. Makowski reiterated his point that bin Laden was anxious to sink a US warship. "Warship?" the officer from Washington asked, nonplussed. It was obvious that the counterterrorism official hadn't read Makowski's responses on the agency's forms.

Makowski left the meeting with a sense of foreboding. He predicted that if men and women like the counterterrorism officer were coordinating the agency's response to bin Laden, "the latter had many happy years to live while the West faced some major acts of terrorism." Still, at the meeting, the CIA did agree to pay the UOP $24,000 to help Makowski dig up more intelligence.

The CIA later told Vincent that it believed al-Qaeda had discarded the idea of attacking a US Navy warship because it was too hard to pull off. Makowski's sources told him that the CIA had been fed a line. Makowski had seen the CIA get snookered before. He'd heard CIA interlocutors treat as fact a rumor that bin Laden had been sick. Other sources had warned Makowski that misinformation about bin Laden's health had been planted to throw the Americans off his trail.

On October 12, 2000, a skiff with a crew of two drew up alongside the USS *Cole*, a guided missile destroyer, as the warship was refueling in the harbor in Aden, Yemen. A load of explosives was set off. The detonation ripped a forty-foot hole in the ship's hull. Seventeen American servicemen were killed and thirty-nine wounded. If the suicide squad had set off the explosion several yards farther down the ship's hull, where munitions were stored, the *Cole* would have sunk and the loss in human lives would have been much larger. Its crew numbered 350.

It is unclear whether the CIA had warned the navy about reports that al-Qaeda sought to attack a US warship. What is clear is that the navy hadn't put in place a more robust force protection plan for its ships in the Middle East. When the skiff pulled up to the *Cole*, no one was on the bridge.

Makowski learned immediately from Massoud's intelligence network that al-Qaeda was responsible. He passed those details to Vincent and the CIA. The CIA itself, however, wouldn't reach the same conclusion until December, two months after the attack. Makowski was befuddled by the agency's apparent unwillingness to take bin Laden more seriously.

Bin Laden, of course, wasn't satisfied. On September 11, 2001, suicide bombers flew two planes into the World Trade Center in lower Manhattan, one plane into the Pentagon, and a fourth that fell from the sky into a field in rural Pennsylvania after passengers fought with the hijackers. A new American president, George W. Bush, vowed revenge and would soon declare a "Global War on Terror."

Makowski was in Warsaw when the attacks took place. He'd been mourning the death of Ahmad Shah Massoud, who himself had been killed by an al-Qaeda suicide bomber two days before 9/11. Makowski was having tea in his Warsaw apartment when he saw on CNN United Airlines flight 175 plow into the second tower of the World Trade Center.

"This was certainly not the old CIA I had known when they and I stood on opposite sides of the barricades," Makowski wrote in a memoir of his years in Afghanistan. "Nor was it the CIA which had turned the jihad around in the 1980s and helped it win."

Makowski was miffed that the CIA appeared so dismissive of the intelligence he'd generated. Part of this was ego-driven. He had a high opinion of his work. He was also right that some CIA officers believed that a second-tier power like Poland could never come up with the goods. A generation of American spies who'd grown up respecting Polish tradecraft had left the scene. John Palevich had retired in 1994. Bill Norville was working in another arena. Some of the newer American officers viewed Poland as, to quote US ambassador Rey, just "a small country."

But it wasn't simply that the CIA refused to listen. There was no single villain here; bureaucracy was also to blame. The stovepiped nature of information management at the CIA stopped Makowski's intelligence from reaching officers who could act on it. Michael Scheuer, who from 1996 to 1999 headed the CIA's special "Alec Station," which tracked bin Laden, told a reporter that he'd been unaware of Poland's intelligence on the terrorist leader. But others in the CIA were privy to Alex's harvest and believed it was accurate. The trouble, one former high-ranking CIA officer said, was that Makowski appeared to be relying on a single source, so his intelligence wasn't distributed widely.

Why did Makowski volunteer to help the United States? "I thought I owed it to America," Makowski said, "for my high school years, for Harvard Law School, not to mention New York. It might sound long-winded but I spent nine years of my life in the United States. After 9/11, this motivation obviously became much stronger."

Makowski greatly regretted letting bin Laden slip from his grasp. In his memoirs, he didn't spare himself criticism. "Maybe I could have been more pushy, argumentative and so on. Leave no loose ends, be a damn nuisance and never give up," he wrote. "Sometimes, it's not enough just to be doing the right thing."

CHAPTER SEVENTEEN

BLACK SITE BARGAIN

The 9/11 attack found Poland keen to do right by the United States. Thousands of families put candles in their windows to commemorate America's dead. Young people wore T-shirts reading I AM A NEW YORKER. Poland's government, led by ex-Communist president Aleksander Kwaśniewski and Prime Minister Leszek Miller, saw the attacks as an opportunity to purge any lingering doubts about their loyalty to America.

"We really wanted to deliver," recalled Ambassador Jerzy Koźmiński. "We were ready to do anything." Poland quickly volunteered for the NATO mission to invade Afghanistan. Alex Makowski switched his focus. Instead of spying for the Americans, he worked to ensure the safety of Poland's troops as they deployed in Ghazni province. Then the CIA had a request.

Six days after 9/11, President George W. Bush signed a covert action Memorandum of Notification authorizing the CIA to capture suspected terrorists. In November, the CIA's station chief in Warsaw approached Zbigniew Siemiątkowski, the new director of the UOP. Siemiątkowski was a bookish former professor who'd been involved in Polish Intelligence as an administrator and reformer since the early 1990s. He'd be the last chief of the UOP. In 2002, he led changes that split the UOP's intelligence and counterintelligence functions in two. Agencja Wywiadu, or the Intelligence Agency, operated like the CIA; Agencja Bezpieczeństwa Wewnętrznego, or the Internal Security Agency, was modeled on the FBI.

Warsaw station chief D, who won't be identified because he's still employed by the CIA, asked Siemiątkowski whether Poland would allow the United States to hold a few terrorist suspects on Polish territory. "In Poland, we were united in wanting to do anything we could," Siemiątkowski said. Chief D informed US ambassador Christopher Hill that he'd approached the Poles.

November had been a tragically messy month in Afghanistan. Following the 9/11 attacks, US Special Forces had entered the country and joined with the Northern Alliance to unseat the Taliban regime. Hundreds of Afghan and al-Qaeda fighters had been captured and were being held in the Qala-i-Jangi fortress near the northern city of Mazar-i-Sharif. CIA officers were interrogating them there.

On November 25, the prisoners revolted and fighting quickly escalated into one of the bloodiest battles in the conflict. It took six days for the Northern Alliance, backed by US and British Special Forces, to quell the uprising. Only eighty-six prisoners out of some five hundred survived. The sole American fatality was CIA officer Johnny Spann, the first US casualty in the 2001 invasion of Afghanistan.

The revolt brought home to the CIA the necessity of finding a secure place for questioning what it began calling "high-value detainees." Among those held in the fortress was John Walker Lindh, known as "the American Taliban." The Bush administration worried about the possibility of a new terrorist attack and believed that al-Qaeda members might know the plans. From a failure to imagine 9/11, the

CIA veered 180 degrees and began contemplating all sorts of horrible scenarios, from ticking time bombs to dirty nukes.

The CIA's original idea was to imprison suspects on US military bases overseas. The agency soon realized that warehousing the captives in facilities run by other governments would free the CIA from having to declare the prisoners to the International Committee of the Red Cross. Keeping the prisons secret meant CIA officers could use more aggressive interrogation techniques to elicit information, without having to fret about prisoners' rights.

Discretion was of the utmost importance. The CIA had authorized Station Chief D to inform Ambassador Hill of the request because it feared he would hear about the program from chatty Polish contacts. D requested that Hill refrain from sharing the information with anyone else at the State Department.

Six weeks later, on January 10, 2002, Hill accompanied Polish prime minister Miller to the White House. At a meeting in the Oval Office, Hill pulled President George W. Bush aside. "I just want to make sure that you're aware of this," Hill said, speaking about the CIA program. Bush nodded. "Shhh," he said. Back in Warsaw, Hill asked Chief D to tell him when the detainees actually began coming to Poland. D agreed.

Within the CIA's Counterterrorism Center, there was a debate about whether Poland was an appropriate location for what later came to be known as a black site. The center's lawyers warned that CIA officers might face legal action in countries that "take a different view of the detention and interrogation practices employed by" the CIA. Poland was of particular concern. Many of its leaders had suffered through decades of Soviet rule. Many had been beaten and jailed for opposing the Soviet Union's domination of their country. They might look askance at their country being turned into a depository where people were incarcerated and interrogated by yet another foreign power. Within the CIA, these concerns didn't prevail. Nor, interestingly, did they figure much within the upper echelons of the Polish government.

One possible reason: neither Poland's president nor its prime minister had been on the victims' side of the ledger during Communist rule.

On July 17, 2002, President Aleksander Kwaśniewski was in Washington on a state visit. It was shortly before noon and the Polish president was in the Oval Office with President Bush. They'd just concluded a two-hour meeting and were readying for a joint press conference. As their aides filed out, Bush signaled Kwaśniewski to stay behind. "I've got a favor," Bush said.

The American president reiterated the request; the United States had captured terrorist suspects and needed a place to question them without bringing them to the United States. "We were absolutely alone in the Oval Office," Kwaśniewski recounted. "Bush took me aside and whispered. He told me it was important." On the spot, Kwaśniewski acquiesced.

As Kwaśniewski saw it, Poland had no choice. The United States, and particularly the CIA, had been central to Poland's transformation from a Soviet satellite to an American ally. The first Bush administration had supported German reunification on the condition that the new government in Berlin recognize Poland's western borders. The Clinton administration had ushered through NATO's enlargement despite Russian opposition. And the new Bush administration was continuing to support Poland as it went through tough negotiations to enter the European Union.

Overcoming French hesitancy over enlarging NATO and the EU was a constant battle. French president Jacques Chirac leaned on Kwaśniewski for favors at every turn. When Poland's LOT Airlines purchased Boeing instead of Airbus planes, Chirac called Kwaśniewski to berate him. It was the same when Poland chose US-made F-16 fighters over the French Mirage. "You want to be a member of the European family but you don't want to buy our products?" Chirac asked. The French president grew fond of calling Poland "America's Trojan horse."

Kwaśniewski and the rest of the ex-Communists wanted to be

seen as the responsible custodians of the American alliance. "It was an opportunity for them to become friends with America and strengthen their position at home," observed Józef Pinior, a longtime Solidarity activist, former political prisoner, and member of the European parliament. "They couldn't say no to America." As Kwaśniewski put it, agreeing to Bush's request to house terrorist suspects in Poland "was part of a bigger game."

On July 17, Bush hosted a state dinner for Kwaśniewski and his wife, Jolanta. The next day, he lent Kwaśniewski Air Force One for a trip to meet Polish Americans in the Midwest. As an ex-Communist, Kwaśniewski wasn't very popular among Polish Americans. Bush was happy to help Kwaśniewski burnish his credentials with that influential group. A few months later, the CIA began ferrying prisoners to Poland.

On December 5, at 2:56 in the afternoon, a Gulfstream jet, flying from Bangkok, Thailand, landed at a small airport in the northern Polish town of Szymany. It was snowing. The airport manager had ordered staff off the airfield and into the small terminal. All planes and vehicles had been cleared from the runway.

An hour before the plane touched down a team of CIA officers arrived at the airport to assume control of the facility. Polish Border Guards fanned out along the airport's perimeter. A CIA contractor, Jeppesen International Trip Planning, had filed a raft of dummy flight plans to mask the aircraft's intended destination. Poland's air traffic control agency managed the plane's journey into and out of Poland's airspace without a paper trail. The airfield was leased to a firm that functioned as a front for the Polish military intelligence agency, WSI. In fact, the airfield's manager worked for WSI.

Two suspected terrorists were on board the Gulfstream: a Saudi named Abd al-Rahim al-Nashiri and a Palestinian, Abu Zubaydah. Nashiri was considered by some in the CIA to be the mastermind of the October 2000 suicide attack on the USS *Cole*. As for Zubaydah, after he was shot three times and captured on March 28, 2002, in Faisalabad, Pakistan, President Bush told the American people that he was "one of the top operatives plotting and planning death and destruction on the United States." CIA officials suspected that Zubaydah knew of upcoming terrorist attacks.

When the plane landed in Szymany, Polish Border Guards didn't process the pair or the six CIA officers who accompanied them. Bundled off the aircraft, Nashiri and Zubaydah were taken on a short drive to the Intelligence Training Center in Stare Kiejkuty, fifteen miles away. This was the same institution that had graduated Gromek Czempiński, Alex Makowski, Vincent, and other leading Polish spies.

The CIA had set up what would become the most important of the agency's black sites in a two-story villa on the center's campus. The agency spent some $300,000 to renovate the building. The Americans brought in their own paint and modified the building's electrical system to run on 110 volts, not the European standard 220. Initially, the building was fitted to hold three detainees. It would soon get crowded.

Poles were not allowed inside the villa. Polish military guards patrolled the perimeter. By all accounts, no Pole was given access to the detainees. It was like a little piece of America in the heart of Poland's lake country.

Soon after arriving, Nashiri and Zubaydah were both subjected to "enhanced interrogation techniques": slapping, sleep deprivation, holding stress positions, and waterboarding. At one point, an interrogator entered Nashiri's cell and cocked an unloaded pistol in a mock execution. At another, he revved a drill next to Nashiri's blindfolded head.

On February 8, 2003, a third terrorist suspect, Ramzi bin al-Shibh, a Yemeni, arrived in Szymany. Again, the runway was cleared, employees were ordered inside, and CIA officers took control of the airfield.

The CIA believed that bin al-Shibh had been an associate of several of the 9/11 hijackers and had aided their plot by wiring them money and serving as an intermediary between them and the al-Qaeda leadership. Bin al-Shibh had already been in Pakistani custody for five months. In Poland, bin al-Shibh was also subjected to enhanced interrogation techniques.

CIA officers in Poland thought that bin al-Shibh was cooperating. Langley didn't buy it and demanded harsher methods. From mid-February, CIA officers subjected bin al-Shibh to three weeks of additional enhanced interrogation including sleep deprivation, nudity, dietary manipulation, facial holds, attention grasps, abdominal slaps, and facial slaps, among others. Bin al-Shibh began to suffer psychotic episodes. He saw things, couldn't sleep, and attempted suicide. He became paranoid.

The CIA hadn't divulged its plans to use such techniques with Polish authorities. Not much more was shared with Ambassador Hill, either. When Hill asked Station Chief D how the prisoners were being treated, D replied, "Well, we're denying them access to their Korans." That left Hill feeling uneasy. "It didn't sound very nice," he said.

Polish intelligence officers began to catch wind of the rough treatment occurring inside the villa. Little things began to raise eyebrows. The Americans didn't take to the pork sausages that the Poles provided. Some of them threw the sausages over the intelligence facility's fence, leading to rumors in the town that the facility was occupied by Muslims. Polish authorities found a receipt for the construction of a metal cage from a nearby town. When they asked, they were told it was for a tiger, but that didn't explain why it contained a chemical toilet. "Very quickly the Polish authorities understood that the US was operating a prison camp on Polish soil," Józef Pinior said. President Kwaśniewski heard these reports as well. "We were absolutely afraid. We had no access to this building," he said. "No entry."

On March 1, 2003, CIA and Pakistani intelligence officers arrested Khalid Sheikh Mohammed, a Pakistani considered the principal architect of the 9/11 attacks. KSM, as he was known, was first interrogated in Pakistan, then at a CIA site in Afghanistan. By March 3, the CIA decided that they wanted him moved to Poland, where two CIA contractors, psychologists James Mitchell and Bruce Jessen, were waiting to question him.

Already uncomfortable with the mission, the Poles tried to shut it down. In Warsaw, Foreign Intelligence chief Siemiątkowski told CIA Station Chief D that Poland couldn't support the operation anymore. Station Chief D informed Ambassador Hill that KSM had been captured and that the CIA wanted him in Poland. He asked the ambassador to work on the Poles. Hill met with Kwaśniewski. "I told him the next prisoner is a very important one, please let us have one more," Hill said. Hill hinted that KSM might be the one to lead the CIA to Osama bin Laden. Didn't Poland want to be part of that operation? he asked. Kwaśniewski directed Hill to clear the request with Prime Minister Miller.

Hill preferred dealing with Miller. Kwaśniewski was charming, somewhat in the mold of Bill Clinton: enormously fun to be around but at root a little slippery. Miller might have been "Comrade Shaggy," still, as the exoneration of Ryszard Kukliński had shown, he could get difficult things done.

Miller demanded that the United States sign a memorandum of understanding covering the relative roles of the CIA and Polish Intelligence in the management of the site. The Poles asked the CIA to commit on paper to a certain standard of treatment for the prisoners. "What if somebody dies in custody?" Miller asked. But the CIA refused to sign. Miller was concerned about the legality of operating a secret prison on Polish soil. He hadn't notified parliament. "There's nothing in writing," Miller complained. "I am out here on my own."

"We just need this one," Hill responded. But he understood Miller's predicament. "Miller was worried about the rule of law," he recalled. "He had no cover from parliament, no authorization to do this." At the time, Hill recalled, only a few in the Bush administration bothered about the legality or the morality of the program. "We were worried," Hill said, "about the next attack." Under pressure from Hill, Miller reluctantly agreed to keep the prison open for KSM.

Hill relayed the news to Chief D, who'd been working his own angles. The CIA had agreed to increase its annual contribution to Polish Intelligence. Soon after KSM was apprehended, the CIA shipped $30 million in cash in two enormous cardboard boxes via diplomatic pouch from Frankfurt to the US embassy in Warsaw.

By this time, Andrzej Derlatka, the instigator of Operation Unity, had been promoted to deputy chief of Foreign Intelligence, one notch below Intelligence chief Siemiątkowski. In the decade since Poland's revolution, Derlatka had run numerous operations with the CIA and the Defense Intelligence Agency. He'd been in and out of government; he'd worked as an analyst for Lockheed Martin as it sought to sell the F-16 to Poland; he'd dabbled in real estate; and he'd served as Polish Intelligence's liaison officer to NATO headquarters in Brussels as Poland aligned its special services with those of the West.

From the embassy, Station Chief D accompanied the cash to the headquarters of Polish Intelligence, a fifteen-minute drive away. Derlatka and two underlings met the CIA shipment. Siemiątkowski had requested that the CIA send cash so it wouldn't be traceable as a bank transfer. He didn't want Poland's Ministry of Finance to interfere. Deploying several cash-counting machines, Polish officers took days to record the money. Additional payments were made to Poland's military intelligence organization, WSI, which also assisted in the operation.

Derlatka didn't view the money as necessarily linked to the secret prison. The CIA had been subsidizing Poland's intelligence operations for years. "The money was not for the black site but part of a long-term financial support of Polish services," he claimed.

Still, the CIA believed that the additional payment helped. After the cash transfer and Hill's intercession, Poland's leadership expressed a newfound flexibility when it came to the number of detainees and when the facility would eventually be shut down. In a cable back to

CIA headquarters, Station Chief D speculated that Poland's change of heart was "at least somewhat attributable . . . to our gift of [redacted] million."

Khalid Sheikh Mohammed arrived in Poland at six in the evening on March 7, just days after he'd been detained in Rawalpindi, Pakistan. At the villa, he was stripped and placed in a standing sleep deprivation position. After a quick examination, he was cleared for rougher treatment, which began at 7:18. "I want to know what he knows, and I want to know it fast," James Pavitt, the CIA's then chief of clandestine services, demanded from Washington.

Waterboarding began on March 10 and lasted two weeks. Over the course of fifteen separate sessions, KSM would be waterboarded 183 times. The CIA moved KSM out of Poland on March 24, taking him to a secret site in Romania and later to Guantánamo Bay, Cuba, where he remains to this day.

In the late spring of 2003, the Polish leadership decided that the black site needed to be closed. Kwaśniewski called President Bush. "George," he said, "it's time to wrap it up." The Americans reluctantly agreed. Nashiri was removed on June 6 on a Gulfstream V, ultimately arriving at Guantánamo Bay. On September 5, Ramzi bin al-Shibh was also transferred to Guantánamo, and placed on antipsychotic medications. Zubaydah, the sole remaining prisoner at Stare Kiejkuty, departed on September 22, 2003, destination Guantánamo.

The plane that took Zubaydah out of Poland was a lot bigger than a Gulfstream; it was a Boeing 737. As with all the other flights into Szymany, none of the arriving passengers—in this case, seven crew members and five high-ranking CIA officials—went through Polish customs. It was as if the passengers disembarked into a dimension beyond nationality.

With the Americans gone, Kwaśniewski asked Siemiątkowski to visit Stare Kiejkuty and tour the villa. There, the chief of Polish Intelligence discovered what Kwaśniewski delicately called "signs of mistreatment."

In all, at least seven and possibly as many as eleven "high-value detainees" cycled through the CIA's secret prison at Poland's Intelligence Training Center. It was unclear whether the CIA gained any actionable intelligence in the Polish villa or elsewhere. A report by the Senate Select Committee on Intelligence concluded that the use of enhanced interrogation techniques "was not an effective means of acquiring intelligence or gaining cooperation from detainees." But when Jose Rodriguez, then the director of the CIA's Counterterrorism Center, visited Poland, he told Derlatka that the CIA had "obtained information in Poland which opened the gates to other information that would have been impossible to open if not for Poland's help." Derlatka was satisfied that Rodriguez was telling the truth.

In a speech on September 29, 2006, President Bush claimed that intelligence gathered in Stare Kiejkuty had saved lives and disrupted plots. He specifically mentioned KSM, Zubaydah, and bin al-Shibh. All of them had been interrogated in Poland.

CHAPTER EIGHTEEN

BETRAYED

Ever loyal, Poland wasn't done aiding the United States. In early 2003, as US pressure mounted on the Iraqi regime of Saddam Hussein, GROM units began joint operations with the Navy SEALs and other US commandos to protect shipping in the Persian Gulf, cut off Iraq's oil exports, and stop Iraq from breaking UN sanctions.

Poland's political leadership had been vexed by the Bush administration's plan to invade Iraq. The advice it received on whether to participate was contradictory, too. Józef Glemp had been the archbishop of Warsaw during martial law from 1981 and had faced no shortage of difficult decisions as the Catholic Church's representative in Poland during Communism. In an interview shortly before the war erupted, Glemp said he agreed with the Church's position: he opposed the war. But should Poland take part? he was asked. "Definitely yes," he replied. "We are America's ally. We should be a loyal ally." The same advice came from Zbigniew Brzeziński, who in the United States became an eloquent and passionate opponent of the war. But when Koźmiński plumbed Brzeziński for his view, Brzeziński said he thought Warsaw should follow the United States.

President Kwaśniewski and Prime Minister Miller united in their support of the US invasion. They didn't want to alienate France and Germany, which both opposed the invasion. But their fealty to the American alliance won out. Both Kwaśniewski and Miller felt obligated to prove their devotion to the United States. "If it is President Bush's vision," Kwaśniewski told a reporter as the Iraq crisis unfolded, "it is mine."

On the night of March 19, just hours before the invasion of Iraq, GROM became the first Polish unit to engage in combat operations since World War II. Working with Navy SEALs, a GROM team secured Iraq's massive Khor al-Amaya Oil Terminal, which juts a mile into the Persian Gulf. Along with a sister terminal, the KAAOT handled more than 80 percent of Iraq's oil exports.

Taking the terminal was a key step in the invasion. During the First Gulf War in 1990, Saddam had destroyed Kuwait's oil wells, triggering a massive economic and environmental disaster. There were fears he'd do something similar again. Grabbing the KAAOT was also a stepping-stone to the Iraqi port of Umm Qasr, which would be needed to move the US-led force into southern Iraq.

GROM operatives built a model of the facility, and their teams practiced approaches by sea and by air—in case the waters on the night of the invasion were too choppy for GROM's small speedboats. The terminal contained dozens of rooms and a pumping station, along with a dormitory. GROM operatives trained to be extra careful with their firearms once at the terminal. Bullets and oil don't mix.

On the night of March 19, the gulf was calm. GROM teams huddled on board Mark V Special Operations Craft and rigid-hulled inflatables as they sped toward their target. Overhead US Navy helicopters manned by GROM snipers provided cover. With engines muffled, the craft zeroed in.

Almost noiselessly, GROM commandos landed at the KAAOT, boarded the terminal, burst into the pump room, secured it, shut down the oil pipeline, rolled through the living quarters, broke through the door of the engine room, and took over the facility. Seven hours of painstaking, door-to-door searches unfolded during which twenty heavily armed but totally surprised Iraqis were captured. As a GROM participant put it, the Iraqis "had been prepared, but not for such a daring action."

Two days after the launch of the invasion, Ambassador Hill asked Polish minister of defense Jerzy Szmajdziński if details of GROM's operation could be publicized. Chairman of the Joint Chiefs of Staff General Richard Myers wanted to use Polish Special Forces as an example of the role "new Europe" was playing in the "Coalition of the Willing." Szmajdziński was worried about the reaction from "old Europe," which had opposed the war. He asked for more time. Poland's free media wasn't about to wait. The next day, *Rzeczpospolita*, a leading Polish daily, ran a front-page photograph showing GROM fighters with their SEAL team counterparts atop the KAAOT.

Following the takeover of the terminal, GROM's units were subsumed into the US Special Operations Command. Piotr Gastał, a top GROM officer, and his team worked with soldiers from the Third and Fifth Special Forces Groups. "Almost each night there were operations," he said of the year he spent in Iraq. "The teams were so mixed that you could replace a GROM guy with a Navy SEAL and not know the difference other than the accent."

GROM units fought in Mosul, Fallujah, and Baqubah in some of the hottest combat of the war. They chased one of Saddam's sons; they found his Porsches but not him. They worked with the likes of "American Sniper" Chris Kyle, who had his picture taken visiting a GROM base. "We were hunters," Gastał recalled. "We determined when to fight." In the opinion of several US Special Forces officers, GROM had matured into one of the best-trained Special Ops units in the world.

Gastał, too, spoke of a "special bond" with the Americans. "We understood each other naturally," he said. He posited "no BS, straight-forward, a belief in the alliance" as the ingredients that made the relationship work.

Elsewhere, inside Iraq, information provided by Polish assets allowed the US Air Force and Navy to conduct pinpoint strikes. "If you want to hit a precise place, say, in the Ministry of Defense in Baghdad, you need information," Andrzej Derlatka noted. "Now, how do you get that information? Everyone will tell you that it's done by satellite but if you're trying to hit an underground bunker via a chimney, you're going to need people on the ground. Cruise missiles are expensive. They shouldn't go to waste."

On May 1, after toppling the government of Saddam Hussein, the US occupying force carved Iraq into four parts. Poland was awarded command of the South Central Sector—sandwiched in between sectors run by Britain and the United States. It was an unquestionable honor for Poland, so recently a Soviet satellite, to be asked by Washington to assist in such a crucial mission. Said Marek Belka, a former Polish prime minister, "We were given a chance to box above our weight."

However, as they engaged with US officials about America's vision for the new Iraq, Polish officials were struck by a disquieting comparison. In 1989, American diplomats, CIA officers, and above all President George H. W. Bush understood that compromise with the Communists was necessary to make the changes stick. Thanks to the UOP's emerging partnership with the CIA, former Communist officers proved that they were both loyal and useful to the new Poland. But the Poles involved in Iraq saw none of that broad-mindedness among the American planners working there. The Americans wanted to rebuild Iraq from scratch, sweeping away all elements of the old regime. "It was like they'd forgotten history," observed Jerzy Koźmiński. "They wanted to wipe the slate clean."

In February 2003, as the United States prepared to invade Iraq, Koźmiński, by this time an ex-ambassador, was invited to Washington to meet with officials from the National Security Council. They wanted to hear his views on whether Poland's experience in 1989 might be relevant to a post-invasion Iraq. Koźmiński stressed that a key pre-requisite for Poland's successful transition had been involving those from the old regime. Koźmiński noted that the United States hadn't leaned on Poland to fire all its Communists. Koźmiński himself had belonged to a Communist-controlled student organization when he was younger.

At the end of the meeting, Koźmiński asked the NSC officials how far they'd progressed in designing a post-invasion landscape. They didn't have much to say. Koźmiński concluded that the Americans hadn't thought further than the off-the-cuff claim that Vice President Dick Cheney would soon make on *Meet the Press*: that the American-led invaders would "be greeted as liberators." As time passed, Koźmiński grew concerned that no one was drawing any parallels between America's enlightened approach to Poland and the task that awaited it in Iraq.

In Poland, President Kwaśniewski asked Koźmiński to take a position in the Coalition Provisional Authority, the US-led occupying government that assumed control of Iraq after the invasion. Koźmiński would be a deputy to the American Paul Bremer. Kwaśniewski joked that Koźmiński "could be the viceroy of Iraq." Koźmiński declined. Kwaśniewski then offered the post to Marek Belka, who'd recently left the Ministry of Finance.

On May 16, Bremer announced the beginning of the "de-Baathification" program. He ordered that all public-sector employees affiliated with Iraq's Baath Party were to be removed from their positions and banned from any future employment in the government. It wasn't just the army and the secret police that were purged; fifteen thousand teachers lost their jobs. The Americans seemed obsessed with purifying Iraq, cleansing it of Saddam's influence. This obsession went deeper than politics. Even the banking sector was going to be reconstituted. Belka advocated building up new banks while keeping the old ones, as Poland had. The Americans vetoed that idea.

Koźmiński watched uneasily as Bremer took steps that Poland had avoided. Bremer disbanded the Iraqi army; Poland had left its army intact. Bremer dismantled the security forces and police; Poland had fired some officers and kept the rest. Bremer eliminated the Baath Party; Poland had allowed its ex-Communists to regroup under a new name; they even won elections. Koźmiński warned friends from the United States: "Following a revolution if you knock down all the old structures, you're going to have a mess."

In Poland's sector, Polish forces had formed what Bogusław Winid, a top diplomat, called "immensely good contacts" with the Iraqi police, who seemed eager to cooperate in building a new nation. But following Bremer's order, they were fired. "Immediately," Winid observed, "we created an opposition." This happened across Iraq. Bremer's de-Baathification program gave rise to a group of well-trained and well-armed people itching to kill Westerners.

"The Baath Party ban was the biggest mistake," observed former prime minister Leszek Miller. As an ex-Communist politician, he'd directly benefited from Poland's more flexible, less punitive approach to its revolution. "They should've involved everyone in building up a new Iraq, like they involved us in building the new Poland. The Americans botched it."

Koźmiński, Belka, Miller, Kwaśniewski, and others were baffled at US policy in Iraq. How could the nation that had so brilliantly assisted Poland's transition to democracy so quickly forget the lessons of the recent past? To be sure, there were those who argued that Poland and Iraq were so radically different that applying lessons from one to the other didn't fit. The Iraqis weren't Europeans; they were Shiites and Sunnis with no tradition of democracy. But that view ignored the many similarities: the populations of both countries were well educated and had lived under authoritarian governments.

The CIA's role in Iraq perplexed the Poles. The Baghdad station chief was known to have opposed de-Baathification, but the Poles were surprised at how little influence the CIA had over Bremer's scheme. In Poland, the CIA, through the efforts of John Palevich, Paul Redmond, Bill Norville, and Milt Bearden, had played an enormously influential role in convincing the Poles not to blow up their bureaucracy and start at ground zero. Apparently, the CIA had absented itself from that debate in Iraq. Bremer's policy won out. A bloody uprising against the American occupation followed. Belka couldn't wait to get out of Iraq. His opportunity arose a year later, in May 2004, when he returned to Warsaw to become prime minister. Poland kept troops in Iraq until the end of 2008, when it completed its withdrawal.

The Poles' disappointment over the Iraqi operation was magnified by Poland's failure to win any major contracts to rebuild the country and to sell arms, specifically tanks, to the Iraqi army. US officials had promised Kwaśniewski that such contracts would be forthcoming. But American officials even lobbied against Polish companies when they participated in tenders. Years later, when Poland's then foreign minister, Radosław Sikorski, complained about this treatment, an American counterpart responded testily: "We kept our promise. Kwaśniewski got his state visit to the White House." As if that should've been enough.

Daniel Fried, who served on the National Security Council throughout the American occupation of Iraq, observed that the Iraqi quagmire ate into a lot of America's political capital with the Poles. "They followed us because they thought we knew what we were doing," he said. The Poles felt betrayed. What unfolded next only made things worse.

On November 2, 2005, the *Washington Post* published an article headlined "CIA Holds Terror Suspects in Secret Prisons." The *Post* reported that the CIA had been interrogating suspected al-Qaeda operatives in eight countries including "several Eastern European democracies." The Bush administration had convinced the *Post*'s executive editor not to reveal the names of the Eastern European countries. Five days later, however, Human Rights Watch identified two of those nations as Poland and Romania. Officials in both countries denied any involvement. "There was never that type of prison and there never will be," President Kwaśniewski told reporters at the time. "I am certain that no al-Qaeda prisoners were ever held in Poland." Kwaśniewski added that it was preposterous to consider that Poland could house such a site. "Unlike Germany," he said, "Poland has no US bases—extra-territorial sites to which we would not have access and where the US could act freely." That would've been against the law, he said, and he was right. It *was* illegal for a Polish government to surreptitiously cede part of Poland, even a two-story villa on the campus of an intelligence training center, to another government. On November 7, five days after the story ran, the Parliamentary Assembly of the Council of Europe, a pan-European body mandated to enforce human rights accords, appointed a former Swiss prosecutor, Dick Marty, to investigate the claims.

In Warsaw, Polish and US officials attempted to kill the story. On December 10, the new Polish government announced an internal probe to "close the issue." Victor Ashe, the former mayor of Knoxville, Tennessee, who'd succeeded Christopher Hill as ambassador, predicted in a cable to Washington that the "'CIA prisons' issue will continue to dog the Polish government, despite our and the Poles' best efforts to put this story to rest."

In January 2006, Dick Marty released an interim report to the Council of Europe. It concluded that senior leaders from Poland and Romania, despite their denials, knew about the CIA's renditions program. Marty said that he'd uncovered a system of "outsourcing" of torture and revealed data for dozens of suspicious flights into and out of Europe, despite the CIA's best efforts to cover its tracks.

On September 6, President Bush addressed the nation and acknowledged the existence of secret prisons operated by the CIA outside the United States. While Bush didn't reveal the locations of these facilities, his administration didn't give Poland advance warning that he was going to make the speech. The Polish government again came under pressure to admit that it had known about the black sites. In June 2007, Marty's second report came out. It contained further damning allegations about the involvement of both civilian and military intelligence and the highest levels of Poland's government. Still, the Polish government continued to deny any knowledge of the villa and the interrogations.

In March 2008, a new Polish prime minister, Donald Tusk, ordered the prosecutor's office in Warsaw to launch a criminal investigation into allegations that officials from the Polish government broke the law by allowing extrajudicial detentions and by handing a part of Poland over to a foreign government. Cracks in the armor of the government's denials began to widen.

On June 22, the *New York Times* published the revelations of Deuce Martinez, a CIA officer who'd spent dozens of hours interrogating Khalid Sheikh Mohammed in Poland. The CIA put the black site in Poland, the *Times* reported, because Polish intelligence officials were eager to cooperate. "Poland is the 51st state," one former CIA official quoted James Pavitt, director of the agency's clandestine service, as saying. "Americans have no idea." In September, two unnamed Polish intelligence officers told a Polish newspaper that the black site existed and that both Kwaśniewski and Miller knew about it.

In 2010, the European Court of Human Rights began taking cases from men who'd disappeared into the black sites in Poland. Lawyers representing Abd al-Rahim al-Nashiri filed his case in July 2012; Abu Zubaydah's attorneys followed a year later. On July 4, 2014, the court delivered a landmark judgment, finding that Poland was complicit in the CIA program and had exposed both men to serious risk of torture. Poland's appeal was rejected, and the court ordered Poland to pay both men one hundred thousand Euros each in damages.

In Poland, prosecutors got no help from the United States. All of their requests for documents were turned down. Nor did they get much assistance from the Polish government. The first prosecutor was removed from the case and was replaced by someone less aggressive. Then, the whole case was transferred out of the capital to the southern city of Kraków. Still, the prosecutors did succeed in indicting at least one Polish official in connection with the operation.

On March 27, 2012, a secret indictment against Zbigniew Siemiątkowski, the former head of Polish Intelligence, became public. Siemiątkowski was charged with "unlawfully depriving prisoners of their liberty" and allowing corporal punishment in connection with the site at the Intelligence Training Center. Polish newspapers reported that prosecutors were considering charges against Andrzej Derlatka and former prime minister Leszek Miller. Kwaśniewski continued to defend himself against any allegations. "Of course, everything went on behind my back," he said in May.

On December 14, 2014, the US Senate's Select Committee on Intelligence released declassified portions of its sixty-seven-hundred-page report on the black sites. While the report did not mention Poland by name, it was clear that Poland was "Detention Site Blue." The report's release spurred former president Kwaśniewski and former prime minister Miller, after years of denials, to tell at least a portion of the truth. At a joint press conference, they both admitted involvement in the affair.

"The US side asked the Polish side to find a quiet site where it could conduct activity that would allow them to effectively obtain information from persons who had declared readiness to cooperate with the US side," Kwaśniewski told reporters. Kwaśniewski and Miller rejected allegations that they knew about the enhanced interrogation techniques that had been inflicted on the prisoners. Said Kwaśniewski, "We didn't support sadists who had no place to exercise their practices."

Poland's reaction to revelations that torture might have occurred on Polish soil was mixed. Mikołaj Pietrzak, a prominent Warsaw attorney who represented Nashiri at the Court of Justice of the European Union, argued that Kwaśniewski and Miller "sold out our country to prove their friendship to the USA." The ex-Communists, he said, "were overly enthusiastic." As for the Americans, he said, "they considered us to be some kind of backwater shithole where the name of the CIA was enough to make us spread our legs, where dollars brought over in a cardboard box would make us prostitute our constitution." To the United States, Poland wasn't an equal partner; it was, Pietrzak observed, "a weak-willed country that could be abused for instrumental purposes."

From many others, especially those in the government, there was less outrage and more dismay, particularly at the CIA officers who leaked damaging information about Poland. The Poles felt burned for being loyal to the United States. They'd been devoted to the CIA and the agency had left them high and dry. As Kwaśniewski said, "It was a violation of trust." Observed Radosław Sikorski, who was serving as minister of defense when the story broke, "We didn't mind Bush so much. Our problem was that we got embarrassed politically and exposed legally." As the scandal unfolded, Sikorski had to provide an affidavit to a Polish court arguing that Prime Minister Miller had not committed a crime when he allowed the Americans to interrogate terrorist suspects on Polish soil. "Which Polish prime minister will authorize an operation that violates Polish law in the future?" Sikorski asked.

The CIA tried to make it up to the Poles. "I acceded to almost every request to compensate for the damage their cooperation with us cost," said Michael Sulick, who directed the CIA's clandestine services from 2007 to 2010. "We needed to help them out wherever we could." The agency continued to give Poland's services financial and technical support. Sulick found the experience with Poland humbling. "The irony is that we had a superior attitude to our partners. We didn't have leaks. We didn't have spies. And then we had [Russian mole] Aldrich Ames and we leaked like a sieve. In fact, the Poles have been more buttoned up than us." Sulick had a premonition that this type of crisis would befall the two nations. Wrapping up his tour as Warsaw station chief back in 1994, Sulick had warned his counterparts at Polish Intelligence: "We have an incredible relationship now, but at a certain point, we're going to screw you."

"Not like the Soviets would screw you," he added. "We'll think we're well meaning, that everything will work out fine, but despite our best intentions, we will screw you."

CHAPTER NINETEEN

UNDER THE BUS

Against the messy backdrop of Poland's relationship with its key ally, the knotty questions of what constituted patriotism and what it meant to be a true Pole reemerged as political issues in Poland. In September 2005, when the ex-Communist political party led by Leszek Miller lost parliamentary elections to two right-wing parties, those issues returned with a vengeance.

In July 2006, a year after winning, the new prime minister, a hard-right politician named Jarosław Kaczyński, appointed Antoni Macierewicz as deputy minister of defense. This was the same Macierewicz who, as minister of the interior in the early 1990s, had sought to purge ex-Communists from the security services and resumed surveillance of the US embassy. Days after taking up his new post in August 2006, Macierewicz alleged in a TV interview that "a majority of [Poland's] former foreign ministers were agents of the Soviet special services." Macierewicz had scant proof. At the US embassy, Ambassador Victor Ashe watched with alarm. In a cable sent on August 26, Ashe called

Macierewicz "an anti-communist firebrand" with "a history of witch hunting." Macierewicz, he wrote, was "seen by many as almost paranoid in his conspiracy theories about Poland's recent history." But Prime Minister Kaczyński and his twin brother, Lech, who had been elected president in 2005, backed Macierewicz completely.

Macierewicz followed these charges with a report on February 16, 2007, that detailed operations by Poland's military intelligence agency, the WSI. The report revealed the names of numerous sources, both foreign and domestic, who'd cooperated with Poland's spies. This move was truly without precedent. Many Polish assets were exposed, not by an enemy service but by Poland's own deputy minister of defense. Among those outed were Alex Makowski and his network of sources in Afghanistan. Others who were listed as officers of military intelligence included Poland's ambassadors to Austria, Kuwait, and Turkey. They were recalled immediately. Macierewicz's report resulted in the arrests and sentencing of Belarussians and Russians who'd worked as agents for the Poles. "There were real life consequences," said Marek Dukaczewski, the WSI's chief from 2001 until 2005, when he quit in order not to be swept up in Macierewicz's campaign.

Macierewicz claimed that his intent was to weed out ex-Communists, Russian spies, and corruption. In fact, there *had* been malfeasance in the special services as Poland transitioned to a democracy, especially in the WSI. And the WSI *had* been penetrated by agents from Moscow. But Macierewicz's scorched-earth tactics damaged Poland's ability to protect itself and to maintain its alliance with the United States.

Macierewicz's report landed in the midst of the deployment of several thousand Polish troops to Afghanistan and Iraq as part of Poland's support of the US-led wars in those countries. Alex Makowski, who'd continued to commute between Afghanistan and Poland, had been hired by Polish military intelligence to help provide security for Poland's forces in Afghanistan. Exposing his ring of informants put Polish soldiers at risk. The same held true in Iraq. A bomb attack in October 2007 on the Polish ambassador to Iraq, General Edward

Pietrzyk, brought home the deadly implications of Macierewicz's mis-adventure. Traveling in an armored vehicle, Pietrzyk miraculously survived. Polish government officials said they hadn't been prepared for an assault because, after Macierewicz's report, Poland's sources had gone silent.

The underlying rationale for Macierewicz's assault on the WSI appeared to be the same as the one that had motivated him in 1992: a deep-seated belief that Poland's revolution was incomplete, and that the last bacilli of the Communist affliction needed to be expunged from the Polish body politic before Poland could truly be free.

For Macierewicz, it appeared that the crusade to cleanse Poland of Communist influence trumped the security of Polish forces abroad. As he told an interviewer in February 2007, "Indeed, I destroyed post-communist military intelligence. I wanted to do it, and this is what the prime minister and president hired me to do, because they knew I would do it."

When Macierewicz discovered that Alex Makowski was involved in force protection in Afghanistan, he ordered Makowski's aspect of the operation halted immediately. Before 1989, Makowski's exploits spying on Solidarity had been enormously damaging to the move-ment. Macierewicz couldn't believe that a man who'd so bedeviled Solidarity could be trusted in the new Poland. Macierewicz devoted a whole chapter in his report to Makowski's activities in Afghanistan, along with another four pages on Makowski's curriculum vitae. No other individual received as much attention in the document.

Makowski described Macierewicz as "a monkey with a razor" and did his best at damage control. He informed his sources that they'd been outed. He returned to Afghanistan to clean up the mess and explain why the operation had been blown. The Afghans were bewil-dered, but, Alex noted, "they showed a lot of understanding."

Makowski wasn't the only one betrayed by Macierewicz's report. After its release, Macierewicz's superior, then minister of defense Radosław Sikorski, also resigned in protest. The report exposed

Operation Zen, a classified mission undertaken for the United States that Sikorski was managing directly. Sikorski and Makowski had been searching for Ayman al-Zawahiri, a senior al-Qaeda operative.

The United States had tried to execute al-Zawahiri in January 2006 with a Predator drone strike. It ended up killing eighteen people in Pakistan, including nine women and six children, but not the intended target. Sikorski's team generated intelligence that led to another attempt on al-Zawahiri's life, but the Americans missed again. Then Macierewicz released his report and Sikorski had to shut the operation down. Al-Zawahiri ultimately became al-Qaeda's leader after US forces killed Osama bin Laden in 2011.

Macierewicz asserted that his report constituted proof of corruption and other crimes. But only one of hundreds of allegations in the document ever resulted in a conviction. "A serious state doesn't reform its intelligence service in such a way as to lose touch with its agents," Sikorski wrote.

Macierewicz continued to weed out ex-Communists until 2007, when a coalition of centrist parties beat the right wing in parliamentary elections. Donald Tusk was named prime minister. Tusk moved to restore the reputation of the special services and end the attack on ex-Communists. Professionals, like Bogdan Libera, were brought back in to lead the Foreign Intelligence Department.

In 2015, Law and Justice, the far-right party led by Jarosław Kaczyński, won parliamentary elections again. Law and Justice reentered government with an even stronger desire to punish the ex-Communists. This time around, Kaczyński appointed Macierewicz as minister of defense. Kaczyński and Macierewicz continued to allege that the ex-Communists were behind all sorts of crimes.

On April 10, 2010, Kaczyński's twin brother, Lech, Poland's president at the time, had died in a tragic plane crash in Smolensk, Russia, as he and ninety-six others, including political, economic, and military leaders, flew to Russia to commemorate the seventieth anniversary of the Katyn Massacre. Official Polish and Russian investigations blamed pilot error. But Kaczyński and Macierewicz concocted a conspiracy theory that the president and his entourage had been assassinated by Russians, Polish liberals, and their ex-Communist allies. Those claims took on a quasi-religious gloss after right-wing Catholic priests began repeating them in church.

At the Ministry of Defense, Macierewicz intensified his battle against all those who'd served Communist Poland—even though Communism had collapsed almost thirty years before. On December 18, 2015, Macierewicz ordered a nighttime raid on a NATO counterespionage center in Warsaw. No other NATO member had ever attacked a NATO installation on its territory before. Macierewicz justified the raid by claiming that he was trying to rid the center of Polish officers who'd joined the army during Communist times.

On December 16, 2016, urged on by Macierewicz, the Polish parliament slashed the pensions of forty-three thousand former employees of the Communist-era security services—from spies and police detectives to beat cops and janitors. Even people who'd worked for a few months and then made the transition to a free Poland saw their pensions drop below the poverty line. Macierewicz's goal was to pauperize the officers who'd built Poland's "special relationship" with America.

"Going after the ex-Communists should have been done many years earlier," Macierewicz said. "They collaborated with our occupiers. They were traitors. It's simple justice."

Ricardo Tomaszewski, the officer whom CIA officer John Palevich first contacted in Lisbon, saw his pension cut from more than $1,000 a month to less than $250. He had to sell his apartment in a suburb of Gdańsk and squeeze into a one-room rental with his wife. The couple could barely afford to eat. "What interests me is how miserable life is these days," he said. "It apparently doesn't matter what we did for Poland in the past."

Andrzej Maronde, who as Baghdad *rezydent* helped save the six Americans in Iraq and deliver the Baghdad map, had his pension slashed to $300 a month. The pension of Andrzej Derlatka, the first intelligence officer to float the notion of NATO membership, also dropped to $300. Derlatka and his three children didn't starve thanks to income from his wife, a college professor.

Bogdan Libera, the former chief of Polish Intelligence about whom CIA director George Tenet had once raved, found himself labeled an "*ubek*," Polish slang for a member of the secret police. "Those were the same people who took away my father," he said with a grimace. "This is a great injustice. It's evil. It's not just taking away money, it's taking away dignity. It's done by people who don't know history."

Andrzej Milczanowski, the first dissident to lead Poland's intelligence service, tried to lobby on behalf of the former officers with whom he created Free Poland's first foreign spy agency. He reminded the government that it had promised to maintain the pensions of those who'd served Communist-era Poland. That decision, he said, had expedited Poland's peaceful transition to democracy. Milczanowski was ignored. "This makes my blood boil," he said. "If they'd done this earlier they would've had a revolution on their hands." But now the officers were mostly retired, in their sixties and seventies, and often infirm. "It's easy to victimize them now," Milczanowski said. "They're harmless."

In 2007, the Macierewicz Report had exposed Poland's military intelligence operations. In 2015 the Polish government began outing civilian intelligence officers who'd entered the service during the Communist era. Jan Olborski was one. Olborski had joined the Foreign Intelligence Bureau in 1985. After the changes in 1989, he served as *rezydent* in Belarus and worked in Estonia as well. In June 2016, the government released Olborski's real name and pseudonyms. "This would've been a coup for any counterintelligence agency," Olborski said. "But we did this to ourselves."

Forced to return to Poland from overseas. Olborski left the service. During his service as a spy, he'd counted on a pension of more than $1,000 a month. When he retired, he received less than $300. To make ends meet, he drove a laundry truck. "I can live without caviar and champagne," he said. "I had that in a previous life."

Gromosław Czempiński had done well since he'd retired from the service in 1996. He'd worked as a consultant for Deloitte as Poland's economy transited from one run by the state to a market-oriented one. He'd purchased a condo in Florida to pursue a passion for deep-sea fishing. The cuts in his pension didn't hurt him, but a series of criminal investigations made life difficult. Czempiński was arrested in 2011 on charges of profiting from privatization deals. His case never went to trial. When the right-wing Law and Justice Party took power again in 2015, prosecutors resumed investigating Czempiński for economic crimes. He was never indicted, nor was he ever cleared. The interminable probes seemed to be the point. Under constant investigation, Czempiński couldn't find meaningful work. "I feel like a man with one arm," he said.

Czempiński lobbied the CIA to come to the aid of his men and pressure the Polish government to end its crusade against those once associated with the Communist system. He organized a documentary film team and tried to convince CIA officers, current and retired, to sing the praises of Poland's spies. But the agency declined to cooperate and the former officers, accustomed to the shadows, balked at the prospect of appearing on camera. In 2020, Czempiński contracted COVID-19. He survived but, at seventy-five, he was a lion in winter.

Suicides became commonplace among former officers. Sławomir Petelicki, GROM's street-fighting mastermind, was one casualty. Petelicki had always been high-strung. After he retired in 1999, he faced financial difficulties and struggled to support his younger wife and children. On June 6, 2012, Petelicki was found in the parking lot of his apartment building, dead of a self-inflicted gunshot wound to the head.

After all the risks they took to establish an alliance with the United States, Poland's intelligence professionals wondered where their reward was. One might conclude that for Poland, it added up to a black eye in the international community, and for the intelligence professionals, a meager government stipend that wouldn't even pay the rent.

In January 2014, Radosław Sikorski, who by then had become Poland's minister of foreign affairs, was caught on tape dismissing Poland's alliance with the United States as "worthless" and worse. "We'll get in conflict with the Germans, Russians, and we'll think that everything is super because we gave the Americans a blow job," he allegedly said in a recording leaked to the weekly *Wprost*. Edward Lucas, a British journalist, wasn't so harsh. He compared Polish–American relations to a "companionable marriage where convenient sharing of chores, rather than romantic passion, has become the main bond."

Still, the obvious resentment needs to be weighed against the result of Poland's labors. In 1990, while Gromosław Czempiński was saving six Americans in the sands of Iraq, at least two divisions of Soviet troops along with Soviet nuclear weapons were deployed on Polish soil. The future was in the balance. By 2020, more than eleven thousand US soldiers, airmen and women, missile defense systems, and an array of secret American intelligence installations had taken their place in a Poland integrated into the European Union. "We helped make an alliance with the United States," Czempiński said. "No one can take that away from us."

PART FOUR

MARRIAGE WITH HIPPOS

CHAPTER TWENTY

SAME BED, DIFFERENT DREAMS

Throughout and beyond the events of *From Warsaw with Love*, Poland stayed married to the American hippo. In the mid-2000s, even as the administration of President George W. Bush humiliated the Poles over the black sites, Poland deployed intelligence officers in Iran to take, as one CIA official put it, "a lot of dangerous walks near Iranian research institutions." The Poles were equipped with a small, ultrasensitive device provided by the United States to collect air samples. CIA officers called them "rocks." When analyzed, the air samples could reveal the presence of uranium, the specific chemical form of the element, and, by detecting impurities, even its origin. Based on the air samples, researchers could tell whether nearby Iranian research institutes were engaged in uranium enrichment or other nuclear activities. If uranium in the form of metal was found in the samples, it would be particularly significant. Uranium metal has limited peaceful uses; it's used to make nuclear bombs.

"This was a high-stakes operation," noted one former

high-ranking US diplomat. "The Poles took enormous risks on our behalf." Polish officers obtained air samples near facilities in Tehran where they could sit in an apartment overlooking the facility or at a coffee shop frequented by workers of nearby nuclear installations, who may have brought in slight radioactive contamination on their clothing. They also ventured out to isolated locations, such as a secret nuclear facility site in Natanz, two hundred miles south of the capital. They dropped the "rocks" near those installations and picked them up later on. Polish officers could easily have been detained, shot, or disappeared during those missions. Włodzimierz Sokołowski, the intelligence officer known as Vincent, directed the operation from Warsaw.

The intelligence turned up by Poland's spies played into a debate in Washington about whether Iran had stopped its nuclear weapons program. On December 3, 2007, a National Intelligence Estimate issued by the Bush administration judged "with high confidence" that Iran had halted its program in the fall of 2003. It also assessed with moderate confidence, based in part on the air samples, that the program hadn't resumed as of mid-2007.

For their service, in 2008, the US Department of Defense, acting on a recommendation from the CIA, awarded Vincent and five other officers the Legion of Merit. In its dedication, signed by then secretary of defense Robert Gates, the award credited Vincent with "superior and unwavering support" of combined operations with the United States. Vincent, it read, "supervised the coordination, planning, preparation and conduct of several extremely sensitive and hazardous missions" that achieved "unprecedented successes." Those missions, Gates wrote, "served to further the security of the United States."

Poland apparently continued this work for the administration of Barack Obama. Intelligence collected by the Poles was used by Obama administration officials to pressure Iran to commit to end its nuclear weapons program. In 2015, despite lingering fears that Iran continued to cheat, the Obama administration joined with China, France,

Russia, the United Kingdom, and Germany to sign an agreement with Tehran to limit Iran's nuclear program.

In a reminder of the high-stakes nature of Poland's work for America, in October 2018, a Polish defense attaché, Colonel Dariusz Kalbarczyk, a veteran of combat operations in Afghanistan and assigned to Poland's embassy to Iran, died after he was apparently hit by a car under mysterious circumstances in Tehran. No one was ever charged in his death.

Iran was just one nation where Polish intelligence officers continued to spy for America. Even after North Korea expelled Polish military officers from the Neutral Nations Supervisory Commission in 1995, Polish Intelligence kept providing the United States with assistance. On October 30, 2006, Kenneth Hillas, the deputy chief of mission at the US embassy, met with a Polish counterpart. Hillas praised Poland for its "excellent cooperation" on North Korea. "Huge help from Polish Services," Hillas enthused, according to a readout of the meeting published by *Gazeta Wyborcza*. It was a good thing Poland hadn't downsized its embassy in Pyongyang.

The former Soviet Union remained a focus of Polish operations. Polish officers provided the United States with material on the rise of Alexander Lukashenko, a former manager of a state-owned farm, who won the presidential election in Belarus in 1994 and remains in power today. "Local officials would ask us if we were democrats or communists," recalled Jan Olborski, the former *rezydent* of Polish Intelligence in Belarus. "Of course, we'd say communists and they'd hug us and tell us what they knew."

In Russia, Polish Intelligence had focused early on an ex-KGB officer named Vladimir Putin. The Polish agency had predicted the aggressive turn in Russia's foreign policy once Putin became Russia's president in 2000. Polish spies and diplomats dug up some of the best intelligence on the fraught relations between Russia and the former republics of the old Soviet Union. When war erupted between Russia and Georgia in October 2008, Poland provided the United States with the clearest insights. "We knew more than the US and they were asking us for information," wrote Radosław Sikorski, who served as minister both of defense and of foreign affairs. During the Georgian war, Polish military intelligence collected data showing substantial improvement in Russia's armed forces. Putin had spent time and money bolstering the old Red Army and it was paying off. Poland was also a key source on developments in Ukraine, including Russia's annexation of Crimea in February 2014. As Michael Sulick, the former director of the CIA's clandestine services, put it, throughout the 2000s, Poland continued to "assist us in just about every major foreign policy issue that we had."

Nonetheless, NATO was slow to appreciate Poland and its contributions to the alliance. Poland entered NATO in 1999, but it took NATO planners a whole decade to work out a contingency plan in the event of a Russian invasion of Poland.

Americans had spent years actively participating in Polish debates that went to the very core of what it meant to be a Polish patriot, and what it meant to be a democracy. Did they overstep? Probably. But they clearly cared.

Yet, starting in the 2010s, many in the US government considered that Poland had crossed the Rubicon in terms of its democratic and economic transformations and had become a normal country. As a result, America disengaged from Poland, to the detriment of Poland's democracy and of the alliance as well. After 2015, the right-wing Law and Justice Party took Polish politics in an undemocratic direction and sought to eliminate judicial independence. Party loyalists attacked what they called the "ideology" of LGBT rights. Poland's president, Andrzej Duda, claimed that gay rights posed a greater danger to Poland than Communist ideas once had. Neither the US government nor the CIA pushed back.

In 2015, when Defense Minister Macierewicz ordered the raid on the counterintelligence center in Warsaw, the Obama administration didn't comment. NATO called the event "an issue for the Polish authorities." Daniel Fried, who served both Republican and Democratic administrations and had worked for years in Poland, argued that Warsaw's authoritarian lurch under Law and Justice was nothing compared to the bad old days of Communism. For better or worse, the United States left the Poles to battle their demons alone.

To George H. W. Bush and his successor, Bill Clinton, Poland had been central to the remaking of European security. But European security had lost its importance to Washington. As Radosław Sikorski observed, by the late 2010s, "Poland has as much significance to the US as Estonia has to us. It's a likeable country but barely on the radar."

There was also a sense that the "special relationship," fostered by the CIA and Poland's intelligence services, was less special that it had been. Some changes were inevitable. One of the downsides of becoming America's ally was that now everyone knew that Poland was, in fact, an American ally. Poland's spies could no longer move unfettered in dangerous places where they'd once roamed free. "Poland is now perceived no longer as an independent country but as a country actively helping the United States in intelligence," observed military intelligence chief Marek Dukaczewski. "That has affected our ability to operate."

Poland's interests were changing, too. Poland's participation in the European Union became more important in some ways, such as trade, than its alliance with the United States. The old quip "Poland is the most pro-American country in the world—including the United States" was no longer as precise as it had once been. Poland remained the most consistently pro-US nation in Europe, but the ardor had cooled.

The administration of President Donald Trump and his "America First" policy amplified America's tendency to pull back from deeper engagement. In fact, Trump talked up the alliance with Poland as a means to punish America's other Atlantic partners and to threaten NATO itself. When he announced in July 2020 that the United States planned to withdraw twelve thousand troops from Germany, he suggested that they'd be moved to Poland. Trump floated the idea of maintaining only bilateral alliances and used US ties with Poland as an example. Appealing to Trump's vanity, Poland's president Duda promised to name a planned American base "Fort Trump."

Instead of leaning on Poland's government to end its purge of the ex-Communists, respect an independent judiciary, or drop its criticism of LGBT rights, Trump saw in Warsaw's reds-under-the-bed fixation a fellow traveler with a shared paranoia about the dangers of a diverse, multicultural world. Trump chose Warsaw as the site for a fiery speech in July 2017 during which he railed against "radical Islamic terrorism" and political correctness. As the crowd chanted "Trump! Trump! Trump!" the American president laid forth a vision of Poland and the United States as bastions against a globalizing world and the twin dangers of immigrants and terrorists. "The fundamental question of our time is whether the West has the will to survive," Trump said. Trump supported Duda's reelection campaign, feting him in the White House in June 2020 just days before the Polish vote. When Duda criticized the notion of LGBT rights, Trump was silent.

The Poles were the only people in Europe who supported Trump's reelection. A survey in October 2020 found that 41 percent of Poles believed Trump would be a better president than Joe Biden, compared to only 15 percent who favored Biden over Trump. On the day of the election, Polish state-run TV reported that Trump had won. Up until January 6, 2021, when a mob of Trump supporters attacked the US Capitol while Congress was certifying Biden's victory, state-run Polish TV cast doubt on who actually had won. President Duda was slow to congratulate Biden on his win.

Nonetheless, Biden's victory actually provides the two nations with an opportunity to reset and strengthen an alliance that was born in the first flush of freedom after 1989. As a senator in the late 1990s, Biden overcame initial doubts to become a vocal supporter of NATO's enlargement. As vice president under Obama, Biden was the architect of the European Reassurance Initiative. It was this initiative that resulted in the deployment of thousands of US troops on Polish soil. Biden's approach to Ukraine, Belarus, and Russia is also far more aligned with Polish interests than Trump's, given Trump's quixotic bromance with Russian leader Putin.

Even the insurrection in Washington on January 6, 2021, could furnish the United States with an opening to engage Warsaw more meaningfully. Admitting that the United States, too, needs to heal its democracy and that America, too, has its share of extremists could set the scene for a deeper discussion with Poland about its challenges as well.

From his home outside Seattle, John Palevich expressed relief that Biden had ended what he called Trump's "clown act in the White House." He waxed philosophical on Poland's slide into authoritarianism. Some type of revanchism after Poland's liberation was always inevitable, he said. But it won't last. "They have to go through with this," Palevich said. "After a while, it'll swing back the other way." The same might be said of the United States.

CHAPTER TWENTY-ONE

WHAT IS TO BE DONE?

Vladimir Putin's 2022 invasion of Ukraine has made this story—a meditation on alliances—suddenly very relevant. Poland is a front-line nation, sheltering millions of Ukrainian refugees and bolstering Ukraine's defenses. In 1990, Poland had to prove it could be a worthy ally of the United States. By 2022, it had become a bulwark of the NATO alliance. Embedded in Poland's story are lessons for every country seeking to navigate today's messy geopolitical landscape. To my mind, there are three.

Lesson No. 1: Alliances are not optional in a dangerous world.

Poland's ex-communist intelligence officers were early advocates of NATO membership. Stuck between erstwhile overlords, Germany and Russia, they agitated for an alliance with America. Once Poland's politicians came around, they, too, understood that only formal membership in NATO would do.

Poland profited mightily from its alliance with the United States and entry into NATO. US support helped Poland's young government run the perilous shoals of economic reform and democratization. It laid the groundwork for Poland's accession to the European Union, which integrated Poland's economy into a market of half a billion people. The alliance was just as significant for what it avoided: Russia's preternatural compulsion to foment chaos in the nations on its periphery, which it did in Georgia in 2008 and in its 2022 invasion of Ukraine.

For the United States, this book underscores that alliances are not optional, either. Poland did yeoman's work for America; its operatives saved American lives; its soldiers fought side by side with American troops; its intelligence officers spied for the United States in places where Americans dared not go; they even volunteered information when they had no reason to do so.

The United States failed, however, to listen to its Polish ally when Polish spies and diplomats had important intelligence to share. Take the story of bin Laden or the rebuilding of Iraq. Going forward, US strategy must be coordinated with its allies across the globe. This has nothing to do with making allies feel good. It's because allies have much to contribute. Without friends, how else can America obtain security, confront climate change and global pandemics, promote more equitable economic growth, and fend off challenges from China and Russia, or North Korea and Iran?

President Donald Trump treated America's allies shabbily. According to John Bolton, who served as one of Trump's national security advisors, Trump couldn't comprehend why the United States even needed alliances in the first place. Joe Biden's election constitutes a chance to relearn the lesson that the United States is a superpower because, not in spite, of its friends.

Lesson No. 2: Choose your allies wisely.

Poland was railroaded into a forced marriage with Russia for more than four decades. Despite sharing a "Slavic soul," the alliance never jelled. Moscow's interests were not aligned with Warsaw's; Soviet strategists blithely planned for Poland's obliteration in the event of World War III. Throughout the Cold War, Poles chafed under the yoke of Soviet domination.

The alliance with America made more sense for Warsaw. As Andrzej "Globus" Derlatka, the studious Polish spy, observed, Poland's Communist-era intelligence officers "never perceived American intelligence officers as enemies, only as opponents." More broadly, to all Poles, he said, "the USA was mentally not an enemy. It was a nation of true freedom, democracy, unlimited possibilities and individualism. And the Poles loved it, too."

As Derlatka's Operation Unity showed, Poland's ex-Communist spies came early to the conclusion that integration with NATO was Poland's way out of its bad Russian marriage. Those who fought for the alliance—Czempiński, Ambassador Koźmiński, Alex Makowski, and their American counterparts, John Palevich, Bill Norville, and Daniel Fried—can be satisfied that the alliance they forged has been a success. Poles now travel and work seamlessly throughout Europe. Polish military interoperability with NATO partners proceeds apace.

For the United States, an alliance with Poland made perfect sense as well. Americans have always felt, as Fred Hart noted, that something just "clicked" with Poles. Describing the connections that have brought the two nations together since the Revolutionary War, US ambassador Victor Ashe mused in 2009 that "the Poles are like family, not shy about pointing out perceived slights, but with us when we need them." From this vantage point, the unlikely alliance wasn't so unlikely after all.

Like Poland, smaller nations have momentous decisions to make as they seek relationships with more powerful partners. In Asia alone, Myanmar, Vietnam, Taiwan, and South Korea face a choice between the United States and China. On the surface, they share a Confucian culture with China; China's economy might provide more immediate benefits, too. And in Vietnam's case, at least, China's authoritarian political model has more traction than America's noisy democracy. However, China's history of invading Vietnam, its claim that Taiwan, an independent country of some twenty-three million, actually belongs to China, and the high-handed ways it's dealt with South Korea and Myanmar should give all of them pause. America might be a somewhat feckless partner, but it's probably a wiser choice than a nation apparently intent on dominating Asia with an iron fist.

Lesson No. 3: Know what makes alliances last.

The story of America's alliance with Poland illustrates how far America's friends will go for the United States. It also shows what happens when the United States asks for too much. For alliances to endure, they need to be about more than boots on the ground. They need to be about values. And this is where both countries have let each other down.

In pursuing NATO membership, the Poles made their share of mistakes. It's safe to assume that Poland didn't enter an alliance with the United States to warehouse America's prisoners and allow US operatives to waterboard them on Polish soil.

Poland has an excuse. It is deadly serious about its partnerships. Anyone living in its neighborhood would do the same or vanish. Poland received scant support in the nineteenth century and its allies abandoned it during World War II. Poland never wants to repeat that history. "We are enthusiasts about our alliances," observed Radosław Sikorski. "Poland is always faithful once we establish links. We fight to the end with the assumption that our ally will be just as devoted to us as we are to them."

The CIA has less of an excuse. The black site episode exacted a heavy toll. But the agency also let Poland down when it opted not to criticize the campaign in 2015 against the men who first forged an alliance with the United States. How was it that the same organization that had hectored Poland for years over the fate of one officer, Ryszard Kukliński, was incapable of speaking up for a whole generation of Polish officers when they were too old to fight?

More broadly, the US government failed Poland by refusing to slam the Polish government's moves to strip the judiciary of its independence and legislate locally against homosexuality. The United States and its friends in Poland didn't work to win the Cold War for an authoritarian theocracy to replace a Communist state.

This lesson can be extrapolated to other partnerships. The United States needs to meet its friends where they are. With Poland, Washington can afford to be more pointed than it can with, say, Vietnam. The government in Hanoi has a far different history with America; American policy makers need to be mindful of that gap. The challenges of each potential ally differ wildly. And while values must be at the core of each friendship, one size doesn't fit all.

In short, alliances are necessary. Allies need to be chosen wisely. And it's essential to know what makes them last. For all of this to succeed, the United States needs to ensure that it remains the best hippo it can be. After all, there's more than one hippo out there.

AFTERWORD

I came to write this book in a circular manner. In 1992, the *Washington Post* sent me to Warsaw to serve as its chief correspondent in Eastern Europe. Basically, the job was to cover the wars that followed the collapse of Yugoslavia. The *Post*'s Eastern European bureau was still located in Warsaw, however: a throwback to the days when Poland, not Bosnia, was the central story in the region.

In 1994, I was in Warsaw on a respite from war duty in Sarajevo. I started hearing rumors that Polish spies had saved a group of Americans in Iraq in 1990. I got a tip that people at some of the construction companies involved in Iraq at the time might know something. I interviewed twelve of them and came up empty. Then I met a manager of a thirteenth firm. He recalled that they'd employed an engineer who'd told a crazy story about driving Americans out of Iraq but nobody took him seriously. The *Post*'s indefatigable researcher, Halina Potocka, found Eugeniusz in a small town in western Poland. He recounted his story, which I wrote up and, with a request for comment, faxed to the office of the spokesman of the UOP, Poland's spy agency.

Within an hour, I was summoned to the ministry at Rakowiecka

25, a Stalinist-era office block opposite a big prison in the center of Warsaw. After being escorted down long, dimly lit corridors and into a massive office, I was introduced to a looming presence with a pencil-thin mustache and piercing blue eyes. This was my first meeting with Gromosław Czempiński. For the next few weeks Czempiński and I haggled over the story. His concern was real; he wanted to protect his officers and those in Iraq who'd assisted in the operation. Others in the Polish government were helpful in connecting the dots. They were impatient with the Clinton administration and wanted to speed up the timetable for Poland's entry into NATO. On January 17, 1995, the *Post* ran the story. Poland entered NATO in 1999. I don't know whether the story played any role in NATO enlargement. By that time, I'd been sent to report on China.

My first two books focused on China. But in the back of my mind, I'd always thought the adventure in Iraq could form the backbone of a good yarn. I reconnected with Czempiński in 2011 when the Polish translation of one of my books was up for an award. (I didn't win.) I mentioned my interest in doing the book and Czempiński said he'd help if he could. He appeared less than eager. The operation had already been the subject of a so-so movie in Poland called *Operacja Samun*, Operation Desert Wind.

The hard-right turn in Polish politics and the assault on his former comrades in Polish Intelligence in 2015 changed Czempiński's mind. He became more interested in the project. At the CIA, there was movement as well. After I sent inquiries to the agency's public affairs office, it set up a meeting in December 2017 with a historian at the CIA-operated Center for the Study of Intelligence. The agency, the public affairs officer said, was looking forward to helping me tell the story of how such a special intelligence relationship had begun.

A day before the meeting, however, CIA public affairs reached out to say it'd been canceled. During a subsequent phone call, a spokesperson explained that "equities within the building," which I took to mean the clandestine services, had objected to any agency assistance on the book project. The CIA valued its intelligence partnership with Poland and didn't want to get involved in a domestic squabble pitting anti-Communists like Defense Minister Antoni Macierewicz against those ex-Communist officers who'd actually built the alliance with America in the first place. There was a certain logic to the CIA's decision. But it was strange as well, given the agency's history of weighing in on these issues in Poland. Perhaps, some suggested, the moral drift the CIA faced following 9/11 and the agency's Polish black site imbroglio played a role.

Despite the agency's official decision to cancel cooperation, numerous retired CIA officers helped anyway, as did two US military officers, Fred Hart and John Feeley—who were saved by the Poles in Iraq. All of their lives had been touched in a positive way by Polish Intelligence. They believed in the story and wanted it told.

NOTES

CHAPTER ONE: TINSELTOWN ESPIONAGE

9   ~~In 1981, when Rockwell:~~ Interview with Marian Zacharski, Vevey, Switzerland, November 11, 2018.

9   **Ford's gaffe helped:** Presidential Campaign Debate Between Gerald R. Ford and Jimmy Carter, October 6, 1976, https://www.fordlibrarymuseum.gov /library/speeches/760854.asp.

10 **"Complete ignorance":** IPN BU 2333/2: Declassified Case Files for Agent "Pay"—Marian Zacharski, Archives of the Institute of National Remembrance, Warsaw.

11 **"I felt like a character":** Marian Zacharski, *Nazywam się Zacharski. Marian Zacharski. Wbrew regułom* (Poznań: ZYSK I S-KA, 2009).

11 **Its electronics industry:** Mirosław Sikora, "Cooperating with Moscow, Stealing in California: Poland's Legal and Illicit Acquisition of Microelectronics Knowhow from 1960 to 1990," in *Histories of Computing in Eastern Europe*, ed. Chris Leslie and Martin Schmitt (New York: Springer, 2019), 165–95.

12 **During a posting:** Piotr Pytlakowski, *Szkoła Szpiegów (Spy School)* (Warsaw: Czerwone i Czarne, 2011).

12 **"Poles,"** *Time* **noted:** "Spy Guide," *Time* magazine, February 6, 1978, 16.

12 **"I just watched":** Interview with Marian Zacharski, Vevey, Switzerland, October 9, 2017.

CHAPTER TWO: TENNIS, ANYONE?

14 **"In the near future"**: IPN BU 2333/2: Declassified Case Files for Agent "Pay"— Marian Zacharski, Archives of the Institute of National Remembrance, Warsaw.

14 **Friends at Hughes:** Penelope McMillan and Evan Maxwell, "L.A. Spy Suspect Caught in Web of Debt," *Los Angeles Times*, July 9, 1981.

15 **"He slowly became":** *Meeting the Espionage Challenge: A Review of United States Counterintelligence and Security Programs*, Report of the Select Committee on Intelligence, US Senate, Report 99–522 (Washington, DC: US Government Printing Office, 1986).

16 **"Great!" he wrote:** Zacharski, *Nazywam się Zacharski*.

16 **He "showed great initiative":** IPN BU 2333/2: Declassified Case Files for Agent "Pay"—Marian Zacharski, Archives of the Institute of National Remembrance, Warsaw.

17 **"I played along":** Interview with Marian Zacharski, Vevey, Switzerland, October 9, 2017.

17 **"He hooked me":** "A Modern American Tragedy," *60 Minutes*, CBS, March 14, 1982, https://vimeo.com/74330429.

18 **It estimated that Warsaw:** *Soviet Acquisition of Western Technology*, Central Intelligence Agency, Washington, DC, April 1982; declassified May 15, 2006.

18 **When Bell asked him:** *Security Awareness in the 1980s, Feature Articles from the Security Awareness Bulletin, 1981 to 1989*, Security Awareness Division, Educational Programs Department, Department of Defense Security Institute, Richmond, Virginia, 1989.

18 **"He wasn't my only source":** Interview with Marian Zacharski, Vevey, Switzerland, October 9, 2017.

18 **"Zacharski provided other information":** IPN BU 01824/139: Declassified Case Files, Activities to Free Marian Zacharski, Archives of the Institute of National Remembrance, Warsaw.

19 **He worried about:** IPN BU 2333/2: Declassified Case Files for Agent "Pay"— Marian Zacharski, Archives of the Institute of National Remembrance, Warsaw.

20 **In his memoirs, Czesław Kiszczak:** Witold Bereś and Jerzy Skoczylas, *Generał Kiszczak Mówi . . . Prawie Wszystko (General Kiszczak Tells . . . Almost All)* (Warsaw: BGW, 1991), 188.

20 **Yuri Andropov, the general secretary:** IPN BU 3246/535: Declassified Case Files for Operation "Jukon," Archives of the Institute of National Remembrance, Warsaw.

CHAPTER THREE: THE AMERICAN BEAR

22 **In the 1970s:** Interview with John Palevich, Bellevue, Washington, July 3, 2018.

26 **In a report on Palevich:** IPN BU 01903/2: Personnel File of John Palevich, Archives of the Institute of National Remembrance, Warsaw.

26 **John and Bonnie hung out:** "Halberstam of the Times Marries Polish Actress," *New York Times*, June 14, 1965, 44.

27 **By that time, several:** Philip Agee and Louis Wolf, eds., *Dirty Work: The CIA in Western Europe* (New York: Dorset Press, 1978), 162.

27 **"The agency never had":** Interview with Burton Gerber, Washington, DC, March 30, 2018.

29 **He shared an office:** Leszek Szymowski, "Deserters in a Risky Game," *Onet Wiadomści*, August 3, 2010, https://wiadomosci.onet.pl/na-tropie/dezerterzy -w-ryzykownej-grze/0wfgk.

30 **The CIA remembered:** "Favors from a Cold War," *Time*, February 20, 1995, 30.

30 **The officer was expelled:** Phone interview with reporter Tomasz Awłasewicz, March 15, 2021, and John Darnton, "Poland Describes 9 as Agents of C.I.A.," *New York Times*, January 29, 1982, A10, https://www.nytimes.com/1982/01/29 /world/poles-describe-9-as-agents-of-cia.html.

30 **Desperate, Markiewicz approached:** Ksawery Wyrożemski's father, of the same name, was also a CIA officer. He died on a mission in 1967 in the Congo and was formally recognized as a CIA employee on May 28, 2016, with a star at the agency's headquarters in Langley.

31 **Added Ski:** Interview with Waldemar Markiewicz and Ksawery Wyrożemski, Warsaw, Poland, May 8, 2019.

31 **Zacharski notified Warsaw:** IPN BU 2333/2: Declassified Case Files for Marian Zacharski, Archives of the Institute of National Remembrance, Warsaw.

32 **"I'm disgusted":** Zacharski, *Nazywam się Zacharski.*

CHAPTER FOUR: TRUE CONFESSIONS

34 **"We know everything":** Criminal Case Files, 1907–1993, US District Court for the Central District of California, Folder Title, 81–679, Box No. 129, National Archives and Record Administration, The National Archives at Riverside.

34 **The only way:** "A Modern American Tragedy," *60 Minutes*, March 14, 1982, https://vimeo.com/74330429.

35 **To build a decent case:** Scott Winokur, "Obstacles at Every Turn in Bringing Spy to Justice," *San Francisco Examiner*, September 1, 1987, A1.

37 **"And they were terrible witnesses":** Ibid., A4.

38 **Jaruzelski's ramrod posture:** Blaine Harden, "Jaruzelski to Resign, Urges Prompt Vote," *Washington Post*, September 20, 1990, https://www.washingtonpost .com/archive/politics/1990/09/20/jaruzelski-to-resign-urges-prompt-vote /8c65e598-4d4d-4dfe-a6a6-fe5f5ac41775/.

38 **In L.A., potential jurors:** Criminal Case Files, 1907–1993, US District Court for the Central District of California, Folder Title, 81–679, Box No. 4, National Archives and Record Administration, The National Archives at Riverside.

38 **"It was," he later:** Interview with Edward Stadum, San Francisco, December 5, 2019.

38 **While an audience of men and women:** William Overend, "3 Deny Guilt in Sale to Soviets of FBI Secrets," *Los Angeles Times*, October 23, 1984, 1.

39 **The Senate's Select Committee:** *Meeting the Espionage Challenge: A Review of United States Counterintelligence and Security Programs*, Report of the Select Committee on Intelligence, Report 99–522, US Senate (Washington, DC: US Government Printing Office, 1986).

40 **They claimed that Zacharski:** Ibid.

41 **"He had excellent tradecraft":** Interview with John Palevich, Bellevue, Washington, November 30, 2017.

CHAPTER FIVE: THE BRIDGE OF SPIES

42 **His minders ordered:** Interview with Ryszard Tomaszewski, who helped manage Zacharski's case, Warsaw, Poland, October 10, 2017.

43 **"It is hard to believe":** Tomasz Awłasewicz, *Łowcy szpiegów: Polskie służby kontra CIA (Spy Hunters: Polish Services vs. the CIA)* (Warsaw: Czerwone i Czarne, 2018), 135–36.

43 **"They hated him":** Interview with John Kornblum, Berlin, Germany, May 4, 2019.

44 **The Justice Department:** Ibid.

44 **Finally, President Reagan:** George E. Curry, "US Swaps 4 Spies for 25 Prisoners," *Chicago Tribune*, June 12, 1985.

46 **Four Eastern Europeans:** Ibid.

46 **His greatest desire:** IPN BU 01824/139: Activities to Free Marian Zacharski, Archives of the Institute of National Remembrance, Warsaw.

48 **"While the government was":** Lech Wałęsa, *The Struggle and the Triumph: An Autobiography* (New York: Arcade Publishing, 2016), 108.

48 **Polish military intelligence:** Przemysław Gasztold, "Polish Military Intelligence and Its Secret Relationship with the Abu Nidal Organization," in *Terrorism in the Cold War: State Support in Eastern Europe and the Soviet Sphere*, eds. Adrian Hänni, Thomas Riegler, and Przemysław Gasztold (London: I. B. Tauris, 2020), 85–106.

48 **During a visit:** Elaine Sciolino, "US Says Poles Aided Terrorists," *New York Times*, January 25, 1988, https://www.nytimes.com/1988/01/25/world/us-says-poland-aided-terrorists.html.

49 **"One threshold after another":** MEMORANDUM FOR: Director, National Foreign Assessment Center, FROM: Director of Central Intelligence, May 4, 1987, Doc. No. CIA-RDP95M00249R000801120044–2.

50 **"We are observing many cases":** Tadeusz Witkowski, "Arithmetic of the K Division," *Nasz Dziennik*, December 9, 2013, http://www.rodaknet.com/rp _witkowski_32.htm.

50 **Intelligence Command tagged:** IPN BU 003175/1128: Personnel File of Krzysztof Smoleński, Archives of the Institute of National Remembrance, Warsaw.

51 **"It was," Smoleński observed:** Interview with Krzysztof Smoleński, Warsaw, Poland, May 20, 2017.

CHAPTER SIX: PLAYING FOOTSIE

58 **The *rezydent* exacted revenge:** Interview with Andrzej Derlatka, Warsaw, Poland, November 12, 2018.

62 **Polish officials intimated:** Interview, Warsaw, Poland, October 13, 2017, and email correspondence with Henryk Jasik.

62 **He'd even won a prize:** IPN BU 003175/96: Personnel File of Andrzej Derlatka, Archives of the Institute of National Remembrance, Warsaw.

63 **In May 1990, after political:** Ibid.

65 **Bush saw Jaruzelski:** George H. W. Bush and Brent Scowcroft, *A World Transformed* (New York: Alfred A. Knopf, 1998), Kindle edition, 214.

66 **A day later:** Ibid., 208.

68 **"It was all the more":** Interview with Wojciech Raduchowski-Brochwicz, Warsaw, Poland, May 17, 2016.

68 **Speaking to reporters:** John Daniszewski, "Mazowiecki Meets Head of KGB; Walesa Urges U.S. Aid; Rail Strike Ends," Associated Press, August 26, 1989, https://apnews.com/article/87e6ff914a7d931e86f455f77e75b688.

70 **The CIA tried Hungary:** Milton Bearden and James Risen, *The Main Enemy: The Inside Story of the CIA's Final Showdown with the KGB* (New York: Random House, 2003), 418.

70 **In November 1989:** Thanks to Tomasz Kozłowski for his groundbreaking work on this subject in the unpublished article "'Why Can't We Be Friends?': Establishing a Relationship Between Polish and American Intelligence Agencies in the Context of 1989 Political Transformation."

70 **Reporting to Warsaw:** Cryptogram No. 47, January 25, 1990, sheet 153 *et seq.*, Institute of National Remembrance, 003171/230, vol. 1.

71 **Howard had been:** An alcoholic, Howard died of a broken neck from a fall in his Russian dacha in 2002.

71 **Many officers in the Hungarian:** Cryptogram No. 47, January 25, 1990, sheet 153 *et seq.*, Institute of National Remembrance, 003171/230, vol. 1.

72 **"Expect the Americans":** IPN BU 0449/8/6: Declassified Case Files—The American Project to Establish Contacts Between Polish and American Intelligence Services, Archives of the Institute of National Remembrance, Warsaw.

CHAPTER SEVEN: THE BEAR COMES KNOCKING

74 **Ricardo steered him:** This account is based on Tomaszewski's report in the recently declassified Polish document IPN BU 3246/535: Declassified Case File for Operation "Dialog," Document 20, "Lisbon, 01.03.1990, Report re. attempt by CIA to establish contact with R. Tomaszewski," Archives of the Institute of National Remembrance, Warsaw.

77 **There was "little logic":** Ibid.

77 **"Palevich is known":** Palevich had been identified as a CIA officer in 1976 in a publication linked to a KGB propaganda operation. He was again identified as a CIA officer in Philip Agee and Louis Wolf, eds., *Dirty Work: The CIA in Western Europe* (Secaucus, NJ: L. Stuart, 1978), 162.

78 **Kiszczak informed both:** IPN BU 3246/535: Declassified Case Files for Operation "Dialog"; Doc. 33, "Cryptogram no. 0655, accepted at the Codes Section on 17.03.90 at 17:00," Institute of National Remembrance, Warsaw.

79 **He shared with Poland's:** Email communication with Henryk Jasik.

79 **Following the demolition:** Timothy Snyder, *The Reconstruction of Nations: Poland, Ukraine, Lithuania, Belarus, 1569–1999* (New Haven, CT: Yale University Press, 2003), 234.

79 **As he told Bush:** MemCon Meeting with Prime Minister Tadeusz Mazowiecki of Poland, March 21, 1990, 1990-03-21—Mazowiecki.pdf, George H. W. Bush Presidential Library, National Archives and Records Administration.

80 **"Poland is going to":** Antoni Dudek, *Od Mazowieckiego do Suchockiej (From Mazowiecki to Suchocka)* (Kraków: Znak Horyzont, 2019), 106.

80 **Again, Mazowiecki agreed:** BU 0449/1/DVD, vol. 21, Information note regarding the President's official visit Council of Ministers of the Republic of Poland . . . , 51–52, 62, Institute of National Remembrance, Warsaw.

80 **On March 26:** Tomasz Kozłowski, "Odbudowa relacji polsko-izraelskich i operacja 'Most' (The Reconstruction of the Polish-Israeli Relations and Operation Bridge)," *Studia Polityczne*, no. 40 (2015): 35–53.

81 **The Poles were:** Jan Gross, *Neighbors: The Destruction of the Jewish Community in Jedwabne, Poland* (Princeton, NJ: Princeton University Press, 2001), Kindle Edition, Location 1209 of 2453.

82 **Jan Dowgiałło, Poland's new:** Archives of the Sejm, Bulletin No. 670/X, Committee on Foreign Economic Relations and Maritime Economy and the Committee on Foreign Affairs—meeting of September 15, 1990, 16–24.

83 **Redmond memorized all the names:** Interview with Paul Redmond, Marblehead, Massachusetts, April 3, 2018.

CHAPTER EIGHT: SHALL WE DANCE?

85 **He also reiterated:** Report by Henryk Jasik on the meeting with the CIA representatives, May 8, 1990, sheets 2–11, Institute of National Remembrance, 3558/89, vol. 2.

86 **"We knew the USSR":** Interview with Krzysztof Smoleński, Warsaw, Poland, May 20, 2017.

87 **In 1986, he'd been:** Alison Smale, "Soviets Expel Five Americans, U.S. Vows Retaliation," AP News, October 19, 1986, https://apnews.com/a78ce880a2704 7564b371fbb1ffc33cd.

90 **As one American officer:** Alex Storozynski, *The Peasant Prince: Thaddeus Kosciuszko and the Age of Revolution* (New York: St. Martin's Press, 2009), 113.

94 **"But we could guess":** Kita made these comments in an interview with the British journalist Julian Borger, who shared his notes. Interview in Warsaw, Poland, February 7, 2014.

97 **"That's more like it," Milczanowski replied:** Interview with Andrzej Milczanowski, Szczecin, Poland, May 16, 2018.

CHAPTER NINE: DON'T BLOW IT UP

98 **But as one remarked:** Thanks to Tomasz Kozłowski of IPN for this anecdote.

99 **Vetted officers had to:** Andrzej Rzeplinski, "Security Services in Poland and Their Oversight," in *Democracy, Law, and Security: Internal Security Services in Contemporary Europe*, edited by Jean-Paul Brodeur, Peter Gill, and Dennis Tollborg (Burlington, VT: Ashgate, 2003).

99 **"We needed rough men":** Interview with Wojciech Raduchowski-Brochwicz, Warsaw, Poland, May 17, 2016.

100 **Of that group:** Andrzej Rzeplinski, "Security Services in Poland and Their Oversight," in Brodeur, Gill, and Tollborg, *Democracy, Law, and Security*.

100 **"They were people sophisticated":** "Children of General Szlachcic," *Onet Wiadomości*, June 26, 2012, https://wiadomosci.onet.pl/kiosk/dzieci-generala -szlachcica/jmvbp.

101 **Havel looked at the names:** Interview with Milton Bearden, Austin, Texas, February 7, 2018.

102 **Ultimately, the CIA:** Dudek, *Od Mazowieckiego do Suchockiej*, 106.

104 **Instead, he learned to fly:** Interview with Gromosław Czempiński, Warsaw, Poland, May 16, 2016.

107 **"We couldn't touch":** "Gromosław Czempiński on raising his son with Down syndrome: "He taught me great tolerance," *Newsweek Polska*, April 8, 2014, https://www.newsweek.pl/polska/gromoslaw-Czempiński-rodzina-syn-piotr -niepelnosprawne-dzieci-zespol-downa-choroby/1873c3n.

110   "He married fire and water": Piotr Pytlakowski, *Szkoła szpiegów (Spy School)* (Warsaw: Czerwone i Czarne, 2014).

CHAPTER TEN: BAGHDAD SURPRISE

113   With the Cold War: Interviews with John Feeley, Monterey, California, January 10, 2018.

120   "I was devastated": Fred Hart, "The Iraqi Invasion of Kuwait: An Eyewitness Account," USAWC Personal Experience Monograph, US Army War College, Carlisle Barracks, Pennsylvania, May 1, 1998, 39.

121   Feeley needed to be kept safe: Telephone interview with Joe Wilson, February 17, 2017.

125   Norville made it clear: Interviews with Krzysztof Smoleński (Warsaw, Poland, May 20, 2017) and Bill Norville, (Rutherford, New Jersey, February 5, 2018).

126   In the files of the Ministry: IPN BU 003175/271: Personnel File of Henryk Jasik, Archives of the Institute of National Remembrance, Warsaw.

127   "We needed a spectacular": Interview with Andrzej Milczanowski, Szczecin, Poland, May 16, 2018.

130   "He was the right man": Interview with Bill Norville, Rutherford, New Jersey, February 5, 2018.

CHAPTER ELEVEN: NO EXIT

133   Nick was wound tight: Interview with Fred Hart, Fort Mitchell, Alabama, June 12, 2017.

137   While the Americans dallied: "U.S. Diplomats Tied to Russian Spy Ring," *New York Times*, March 4, 1964, https://www.nytimes.com/1964/03/04/archives/us-diplomats-tied-to-russian-spy-ring.html.

139   "Downs was doubly miffed": Hunter Downs declined an interview request.

142   He was manning: Interview with Gromosław Czempiński, Warsaw, Poland, May 16, 2016.

CHAPTER TWELVE: DIDN'T GET THE MEMO

145   "Traveling under this cover": Fred Hart, "The Iraqi Invasion of Kuwait: An Eyewitness Account," USAWC Personal Experience Monograph, US Army War College, Carlisle Barracks, Pennsylvania, May 1, 1998, 51.

152   Webster's trip marked: Webster was not the first US intelligence chief to visit Eastern Europe. Defense Intelligence Agency chief Gen. Harry E. Soyster visited Poland September 14–19, 1990, and conducted talks with Polish military intelligence on European security matters.

152 **"Mr. Poland" had been honored by the Poles:** Interviews with John Palevich, Bellevue, Washington, July 3, 2018, and Gromosław Czempiński, Warsaw, Poland, May 16, 2016.

CHAPTER THIRTEEN: THE FLOODGATES OPEN

155 **That was *six* years:** Marek Handerek, "Poland and North Korea in the 1980s—From Partnership to Stagnancy," in *Korean Society Today: Proceedings of the International Conference on Korean Studies*, ed. A. Fedotoff and Kim So Young (Sofia: St. Kliment Ohridski University Press, 2018), 25–40.

156 **That installation, intelligence officer Piotr:** Google Map satellite photographs of the installation appear to be doctored. See https://www.google.com/maps/place/12–100+Stare+Kiejkuty,+Poland/@53.6307514,21.0768597,365m/data=!3m1!1e3!4m5!3m4!1s0x46e2081c9e8fa2ad:0x8cb1da445ffe6881!8m2!3d53.624332!4d21.0693747.

157 **They recruited her:** Interview with Piotr Wronski, Warsaw, Poland, May 8, 2019.

158 **In 2000, the Poles shut:** "Poland Expels Russian 'Spies,'" BBC, January 20, 2000, http://news.bbc.co.uk/2/hi/europe/612154.stm.

159 **"At a time when":** Thanks to Tomasz Kozłowski for this anecdote. K. Kozłowski and M. Komar, *Historia z konsekwencjami (History with Consequences)* (Warsaw: Świat Książki, 2009), 272.

159 **But no nation before:** Steven Greenhouse, "Poland Is Granted a Large Cut in Debt," *New York Times*, March 16, 1991, https://www.nytimes.com/1991/03/16/business/poland-is-granted-large-cut-in-debt.html.

162 **As a cable from the US embassy:** "New Deputy DefMins: Macierewicz Stirs Up Controversy, While Winid Gets to Work," US embassy, Warsaw, August 26, 2006, *Public Library of US Diplomacy*, WikiLeaks, https://wikileaks.org/plusd/cables/06WARSAW1798_a.html.

163 **"There is a crazy":** Mary Battiata, "Polish Police Files Provoke Political Mudslinging," *Washington Post*, July 9, 1992, https://www.washingtonpost.com/archive/politics/1992/07/09/polish-police-files-provoke-political-mud-slinging/6a04e051-e744–4ceb-93c1–507385de2610/.

163 **That panel determined:** Ibid.

CHAPTER FOURTEEN: SLOUCHING TOWARD NATO

165 **On February 9, 1990:** Memorandum of Conversation Between James Baker and Mikhail Gorbachev in Moscow, US Department of State, February 9, 1990, National Security Archive, George Washington University, https://nsarchive.gwu.edu/dc.html?doc=4325679-Document-05-Memorandum-of-conversation-between.

165 **German, French, and British:** Svetlana Savranskaya and Tom Blanton, "NATO Expansion: What Gorbachev Heard," Briefing Book no. 613, National Security Archive, George Washington University, December 12, 2017, https://nsarchive.gwu.edu/briefing-book/russia-programs/2017-12-12/nato-expansion-what-gorbachev-heard-western-leaders-early.

166 **Simons convinced him:** Interview with Thomas Simons, Cambridge, Massachusetts, April 3, 2018.

167 **Zbigniew Brzeziński supported the idea:** Zbigniew Brzeziński, "The West Adrift: Vision in Search of a Strategy," *Washington Post*, March 1, 1992, https://www.washingtonpost.com/archive/opinions/1992/03/01/the-west-adrift-vision-in-search-of-a-strategy/22e316b6-8e54-4ef0-aba7-979f471d91fb/.

168 **Jack Matlock, the former US ambassador:** Jack F. Matlock Jr., "Who Is the Bully?," *Washington Post*, March 14, 2014, https://www.washingtonpost.com/opinions/who-is-the-bully-the-united-states-has-treated-russia-like-a-loser-since-the-cold-war/2014/03/14/b0868882-aa06-11e3-8599-ce7295b6851c_story.html?utm_term=.ca4a7c5314b9.

169 **He'd already visited Lithuania:** Michael J. Sulick, "As the USSR Collapsed: A CIA Officer in Lithuania," *Studies in Intelligence* 50, no. 2 (2006).

170 **"The Spy Who Went into Retailing":** Stephen Engleberg, "The Spy Who Went into Retailing," *New York Times*, January 22, 1991, https://www.nytimes.com/1991/01/22/business/the-spy-who-went-into-retailing.html.

171 **"What are they doing?":** "AMBASSADOR NICHOLAS A. REY, Interviewed by: Charles Stuart Kennedy," Foreign Affairs Oral History Project, Association for Diplomatic Studies and Training, Initial interview date: September 5, 2002.

172 **"The milk from that goat":** Interview with Bogdan Libera, Piaseczno, Poland, November 19, 2019.

173 **Given America's longtime:** Through a spokesman, George Tenet declined an interview request.

176 **"We want to get":** "AMBASSADOR NICHOLAS A. REY, Interviewed by: Charles Stuart Kennedy," Foreign Affairs Oral History Project, Association for Diplomatic Studies and Training, Initial interview date: September 5, 2002.

176 **"Countries like Poland tend":** Interview with Daniel Fried, Washington, DC, October 1, 2018.

CHAPTER FIFTEEN: THE PRIME MINISTER IS A SPY!

180 **On November 19:** Ramiz Alia—a former Communist leader in Albania—was elected president in 1991 by parliament.

181 **If they were false:** Interview with Jerzy Koźmiński, Warsaw, Poland, May 15, 2018.

182 **Rey observed that Wałęsa:** "AMBASSADOR NICHOLAS A. REY, Interviewed by: Charles Stuart Kennedy," Foreign Affairs Oral History Project, Association for Diplomatic Studies and Training, Initial interview date: September 5, 2002.

184 **"It didn't happen":** John Pomfret, "Poles Ponder Patriotism After Spy's Appointment, Firing," *Washington Post*, September 3, 1994.

186 **Top secret bumped up:** Interview with Jerzy Koźmiński, Warsaw, Poland, May 14, 2018.

187 **Kita knew that GROM:** Julian Borger, *The Butcher's Trail: How the Search for Balkan War Criminals Became the World's Most Successful Manhunt* (New York: Other Press, 2016), chapter 5.

190 **"A screenwriter couldn't have done it better":** Interview with Jerzy Koźmiński, Warsaw, Poland, May 14, 2018.

CHAPTER SIXTEEN: MISSING BIN LADEN

191 **Makowski, the Warsaw Pact spy:** Interview with Aleksander Makowski, Warsaw, Poland, November 12, 2018.

193 **The Ulster Volunteer Force:** "Massive UVF Arms Supply Is Found on Polish Vessel," *Herald* [Scotland], November 24, 1993, https://www.heraldscotland.com/news/12710021.massive-uvf-arms-supply-is-found-on-polish-vessel/.

195 **"A few years back":** Aleksander Makowski, *Tropiąc bin Ladena; w Afgańskiej Matni 1997–2007 (Tracking bin Laden: The Afghan Quagmire 1997–2007)* (Warsaw: Czarna Owca, 2012) and interview with Makowski, Warsaw, Poland, November 12, 2018.

197 **In addition, a member:** Makowski's account of this meeting was confirmed by ex-CIA officer Ksawery Wyrożemski and ex-UOP officer Włodzimierz Sokołowski.

198 **When the skiff pulled up:** Roy Gutman, *How We Missed the Story: Osama bin Laden, the Taliban, and the Hijacking of Afghanistan* (Washington, DC: United States Institute of Peace Press, 2013), 225–31.

199 **Michael Scheuer, who from 1996 to 1999:** Roy Gutman, "CIA Balked at Chance to Kill bin Laden in '99," McClatchy Newspapers, August 28, 2012, https://www.mcclatchydc.com/news/nation-world/world/article24735439.html.

200 **"Sometimes, it's not":** Makowski, *Tropiąc bin Ladena (Tracking bin Laden).*

CHAPTER SEVENTEEN: BLACK SITE BARGAIN

201 **Six days after 9/11:** *Study of the Central Intelligence Agency's Detention and Interrogation Program*, Report of the Senate Select Committee on Intelligence, US Senate, December 9, 2014, 11.

203 **Keeping the prisons secret:** Ibid., xviii.

203 **D requested that Hill:** Interview with Christopher Hill, Denver, Colorado, January 25, 2019.

203 **D agreed:** Ibid.

203 **The center's lawyers:** *Study of the Central Intelligence Agency's Detention and Interrogation Program*, 74.

204 **On the spot:** Interview with Aleksander Kwaśniewski, Warsaw, May 9, 2019. Former president Bush, through a spokesman, declined an interview request.

205 **A CIA contractor:** "CIA Above the Law: Secret Detentions and Unlawful Inter-State Transfer of Detainees in Europe," Council of Europe, Strasbourg, France, June 1, 2008, 192.

205 **As for Zubaydah:** Remarks by the President at Connecticut Republican Committee Luncheon, Office of the Press Secretary, The White House, April 9, 2002, https://georgewbush-whitehouse.archives.gov/news/releases/2002/04/20020409-8.html.

207 **In Poland, bin al-Shibh:** *Study of the Central Intelligence Agency's Detention and Interrogation Program*, 76.

207 **When they asked, they were:** Interview with Józef Pinior, Wrocław, Poland, May 19, 2018.

209 **Deploying several cash-counting:** Interview with Andrzej Derlatka, Warsaw, Poland, November 12, 2009.

209 **In a cable back to CIA:** *Study of the Central Intelligence Agency's Detention and Interrogation Program*, 74.

210 **Over the course of fifteen:** Ibid., 85.

211 **But when Jose Rodriguez:** Interview with Andrzej Derlatka, Warsaw, Poland, November 12, 2009.

CHAPTER EIGHTEEN: BETRAYED

213 **"If it is President Bush's vision":** David E. Sanger, "Threats and Responses: The Continent; To Some in Europe, the Major Problem Is Bush the Cowboy," *New York Times*, January 24, 2003, https://www.nytimes.com/2003/01/24/world/threats-responses-continent-some-europe-major-problem-bush-cowboy.html.

214 **As a GROM participant:** Naval, "GROM and SEAL Joint Operation: Umm Qasr Offshore Oil Terminal," SOFREP, March 26, 2014, https://sofrep.com/news/grom-seal-joint-operation-umm-qasr-offshore-oil-terminal/.

214 **They worked with the likes of:** Chris Kyle with GROM member, https://www.pinterest.com/pin/466474473903816016/?nic_v2=1a27lDElx.

215 **Said Marek Belka:** Interview with Marek Belka, Łodz, Poland, May 7, 2019.

216 **Koźmiński concluded that:** "Dick Cheney on Meet the Press," NBC News, March 16, 2003, https://www.nbcnews.com/id/wbna3080244.

218 **"We kept our promise":** Radosław Sikorski, *Polska Może Być Lepsza (Poland Can Be Better)* (Warsaw: Znak, 2018).

218 **The *Post* reported that:** Dana Priest, "CIA Holds Terror Suspects in Secret Prisons," *Washington Post*, November 2, 2005, https://www.washingtonpost.com/archive/politics/2005/11/02/cia-holds-terror-suspects-in-secret-prisons/767f0160-cde4–41f2-a691-ba989990039c/.

219 **It *was* illegal:** Daniel McLaughlin, "Poland Denies Permitting Secret CIA Prisons," *Irish Times*, December 8, 2005, https://www.irishtimes.com/news/poland-denies-permitting-secret-cia-prisons-1.1172899.

219 **Victor Ashe, the former mayor of Knoxville:** Polish Foreign Minister Miller's Visit to Washington, US Embassy Warsaw, December 13, 2005, *Public Library of US Diplomacy*, WikiLeaks, https://wikileaks.org/plusd/cables/05WARSAW4030_a.html.

219 **While Bush didn't reveal:** *Study of the Central Intelligence Agency's Detention and Interrogation Program*, 75.

220 **"Americans have no idea":** Scott Shane, "Inside a 9/11 Mastermind's Interrogation," *New York Times*, June 22, 2008, https://www.nytimes.com/2008/06/22/washington/22ksm.html.

223 **"Not like the Soviets would":** Interview with Michael Sulick, Raleigh, North Carolina, November 21, 2018. Email correspondence with Sulick as well.

CHAPTER NINETEEN: UNDER THE BUS

225 **Macierewicz, he wrote, was:** "New Deputy DefMins: Macierewicz Stirs Up Controversy."

225 **"There were real life consequences":** Interview with Marek Dukaczewski, Warsaw, Poland, November 14, 2019.

Polish government officials said: Zoltán Dujisin, "Poland: Washing the Dirty Laundry," *IPS News*, June 19, 2008, http://www.ipsnews.net/2008/06/poland-washing-the-dirty-laundry/.

226 **"I wanted to do it":** "Macierewicz: I Destroyed Post-Communist Military Intelligence," *TCMNET News*, February 28, 2007, https://www.tmcnet.com/usubmit/2007/02/28/2376831.htm.

226 **Macierewicz couldn't believe:** Interview with Antoni Macierewicz, Warsaw, Poland, May 18, 2018.

227 **Then Macierewicz released:** "The Sikorski-Rostowski Interview. 'You Can Charge PiS with a Special Committee on Macierewicz,'" *WProst*, June 22, 2014, https://www.wprost.pl/453226/rozmowa-sikorssaki-rostowski-mozna-zac-pis-komisja-specjalna-ws-macierewicza.html.

228 **"It's simple justice":** Interview with Antoni Macierewicz, Warsaw, Poland, May 18, 2018.

231 **"We'll get in conflict":** "The Sikorski-Rostowski interview."

231 **He compared Polish-American:** A.C., "Polish-American Relations: Not So Chummy Anymore," *Economist*, July 19, 2012, https://www.economist.com /eastern-approaches/2012/07/19/not-so-chummy-any-more.

CHAPTER TWENTY: SAME BED, DIFFERENT DREAMS

236 **Those missions, Gates wrote:** Włodzimierz Sokołowski's Order of Merit, https:// www.facebook.com/436743046393355/photos/pb.100044224279704.-2207520000 ./716973985036925/?type=3.

237 **In a reminder of the high-stakes:** "The mysterious death of a Polish spy in Iran. 'I began to suspect it was murder,'" TVN24, November 20, 2020, https://tvn24.pl/polska/tajemnicza-smierc-polskiego-szpiega-w-iranie -zaczalem-podejrzewac-ze-to-jest-morderstwo-4756788.

239 **"It's a likeable country":** Radosław Sikorski, *Polska Może Być Lepsza* (Warsaw: Znak, 2018), 134.

241 **"After a while, it'll swing back":** Interview with John Palevich, Bellevue, Washington, November 30, 2017.

CHAPTER TWENTY-ONE: WHAT IS TO BE DONE?

243 **According to John Bolton:** Peter Hartcher, "Trump Goes with His Gut, Even Though the World Beyond Him Goes Belly-Up," *Sydney Morning Herald*, October 27, 2020, https://www.smh.com.au/world/north-america/trump -goes-with-his-gut-even-if-the-world-beyond-the-us-goes-belly-up-20201026 -p568kv.html.

245 **"We fight to the end":** Sikorski, *Polska Może Być Lepsza*, 130.

BIBLIOGRAPHY

GOVERNMENT DOCUMENTS AND REPORTS

"Ambassador Nicholas A. Rey, Interviewed by: Charles Stuart Kennedy," Foreign Affairs Oral History Project, Association for Diplomatic Studies and Training, Initial interview date: September 5, 2002.

"Caught Unawares: William Bell and Marian Zacharski," Security Awareness in the 1980s, Feature articles from the Security Awareness Bulletin, 1981 to 1989, Security Awareness Division, Educational Programs Department, Department of Defense Security Institute, Richmond, VA, 1989.

Federal Government Security Clearance Programs, Hearings Before the Permanent Subcommittee on Investigations of the Committee on Governmental Affairs, United States Senate, Ninety-ninth Congress, First Session, April 16, 17, 18, and 25, 1985—United States. Congress. Senate. Committee on Governmental Affairs. Permanent Subcommittee on Investigations.

"Meeting the Espionage Challenge: A Review of United States Counterintelligence and Security Programs," Report of the Select Committee on Intelligence, Report 99–522, US Government Printing Office, Washington, DC, 1986.

MemCon Meeting with Prime Minister Tadeusz Mazowiecki of Poland, March 21, 1990, 1990-03-21—Mazowiecki.pdf, George H. W. Bush Presidential Library, National Archives and Records Administration.

MEMORANDUM FOR: Director, National Foreign Assessment Center, FROM: Director of Central Intelligence May 4, 1987 Doc. No. CIA-RDP95M00249R000801120044-2.

Memorandum of Conversation between James Baker and Mikhail Gorbachev in Moscow, US Department of State, February 9, 1990, National Security Archive, George Washington University, https://nsarchive.gwu.edu/dc.html?doc=4325679 -Document-05-Memorandum-of-conversation-between.

Soviet Acquisition of Western Technology, April 1982, Declassified May 15, 2006, Central Intelligence Agency.

"Study of the Central Intelligence Agency's Detention and Interrogation Program," Report of the Senate Select Committee on Intelligence, US Senate, December 9, 2014.

"The Miroslav Medvid Incident" Report, Findings, Conclusions and Recommendations, Submitted to the Commission on Security and Cooperation in Europe, Washington, DC: US Government Printing Office, 1987.

US v. Zacharski, US District Court for the Central District of California, Case 81-679, 021-1986-0075, National Archives and Record Administration, The National Archives at Riverside.

MEDIA OUTLETS

Online archives of:

Chicago Tribune

Gazeta Wyborcza

Herald (Scotland)

Irish Times

Los Angeles Times

McClatchy Newspapers

NBC News

Newsweek

New York Times

Onet Wiadomości

Rzeczpospolita

San Francisco Examiner

60 Minutes

Sydney Morning Herald

Time

TVN24

Wall Street Journal

Washington Post

Wprost

BOOKS AND ARTICLES

Agee, Philip, and Louis Wolf, eds. *Dirty Work: The CIA in Western Europe.* New York: Dorset Press, 1978.

Awłasewicz, Tomasz. *Łowcy szpiegów: Polskie służby kontra CIA* [Spy hunters: Polish services vs. the CIA]. Warsaw: Czerwone i Czarne, 2018.

Bearden, Milt, and James Risen. *The Main Enemy: The Inside Story of the CIA's Final Showdown with the KGB.* New York: Ballantine Books, 2003.

Bereś, Witold, and Jerzy Skoczylas. *Generał Kiszczak mówi . . . prawie wszystko* [General Kiszczak tells . . . almost all]. Warsaw: BGW, 1991.

Borger, Julian. *The Butcher's Trail: How the Search for Balkan War Criminals Became the World's Most Successful Manhunt.* New York: Other Press, 2016.

Bremer, L. Paul, III. *My Year in Iraq: The Struggle to Build a Future of Hope.* New York and London: Simon & Schuster, 2006.

Bury, Jan. "Operation 'Zachod:' Sex, Lies, and Ciphers." *Cryptologia* 40, no. 2 (2016): 113–40.

Bury, Jan. "Finding Needles in a Haystack: The Eastern Bloc's Counterintelligence Capabilities." *International Journal of Intelligence and CounterIntelligence* 25, no. 4 (2012): 727–70.

Bush, George H. W., and Brent Scowcroft. *A World Transformed.* New York: Alfred A. Knopf, 1998. Kindle edition.

Cienski, Jan. *Start-Up Poland: The People Who Transformed an Economy.* Chicago and London: University of Chicago Press, 2018.

Craig, James. *Shemlan: A History of the Middle East Centre for Arab Studies.* London: Macmillan, 1998.

Dudek, Antoni. *Od Mazowieckiego do Suchockiej* [From Mazowiecki to Suchocka]. Kraków: Znak Horyzont, 2019.

Dzuro, Vladimír. *The Investigator: Demons of the Balkan War.* Lincoln: Potomac Books, University of Nebraska Press, 2019.

Furst, Alan. *The Polish Officer.* New York: Random House Trade Paperbacks, 1995.

Gasztold, Przemysław. "Polish Military Intelligence and Its Secret Relationship with the Abu Nidal Organization." In *Terrorism in the Cold War: State Support in Eastern Europe and the Soviet Sphere,* edited by Adrian Hänni, Thomas Riegler, and Przemysław Gasztold, 85–106. London: I. B. Tauris, 2020.

Gross, Jan. T. *Neighbors: The Destruction of the Jewish Community in Jedwabne, Poland.* Princeton and Oxford: Princeton University Press, 2001.

Gruszczak, Artur. "The Polish Intelligence Services." In *Geheimdienste in Europa,* edited by Anna Daun and Thomas Jäger. Wiesbaden: VS Verlag, 2009.

Gutman, Roy. *How We Missed the Story: Osama bin Laden, the Taliban, and the Hijacking of Afghanistan.* Washington, DC: United States Institute of Peace Press, 2008.

Handerek, Marek. "Poland and North Korea in the 1980s—From Partnership to Stagnancy." In *Korean Society Today*, edited by A. Fedotoff and Kim So Young. Sofia: St. Kliment Ohridski University Press, 2018.

Hart, Fred. "The Iraqi Invasion of Kuwait: An Eyewitness Account, USAWC Personal Experience Monograph." Carlisle, PA: US Army War College, May 1, 1998.

Hill, Christopher R. *Outpost: Life on the Frontlines of American Diplomacy.* New York: Simon & Schuster, 2014.

Hoffman, David E. *The Dead Hand: The Untold Story of the Cold War Arms Race and Its Dangerous Legacy.* New York: Doubleday, 2009.

Hutchings, Robert L. *American Diplomacy and the End of the Cold War.* Washington, DC: Woodrow Wilson Center Press, 2007.

Jones, Seth G. *A Covert Action: Reagan, the CIA, and the Cold War Struggle in Poland.* New York: W. W. Norton, 2018.

Karpeles, Eric. *Almost Nothing: The 20th Century Art and Life of Jozef Czapski.* New York: New York Review of Books, 2018.

Koskodan, Kenneth K. *No Greater Ally: The Untold Story of Poland's Forces in World War II.* New York and Oxford: Osprey Publishing, 2009.

Kozłowski, Krzysztof, and Michal Komar. *Historia z konsekwencjami* [History with consequences]. Warsaw: Swiat Ksiazki, 2009.

Kozłowski, Tomasz. "'Why Can't We be Friends?' Establishing a Relationship Between Polish and American Intelligence Agencies in the Context of 1989 Political Transformation." Unpublished article.

Kozłowski, Tomasz. "*Odbudowa relacji polsko-izraelskich i operacja 'Most'*" [The reconstruction of the Polish-Israeli relations and Operation Bridge]. *Studia Polityczne* 40, 2015.

Kyle, Chris. *American Sniper: The Autobiography of the Most Lethal Sniper in U.S. Military History.* New York: Harper, 2012.

Macintyre, Ben. *The Spy and the Traitor: The Greatest Espionage Story of the Cold War.* New York: Crown, 2018.

Makowski, Aleksander. *Tropiąc Bin Ladena: W Afgańskiej Matni 1997–2007* [Tracking Bin Laden. The Afghan Quagmire. 1997–2007]. Warsaw: Czarna Owca, 2012.

Mitchell, James E. *Enhanced Interrogation: Inside the Minds and Motives of the Islamic Terrorists Trying to Destroy America.* New York: Crown Forum, 2016.

Naftali, Timothy. "US Counterterrorism Before Bin Laden." *International Journal* 60, no. 1 (Winter 2004/2005): 25–34.

Nalepa, Monika. *Skeletons in the Closet: Transitional Justice in Post-Communist Europe.* Cambridge and New York: Cambridge University Press, 2010.

Packer, George. *Our Man: Richard Holbrooke and the End of the American Century.* New York: Alfred A. Knopf, 2019.

Paczkowski, Andrzej. "Civilian Intelligence in Communist Poland, 1945–1989: An Attempt at a General Outline." Unpublished manuscript. Warsaw: Institute of Political Studies and Collegium Civitas.

Polak, Wojciech, and Sylwia Galij-Skarbińska. "A Polish Model of the Intelligence Service Reform in 1990." Zapiski Historyczne 2 (2017): 141–58.

Pytlakowski, Piotr. Szkoła szpiegów [Spy school]. Warsaw: Czerwone i Czarne, 2011.

Rzeplinski, Andrzej. "Security Services in Poland and Their Oversight." In Democracy, Law, and Security: Internal Security Services in Contemporary Europe, edited by Jean-Paul Brodeur, Peter Gill, and Dennis Tollborg. Burlington, VT: Ashgate, 2003.

Savranskaya, Svetlana, and Tom Blanton. "NATO Expansion: What Gorbachev Heard." Briefing Book, no. 613, National Security Archive, George Washington University, December 12, 2017, https://nsarchive.gwu.edu/briefing-book/russia-programs/2017–12–12/nato-expansion-what-gorbachev-heard-western-leaders-early.

Schwarzkopf, Norman. It Doesn't Take a Hero: The Autobiography. New York: Bantam Books, 1993.

Sikora, Mirosław. "Cooperating with Moscow, Stealing in California: Poland's Legal and Illicit Acquisition of Microelectronics Knowhow from 1960 to 1990." In Histories of Computing in Eastern Europe, edited by Christopher Leslie and Martin Schmitt. New York: Springer, 2019.

Sikorski, Radosław. Polska Może Być Lepsza [Poland can be better]. Warsaw: Znak, 2018.

Snyder, Timothy. Bloodlands: Europe Between Hitler and Stalin. New York: Basic Books, 2010.

Snyder, Timothy. The Reconstruction of Nations: Poland, Ukraine, Lithuania, Belarus, 1569–1999. New Haven and London: Yale University Press, 2003.

Stanton, Martin. Road to Baghdad: Behind Enemy Lines, The Adventures of an American Soldier in the Gulf War. New York: Ballantine Books, 2003.

Storozynski, Alex. The Peasant Prince: Thaddeus Kosciuszko and the Age of Revolution. New York: St. Martin's Press, 2009.

Sulick, Michael J. American Spies: Espionage Against the United States from the Cold War to the Present. Washington, DC: Georgetown University Press, 2013.

Sulick, Michael J. "As the USSR Collapsed: A CIA Officer in Lithuania." Studies in Intelligence 50, no. 2 (2006).

Talbott, Strobe. The Russia Hand: A Memoir of Presidential Diplomacy. New York: Random House Trade Paperbacks, 2002.

Taras, Ray. "Poland's Diplomatic Misadventure in Iraq: With Us or Against Us." Problems of Post-Communism 51, no. 1 (2004): 3–17.

Wałęsa, Lech. *The Struggle and the Triumph: An Autobiography.* New York: Arcade Publishing, 1991.

Watts, Larry L. "Intelligence Reform in Europe's Emerging Democracies." *Studies in Intelligence* 48, no. 1 (2001).

Weiner, Timothy. *Legacy of Ashes: The History of the CIA.* New York: Random House, 2007.

Wilson, Joseph. *The Politics of Truth: Inside the Lies That Led to War and the Betrayal of My Wife's CIA Identity.* New York: Carroll and Graf, 2004.

Zacharski, Marian. *Rosyjska ruletka* [Russian roulette]. Poznań: ZYSK I S-KA, 2010.

Zacharski, Marian. *Nazywam się Zacharski. Marian Zacharski* [The name's Zacharski, Marian Zacharski]. Poznań: ZYSK I S-KA, 2009.

ACKNOWLEDGMENTS

Writing books, like putting out a newspaper, is a collaborative process. Many people on both sides of the Atlantic assisted me, often selflessly. In Poland, I was lucky to have worked with and befriended Alex Nowacki, an expert researcher, translator, and interpreter of all things Polish. He was a constant and supportive companion. A whole crew of Polish intelligence professionals—Piotr Brochwicz, Gromek Czempiński, Andrzej Derlatka, Marek Dukaczewski, Henryk Jasik, Bogdan Libera, Alex Makowski, Waldemar Markiewicz, Andrzej Maronde, Wojciech Martynowicz, Ryszard Morcyński, Janusz Omietański, Krzysztof Smoleński, Włodimierz Sokołowski, Ricardo Tomaszewski, Piotr Wronski, and Marian Zacharski, to name but a few—gave me a lot of time and exhibited a lot of patience. I can't name all of them, but they were very supportive of the project. Polish politicians, among them Marek Belka, Aleksander Kwaśniewski, Antoni Macierewicz, Andrzej Milczanowski, Leszek Miller, Jozef Pinior, Zbigniew Semiątkowski, and Radek Sikorski, had no need to submit to my interviews but were willing nonetheless. Polish diplomats and security officials Jerzy Kozmiński, Krzysztof Plominski, Marek Siwiec, and Bogusław Winid, and Polish military officers, especially Piotr Gastał, were also incredibly welcoming.

Crusading attorney Mikolaj Pietrzak offered important perspectives and a uniquely moral insight into the costs of the unlikely alliance between Poland and the United States. And leading Polish journalists Bartosz Weglarczyk and Tomasz Awłasewicz provided some critical, last-minute perspective and tips.

This project was helped enormously by two world-class historians, Tomasz Kozłowski and Przemysław Gasztold, who both spent hours helping me obtain recently declassified documents from the Institute of National Remembrance and to provide sage advice about the documents' importance. Both read early drafts of the book and pointed out errors. Of course, I take sole responsibility for the content in the book. Another historian, Witold Bagienski, gave generously of his time and insights as well.

For camaraderie in Poland, I was lucky to have three dear friends: lifelong colleague Anna Husarska, who also read a version of the book and saved me from embarrassing mistakes, and Robert Konski and Tod Kersten, who provided great meals, music, and conversation on my visits to Warsaw. One of these days we'll go boar hunting. Thanks, too, go to Seth Faison and Siobhan Darrow and their children, Sasha and Lane, for opening their home in Geneva on my trips to meet with the engaging Marian Zacharski.

In the United States, former US intelligence officers Milt Bearden, Burton Gerber, Bill Norville, John Palevich, Paul Redmond, Michael Sulick, and Ksawery Wyrożemski were extraordinarily generous with their time. Ambassadors Victor Ashe, Daniel Fried, Chris Hill, Tom Simons, John Kornblum, and the late Joe Wilson provided perspective and key insights. US Army (ret.) officers John Feeley and Fred Hart were enormously helpful and both waded through drafts of the book to make sure I got their stories right. I look forward to continuing our friendships. Thanks go to Alex Storozynski and his wonderful biography of Tadeusz Kosciuszko, which provided the inspiration for this book's epigraph. Colleagues in the media Julian Borger, Roy Gutman, and Jon Landay were extremely supportive as well. Svetlana Savranskaya at the National Security Archive at George Washington University provided priceless guidance about searching for records in the United States. Staff at the presidential libraries of George H. W. Bush, George W. Bush, and Bill Clinton were happy to process my requests for documents. Perhaps some of the files I and other researchers have asked to see will be declassified before the twenty-first century ends. Tim Anderson at the National Archives at Riverside was helpful in locating the files on Marian Zacharski's case. Nuclear proliferation experts David Albright and Olli Heinonen gave their time and expertise. Thanks also goes to Rajiv Chandrasekaran for providing perspective on the US occupation of Iraq. And to Ye Wa and Joe Esherick, who demanded good footnotes.

Serendipity played its part in this book. If I hadn't known James Nathan, ex-diplomat and longtime friend, I never would've met Grant Hammond of the US Air Force on a trip to Alabama. Grant, in turn, found Fred Hart, one of those saved in Iraq. Mutual friend Orville Schell and his late wife, Baifang, introduced me to Eric Karpeles, which led me to Eric's wonderful book on the Polish artist Józef

Czapski and a deeper appreciation of Poland's twentieth-century travails. Friends, like allies, matter. Thanks to all of you.

In addition to my great editor Serena Jones at Henry Holt, three people stood out in helping me tell a better story. Foremost, my wife, Zhang Mei. She has always been my first reader. She has a great ear for a story and is honest when she's bored. Thank you, Mei! None of this would have been possible without you.

Dick Butterfield, a dear friend and classmate, helped me hone the tale and bring it to a conclusion. My sister, Dana Pomfret, line edited every word twice, pushing me to make the story clearer and more accessible, despite all those Polish names. My agent, Gail Ross, as always, provided expert guidance. Jean-Michel Valette and David Greenbaum showed the long-pull of our deep friendships in reading and commenting on early drafts.

At Holt, in addition to Serena Jones, I've been lucky to have great colleagues: Molly Bloom, Omar Chapa, Amy Einhorn, Carolyn O'Keefe, Anita Sheih, and Maggie Richards. Special thanks goes to Holt's executive editor, Sarah Crichton, for approving the last-minute change of title.

Finally, four people have been much on my mind throughout the writing of this book. The next generation, our children, Dali, Liya, and Sophie, to whom this book is dedicated. And my dad, John D. Pomfret, who lobbied for the title, *From Warsaw with Love*, and gave the cover a big thumbs up. R.I.P., Old John. We love you.

ABOUT THE AUTHOR

Raised in New York City and educated at Stanford and Nanjing Universities, John Pomfret is an award-winning journalist, author, and a Pulitzer Prize finalist.

Pomfret was a foreign correspondent for twenty years with *The Washington Post* and covered wars in Afghanistan, Bosnia, Congo, Sri Lanka, and Iraq. Pomfret was posted to China twice—once in the late 1980s during the Tiananmen Square protests and then from 1997 until 2003 as the *Post*'s bureau chief in Beijing. He served in Eastern Europe for four years, three of them in Warsaw.

Pomfret is the author of the bestselling *Chinese Lessons: Five Classmates and the Story of the New China* (1996). His book *The Beautiful Country and the Middle Kingdom: America and China, 1776 to the Present* (2016) was awarded the Arthur Ross Award by the Council on Foreign Relations. Pomfret has been a bartender in Paris and practiced judo in Japan. He lives with his wife, Zhang Mei, and three children in Berkeley, California.